Fearful Hope

Fearful Hope

Approaching the New Millennium

Edited by

Christopher Kleinhenz

and

Fannie J. LeMoine

THE UNIVERSITY OF WISCONSIN PRESS

The University of Wisconsin Press
2537 Daniels Street
Madison, Wisconsin 53718

3 Henrietta Street
London WC2E 8LU, England

5   4   3   2   1

Library of Congress Cataloging-in-Publication Data

Fearful hope: approaching the new millennium / edited by Christopher Kleinhenz and
    Fannie J. LeMoine.
        236 pp.   cm.
    Includes bibliographical references and index.
    ISBN 0-299-16430-6 (cloth: alk. paper). — ISBN 0-299-16434-9 (pbk.: alk. paper)
    1. Millennialism—Congresses. 2. Millennialism—History of doctrines Congresses.
I. Kleinhenz, Christopher. II. LeMoine, Fannie.
BT891.F43 1999
236'.9—dc21   99-18917

Contents

Illustrations   vii
Preface   ix
Acknowledgments   xiii
Contributors   xiv

1. Introduction: Three Millennial Themes   3
   Christopher Kleinhenz and Fannie J. LeMoine

Part 1. Apocalyptic Visions in the Ancient World

2. The Sense of an Ending in Pre-Christian Judaism   25
   John J. Collins

3. Hope for the Millennium in the Early Church:
   Expectation for This World?   44
   Henry Chadwick

**Part 2. The Apocalyptic Tradition from the Middle Ages
to the Twentieth Century**

4. "To the Scandal of Men, Women Are Prophesying":
   Female Seers of the High Middle Ages   59
   Bernard McGinn

5. Beyond the Apocalypse: The Human Antichrist
   in Late Medieval Illustrated Manuscripts   86
   Richard K. Emmerson

6. Madness and the Millennium at Münster, 1534–1535   115
   H. C. Erik Midelfort

7. Apocalypticism in Russian Literature: A Brief Portrait   135
   David M. Bethea

Part 3. Apocalypticism in Twentieth-Century Thought

8. The Apocalyptic in the Twentieth Century   149
   Paul Boyer

9. End-Time Paranoia: Conspiracy Thinking
   at the Millennium's Close   170
   Michael Barkun

**Part 4. Hope and Faith at the End of the Millennium:
          Two Homilies**

10. Hope in the Face of Crisis   185
    Archbishop Rembert G. Weakland, O.S.B.

11. Christian Faith and Witness amidst Political Oppression:
    A Glance Back to Church Life in East Germany,
    1970–1990   191
    Bishop Johannes Hempel

Appendixes: Reports from the Workshops

A. Apocalyptic Experience and the Conversion
   of Women in Early Christianity   201
   Fannie J. LeMoine

B. Abbot Joachim of Fiore: A Reformist Apocalyptic   207
   E. Randolph Daniel

C. Early Protestant Views of the Book of Revelation   211
   Robert M. Kingdon

D. The American Puritans and Millennialism   214
   Sargent Bush, Jr.

Index   218

Illustrations

1.1 Gustave Doré, "The Giant and the Harlot"   9

1.2 The Triumph of Love   11

1.3 The Triumph of Chastity   12

1.4 The Triumph of Death   13

1.5 The Triumph of Fame   14

1.6 The Triumph of Time   15

1.7 The Triumph of Eternity   16

1.8 The Triumph of Death   17

1.9 John the Evangelist, from the Nuremberg Chronicle   18

1.10 The Advent of the Antichrist, from the Nuremberg Chronicle   19

1.11 The Last Judgment, from the Nuremberg Chronicle   20

1.12 Conference logo, based on Dürer's, "The Four Horsemen of the Apocalypse"   21

5.1 Antichrist Orders the Execution of Enoch and Elijah, from the *Wellcome Apocalypse*   88

5.2 The Conception of Antichrist, from *Jour du Jugement*   89

5.3 The Pregnancy of Antichrist's Mother; Antichrist's Birth; The News Delivered to Hell, from *Jour du Jugement*   92

5.4 Opening of the Antichrist Entry, from *Omne Bonum*   94

5.5 Opening of the Second Coming Entry, from *Omne Bonum*   97

5.6 Head of Antichrist, from *Piers Plowman*   98

5.7 Destruction of Gog and Magog; Antichrist's Tyranny, from the *Carthusian Miscellany*   101

5.8   Death of Enoch and Elijah; Death of Antichrist, from
      the *Carthusian Miscellany*   101
5.9   Antichrist's Persecutions, from *Livre de la Vigne Notre
      Seigneur*   104
5.10 Signs of Doomsday; Antichrist Preaches False Doctrine,
      from *Légende dorée*   106
5.11 Antichrist Bribes His Followers and Persecutes the
      Faithful; Christ's Second Advent, from *Légende dorée*   107

Preface

This volume of essays grows out of a conference held in Madison, Wisconsin, from 21 to 24 September 1997. Entitled "Waiting in Fearful Hope: Approaching the New Millennium," it dealt with millennial expectations from antiquity to the present and in a variety of forms, from biblical and classical texts through contemporary film. Arranging a conference on this topic was an unsettling experience for at least two reasons: it revealed the wide distance separating contemporary academics and mainline religious from a vast popular movement, and it made it impossible to ignore the pervasiveness of apocalyptic themes in our contemporary culture.

Exciting but entirely different conferences could have focused on such topics as the millennium in the Christian communities in the developing world, the millennium as a secular phenomenon, or millenarianism and its accompanying technological dimensions. Certainly the prophetic call to a new age has had wide appeal in this century, whether the call is couched in Judeo-Christian or secular language. For example, the many websites devoted to the millennium range from the scholarly to the popular, from the sedate to the truly unusual. In a major 1996 study of North American religious attitudes conducted by the Angus Reid Group, 42 percent of the U.S. respondents agreed that the world would end in a battle at Armageddon between Jesus and the Antichrist. In other words, almost 100 million Americans embrace a view of history and the coming end of time that many others in our society dismiss or find faintly ridiculous. Such a cavalier dismissal is dangerous, for it ignores the persistence and importance of religious concerns in modern society. It also fails to consider the significance of religious history in shaping contemporary Western culture.

The conference was sponsored by the University of Wisconsin–Madison and the Commission for Lutheran–Anglican–Roman Catholic–United Methodist Relations for Wisconsin and Upper Michigan (LARCUM), an ecumenical religious group. The conference received funding support from LARCUM and the Wisconsin Humanities Council and gift funds from the university. At every step of the way from conception to conclusion, the planners of the conference tried to maintain a careful separation between academic and religious events. The need to be so observant was a strong reminder of the sometimes uneasy distinctions contemporary institutions must draw when examining religious themes within the context of publicly supported discussions.

Care was probably even more necessary in this conference because the topic itself provokes uneasy, even bizarre, reactions. University colleagues who heard about the conference responded either with interest and polite respect or with the faint suggestion that we had entered the land of the familiar bearded sign-carriers of *New Yorker* cartoons—that we too were proclaiming that the end was near. On the other hand, when we discussed the conference during a call-in program on the state public radio network, most of the callers were interested in identifying the number of the beast, a sure sign of strong belief that Satan is alive, well, and highly influential in everyday events.

In planning the conference, we wished to reach as broad a public audience as possible, and we believe we succeeded. Around 1,500 people from all walks of life attended, and the cliché "from all walks of life" characterized this group very well. The conference not only focused on scholarly discussions of the origins and development of this powerful conception of the end of time in Western history, but also examined the secular apocalyptic in modern film and the inspiration of apocalyptic themes in music and art, as well as religious meditations.

Thus, the conference presented a kaleidoscope of topics related to millennial and apocalyptic expectations. Its variety and unusual features illustrate how unexpectedly these themes recur in contemporary culture. It included academic lectures, religious services, musical presentations, film screenings, and a special rare book and manuscript exhibit. There were two ecumenical services: an evensong at Luther Memorial Church with a homily by the Roman Catholic Archbishop of Milwaukee, Rembert Weakland, "Hope in the Face of Crisis," and a homily at St. Paul's Catholic Chapel by the Lutheran bishop Johannes Hempel (of Dresden, Germany) on "Christian Faith and Witness amidst Political Oppression: A Glance Back to Church Life in East Germany, 1970–1990." These meditations provide insight into the power and message of hope as they have experienced it both in their personal lives and in greatly different historical circumstances. Five films were shown and discussed: *The Seventh Seal, Road Warrior, Planet of the Apes, Brazil,* and *Twelve Monkeys.* Musical performances on apocalyptic themes included Olivier Messiaen's *Quartet for the End of Time.*[1]

The conference also featured workshop discussions on subjects as diverse as biblical texts, environmental concerns, and the use of apocalyptic imagery in Nazi propaganda.[2] Short informative "reports" on four of these workshops are provided in the Appendix to this volume. These contributors are Fannie LeMoine (on the martyr Perpetua and the conversion of women in early Christianity), Randolph Daniel (on the apocalypticism of Joachim of Fiore), Robert Kingdon (on early Protestant views of the Book of Revelation), and Sargent Bush (on the Puritans and millennialism). David Bethea, who led a workshop on "The Millennial Impulse in Russian Literature," kindly agreed to contribute an essay for this volume. In chapter 7 he presents an overview of the apocalyptic character of Russian literature in its several manifestations over the past two hundred years, from Pushkin to the present.

The first day of the academic conference was devoted to "Apocalyptic Visions in the Ancient World." John Collins opened the proceedings by tracing apocalyptic thought in pre-Christian Judaism. He was followed by E. P. Sanders, who described the characterization of hope in Jewish and Christian texts of the first century. Henry Chadwick concluded the first day by weaving together the various strands of apocalyptic thought in an address on the millennium and the early Christian church.

"The Apocalyptic Tradition from the Middle Ages to the Twentieth Century" was the major focus of the second day. Bernard McGinn investigated the nature and significance of female apocalyptic prophecy in the Middle Ages, giving special attention to the lives and visionary writings of Hildegard of Bingen and Mechthild of Magdeburg. Erik Midelfort probed the nature of madness and its general manifestations in Reformation Germany, examining in particular the conditions in the city of Münster under the control of Jan Mattijs and Jan of Leiden. In his evening illustrated lecture "Apocalyptic Visions: Visualizing the Apocalypse in Medieval and Renaissance Art," Richard Emmerson introduced a wide variety of manuscript illuminations of the Book of Revelation. For his chapter in this volume, he examines the varying representations of the Antichrist in six illuminated manuscripts and considers their relationship to traditional sources and the interaction of word and image.

On the last day of the conference two speakers examined "Apocalypticism in Twentieth-Century Thought." Paul Boyer provided a wide-ranging and detailed examination of the apocalyptic in twentieth-century America. He discussed continuing belief in a coming Armageddon, the Rapture, and contemporary interpretations of political changes in places as diverse as Russia, Israel, and the United States. Michael Barkun described the fear widespread among contemporary religious groups that anticipate a cataclysmic end of time. His lecture on "End-Time Paranoia: Conspiracy Thinking at the Millennium's Close" demonstrates the pervasiveness of conspiracy theories in modern society.

Notes

1. In addition to the Messiaen *Quartet,* there was a special presentation of "Apocalyptic Chants and Texts" by the Ad Hoc Schola Gregoriana, directed by John K. Leonard, and the Ad Hoc Polyphonic Quartet, directed by Timothy Stalter. The event featured various chants ("Fortis atque Amara," "Plange Quasi Virgo," "Libera Me, Domine," and "Dies Irae") and readings from such biblical texts as Lamentations, Joel, and Zephaniah and from the Homilary of Toledo.

2. The other presenters and their workshops are as follows (in alphabetical order):

Paul Boyer (University of Wisconsin–Madison), "Fundamentalist Politics and the Millennium"

Barry Brummett (University of Wisconsin–Milwaukee), "The Rhetorical Uses of the Apocalypse"

Reverend David Couper (St. John the Baptist Episcopal Church, Portage, Wisconsin), "Work and Spirituality"

Calvin DeWitt (University of Wisconsin–Madison), "Millenarianism and the Environment"

Susanna Elm (University of California–Berkeley), "Apocalyptic Expectations and Ascetic Response: The Case of Montanism in the Fourth Century"

Michael Fox (University of Wiscosnin–Madison), "The End of History in the Hebrew Bible"

Richard Landes (Boston University), "The Tidal Wave Model of Christian Conversion: On the Role of Charismatic Apocalyptic Preachers in the First Rounds of Missionary Success"

David C. Lindberg (University of Wisconsin–Madison), "Images of the Earth in the Year 1000"

George Nickelsburg (University of Iowa), "Waiting for the End at the Shores of the Dead Sea: Demons, Angels, and Apocalyptic Literature at Qumran"

Jon H. Roberts (University of Wisconsin–Stevens Point), "Science and Christian Millennialism"

Jane Schulenburg (University of Wisconsin–Madison), "The Year 1000 and the Retarded Millennium of 1033"

Leonard Thompson (Lawrence University), "The Book of Revelation: Apocalyptic Spirituality in Ordinary Life"

Gerhard L. Weinberg (University of North Carolina–Chapel Hill), "The Millennium and the Nazis"

Acknowledgments

The conference on "Waiting in Fearful Hope: Approaching the New Millennium" was sponsored by the Commission for Lutheran–Anglican–Roman Catholic–United Methodist Relationships in Wisconsin and Upper Michigan (LARCUM), and by the Medieval Studies Program at the University of Wisconsin–Madison. It was funded in part by the Wisconsin Humanities Council, serving on behalf of the National Endowment for the Humanities, with assistance from the Anonymous Fund and the Humanistic Fund, University of Wisconsin–Madison. Additional support was received from Gunderson Funeral Homes of Dane County; the Ellamae Siebert Foundation; Smith and Gesteland, LLP, CPAs and Business Consultants; the Knights of Columbus; the Lewis Lecture Fund of St. Paul's University Catholic Center; Fred and Frances Schlimgen; the Chancellor's Office, College of Letters and Science, and the Graduate School, University of Wisconsin–Madison; the School of Music and the Departments of Classics, Communication Arts, History, Scandinavian Studies, the University of Wisconsin–Madison; the Friends of the University of Wisconsin Libraries; the Elvehjem Museum of Art; Lindsay, Stone and Briggs Advertising; Immanuel Lutheran Church; Luther Memorial Church; the Lutheran Campus Center; St. Andrew's Episcopal Church; St. Paul's University Catholic Center; Grace Episcopal Church; the Ad Hoc Schola Gregoriana; and the Ad Hoc Polyphonic Quartet.

Thanks should be given to the Chair, the Reverend Harvey Lange, and to members of the Millennium Conference Planning Committee as well as to others who generously volunteered their assistance at the conference: Tino Balio, Bruce Bengtson, David Bordwell, Gerald Born, Ron Brant, William Bullock, Philip Certain, Brent Christianson, Faye Darnall, Paul R. Dicks, Jon Enslin, Jean Feraca, Kenneth Frazier, Clarence Harms, Max Harris, Jane Henning, Niels Ingwersen, the Karp Family Players, John K. Leonard, Bernard McGarty, Peter Monkmeyer, Daniel Mortenson, Connie Ott, Yvonne Ozzello, Harvey Peters, Sarah Quinones, Jennifer Rea, Robin Rider, Richard Ringler, Linda Savage, Stephen Smith, David Sorkin, Timothy Stalter, David Susan, Carl Volz, David Ward, Roger White, Diane Witek.

Contributors

MICHAEL BARKUN, Professor of Political Science, Syracuse University

DAVID M. BETHEA, Vilas Professor of Slavic Studies, University of Wisconsin–Madison

PAUL BOYER, Merle Curti Professor of History and Director, Institute for Research in the Humanities, University of Wisconsin–Madison

SARGENT BUSH, JR., Bascom Professor of English, University of Wisconsin–Madison

HENRY CHADWICK, Regius Professor of Divinity, Emeritus, Cambridge University, England

JOHN J. COLLINS, Professor of Hebrew Bible, Divinity School, University of Chicago

E. RANDOLPH DANIEL, Professor of History, University of Kentucky

RICHARD K. EMMERSON, Professor of English, Western Washington University

JOHANNES HEMPEL, Landesbischof Emeritus, Evangelical Lutheran Church of Saxony, Dresden, Germany

ROBERT M. KINGDON, Hilldale Professor of History, and Member, Institute for Research in the Humanities, University of Wisconsin–Madison

CHRISTOPHER KLEINHENZ, Professor of Italian and Chair of the Medieval Studies Program, University of Wisconsin–Madison

FANNIE J. LEMOINE, late Professor of Classics and Associate Dean of the Graduate School, University of Wisconsin–Madison

BERNARD McGINN, Naomi Shenstone Donnelley Professor, Divinity School, University of Chicago

H. C. ERIK MIDELFORT, Julian Bishko Professor of History, University of Virginia

REMBERT G. WEAKLAND, O.S.B., Archbishop of Milwaukee, Wisconsin

Fearful Hope

1 *Christopher Kleinhenz and Fannie J. LeMoine*

Introduction
Three Millennial Themes

Millenarianism is a vast topic of special relevance for our time, yet drawing on a long tradition of millennial and apocalyptic fears and predictions. Three related themes dominate that tradition, especially in the West: preordained patterns in time, rhetorics of crisis, and expectations of radical change.

These three themes are interrelated in special ways in that part of the apocalyptic tradition which links millennial reckoning with the idea of the fullness of time, *plenitudo temporis*. But each of the themes can be distinguished from the others. Thus, rhetorics of crisis are not necessarily associated with an assumption of preordained patterns in time, but develop special force through the power of such imagery in the Judeo-Christian tradition. Similarly, rhetorics of crisis become more persuasive through their abilities to suggest alternate realities. These realities do not necessarily have to be supernatural or linked to a view of a cataclysmic end of time, but they acquire added dimensions through these associations. The ability to expect radical change is a *sine qua non* of hope and fear, and in the Western tradition these expectations have been guided, in part, by the literary and artistic imagination of many centuries.

Those of us who mark time in terms of centuries before and after Jesus' birth have inherited a prophetic tradition that identifies certain periods as times of crisis, moments ordained for the resolution of cosmic events. The

3

language associated with such "crucial" moments both complements and differs from the rhetoric of crisis used by classical authors. Cicero, for example, repeatedly characterizes the Roman Republic as a nation in crisis, attacked by enemies like Catiline or Antony, and in need of extraordinary measures. Cicero's rhetoric encourages taking action—even extreme action, such as execution of citizens without proper trial—to re-establish order. The appeal to the idealized order of former times serves as the impetus for such transgressions of the normal law. On the other hand, the view that moments of crisis are part of a preordained order that will be fulfilled regardless of human action encourages participants to wait—whether in fear of or in hope for a changed world order. Since the rhetoric seems aimed at producing different reactions, it is easy to miss the basic similarity. Identifying a moment as a time of crisis causes people to alter their customary existence. The speaker may be attempting to provoke action or to cause an internal change, as the author of Mark's gospel does when exhorting his hearers to repent: "The time is accomplished, and the kingdom of God is at hand: repent, and believe the gospel" (Mark 1:15, Douay Vulgate).

Central to identifying a certain time as a moment of crisis is the speaker's ability to envision a different time, either in the past or in the future, when things were or will be right. One of Cicero's favorite devices was to invoke the Roman state of the Scipios, that glorious era when Rome defeated Carthage. Appeals to the virtues of this distant past were effective in creating a sense of public readiness to respond to the moral and physical dangers posed by enemies of the state. On the other hand, the Book of Revelation represents John's vision of the end of time, that final conflict between good and evil and the establishment of the Celestial Jerusalem. In this vision good and evil are so clearly delineated with such powerful imagery that these forces are clearly not of ordinary time and place. Indeed, they are so powerful that they become emblematic of crisis itself.

The ability of apocalyptic imagery to arouse hope, inspire courage, and move to action has appeared in many contexts since its origin in the ancient world. Apocalyptic hope has been shown to move people at the deepest level, exhibiting its influence both in religious life and in the public domain. Many have used the bizarre images, mysterious numbers, and symbols of apocalyptic hope to interpret current events and to attempt to predict the future. The tragedies of Jonestown in Guyana and the Branch Davidians in Waco, Texas, suggest the power of apocalyptic rhetoric both to demonize people in authority and to lead to radical and disastrous consequences. Apocalyptic rhetoric is also used to alert people to the need for action to address various pressing human concerns: environmental pollution, ethnic strife, family violence, drug abuse, and a host of other societal ills that today we fear and whose solution we can only dimly imagine. As these modern examples demonstrate both *in bono* and *in malo*, apocalyptic imagery has been used as a powerful tool to influence behavior and effect change in the Western tradition.

The twentieth century has witnessed extraordinary changes, changes far more profound than most people are capable of envisioning and understanding. That reality complements the age-old expectation of radical change embedded in the apocalyptic tradition. Waiting for the end of the world and for the coming of the New Jerusalem was animated by some combination of despair and hatred of the established order. That remains a powerful motive for disaffected groups, such as the followers of Heaven's Gate who were confident of interstellar salvation in the mysterious spaceship following the Hale-Bopp comet. Although their views are clearly extreme, the expectation of radical change or astounding intervention is common. Many people in contemporary society believe that extraordinary changes in the environment or in political structures may occur and fear the possibility of potentially uncontrollable disaster. This popular fear coincides with a questioning of the basic assumption that humans are able to understand the causes and effects that shape history and the world in which we live. In such an atmosphere the possibility, even the certainty, of radical change becomes a defensible or at least tenable intellectual and emotional position.

Visions of heaven and hell and the accompanying scenes of eternal rewards and punishments have occupied a large place in human consciousness over the past two millennia. Apocalyptic rhetoric has been reinforced by visual imagery, especially that rich tradition which has grown up around and is associated with scenes of the Last Judgment. For many the medieval visions of the end of time are emblematic of the word *apocalyptic*. The effectiveness of these scenes relies upon an assumption that time is linear and has been preordained to end in a final cataclysmic crisis. The alternative reality is located in a clearly established temporal frame that gathers every proceeding moment of individual crisis into a final radical transformation of time into eternity. Thus, the scenes of Last Judgment unite the rhetoric of crisis, the assumption of preordained patterns of time, and the expectation of radical change in a conventional apocalypse. The key rhetorical device is to supplant a vision of the way things are with a totally new vision of the way they could be. That can lead to necessary action against the injustices or evils of the present world. It is precisely this vision of an alternative world invested with as much reality as our day-to-day existence (if not more) that gives the medieval Last Judgment scenes their didactic and spiritual power.

Viewers often tend to concentrate more on the vision of hell than on that of paradise, and this may be attributed in large part to the terrifyingly realistic depiction of physical torment. The frenetic activity of the devils and their minions contrasts with the ordered serenity of the heavenly citizens. These scenes are strategically placed either on the facades and in the tympana above the portals of churches or on the interior west wall so that the congregation will be constantly reminded as they enter or go forth from the sanctuary that they must live in fearful hope in the world of contingency. Moments of crisis shape their lives, and they are expected to learn how to respond to these uncertainties from the artistic representations of alternative worlds that lie before them. The presentation of the chaos of hell is only a part of a larger, all-inclusive vision of the universe ordered by God. The chaos and destruction associated with apocalyptic visions from antiquity and the Middle Ages are contained within this larger, beautifully harmonic structure and are controlled by it. For example, the thirteenth-century mosaics in the cupola of the Florentine Baptistery present horrific images of the devils in hell within a beautifully proportioned and harmonic design. However, the apocalyptic visions of modern cinema frequently present alternative realities without any reference to our hope for a rational or divinely ordered universe. Faith in reason and faith in faith have been lost.

The Ordering of Time

Much modern apocalyptic imagery and rhetoric intensify a view of the cosmos as chaotic and without divine plan, and references to the apocalypse add a sense of impending doom without any hope of salvation. For example, the film *Twelve Monkeys* is set within a repetitive and senseless pattern of human disease and destruction. The hero of this film is caught in a continual time warp where he attempts, futilely and repeatedly, to resolve a crisis. Normal expectations of linear time are subverted in this film. The protagonist as a child witnesses his own death and will repeat that vision without understanding and in perpetuity. As viewers of the film, we are forced to rehearse that defining moment in the protagonist's life and in its implications for our own. Time here is seen as never ending, and yet it is to some extent the end of time for the human race, now reduced to a hundred thousand people and forced to live underground. The film suggests how closely apocalyptic imagery can be associated with personal memory, and also that time may be ordered in ways either beyond our understanding or far more arbitrarily than we may assume. As such, *Twelve Monkeys* reminds us that our historical definitions of previous periods are recent and arbitrary. For our concept of periods in history we are indebted to a figure as recent as Petrarch, who assumes that the gulf of the Middle Ages separates his time from the classical past.

Periodization is a way to order, catalogue, and reduce to human dimensions expanses of time beyond our grasp—whether we label the periods Precambrian, Early Stone Age, or the Age of Iron. The idea of a succession of ages, each with its own particular qualities, is ancient. For example, Hesiod uses the analogy of the relative value of metals to describe the decline of the world over time: from a golden age of peace and prosperity to the hard and brutish age of iron. The interpretation of Nebuchadnezzar's dream in the Book of Daniel follows these general outlines in reference to the four successive kingdoms. Both human depravity and human invention coincide in creating this decline. Thus, there is an assumption that human action has a bearing on the passage of time. Time itself was viewed as a continuum, and many medieval chroniclers would begin their narrative with the creation. They might borrow characterizations of time from ancient classical authors who viewed the universe as eternal, rather than created by God, but they did not question the teleological direction in which time was moving. Modern clockwatchers are less certain of any ultimate direction and fear that disasters have no textual key, no comprehensible explanation.

Measuring Time: Text and Image

Speculations on the end of time were pervasive in the thirteenth and fourteenth centuries.[1] The Calabrian Cistercian abbot Joachim of Fiore (c. 1135–1202) had conceived of earthly time as divided into a succession of three periods: the Ages of the Father, the Son, and the Holy Spirit. His periodization influenced the Franciscans and Dante. The Age of the Father was the Old Testament period, and the Age of the Son began with the Christian dispensation. Joachim was convinced that this age was near its end and that the Age of the Holy Spirit was soon to begin. It would be one of untold prosperity and harmony. Dante Alighieri (1265–1321) reflects his interest in and appreciation for Joachim by placing him among the theologians in the Heaven of the Sun in *Paradiso* (cantos 10–13). There the twenty-four theologians whom Dante specifically names form two concentric circles and move in a circular manner similar to that of a clock (10:139–48). The circle signifies eternity, and the clock measures time, two seemingly contradictory movements that Dante succeeds in harmonizing in his poem.

Other elements of millennial thought find their way into the works of Dante. Toward the end of *Paradiso* the Florentine poet notes that only a few empty places for the blessed remain in the Empyrean, thus suggesting the proximity of the end of time (*Par.* 30: 130–32). By the same token, Dante recognizes the corruption of his age and looks forward expectantly to the future coming of a Christo-mimetic leader who will restore order in earthly affairs and usher in an age of peace. The identity of this redeemer figure is uncertain, for Dante refers to him cryptically as the "Greyhound" ("Veltro," *Inf.* 1: 100–111) and as the "Five Hundred, Ten and Five" ("cinquecento diece e cinque," *Purg.* 33: 34–45). Possible candidates include, among others, Can Grande della Scala, Uguccione della Faggiuola, an unidentified but charismatic pope, Dante himself, or even, in the distant future, Garibaldi, Victor Emmanuel II, and Mussolini. However that may be, Dante's poem has a decidedly prophetic tone: for example, in *Paradiso* we find a veiled reference to the coming of a great storm that will cleanse the earth of sinfulness and herald the advent of a new and prosperous age (*Par.* 27: 142–48).

The Book of Revelation gave Dante much of the apocalyptic imagery he uses in the *Divine Comedy,* a work that he fashioned as a new "scripture," disclosing the operation of divine justice in the universe. In the Earthly Paradise atop the Mountain of Purgatory, Dante the Pilgrim sees a series of allegorical tableaux, some features of which evoke the Apocalypse (*Purg.* 32: 109–60). Here, the poet describes the vicissitudes of the church, seen as a chariot drawn by a griffin, a symbol of Christ. Dante's allegory stretches from the time of the persecutions of the early church by the Roman emperors to his own day. The series of tableaux begins with the violent attack of the eagle (the Roman empire) on the chariot (the church), which is then beset by a ravenous fox, which figures the early heresies of the church. Once again the Roman eagle descends upon the chariot, but this time it does no harm, rather it leaves it adorned with much of its plumage. This would represent the so-called Donation of Constantine— that is, the emperor Constantine's giving of temporal riches and power to the church. In the next allegorical enactment, a dragon causes great damage to the chariot, symbolizing the threat that schismatic movements (either the Greek church or Islam) present to the unity of the church. With suddenly increased plumage the chariot begins to undergo a radical transformation into the ten-horned, seven-headed beast described in Revelation; this would represent the corruption of the church by increased temporal possessions. In the final tableau we witness the appearance of a giant (identified with Philip IV of France) who drags the chariot off into the forest and there repeatedly kisses and embraces a harlot, who is identified with the corrupt papacy. This striking image is brilliantly conveyed by the engraving of Gustave Doré (fig. 1.1). In all these elements we may observe how apocalyptic imagery is woven into a strong belief in a preordained temporal sequence that has direct relevance to historical events in Dante's age.

Although the Italian poet Francis Petrarch (1304–1374) is remembered as a pioneer and forerunner of Renaissance humanism, he also conceives

1.1 Gustave Doré, "The Giant and the Harlot" (*Purg.* 32), from Dante Alighieri, *The Vision of Purgatory and Paradise,* (London: Cassell, Petter, and Galpin, [1868])

of the passage of time in allegorical terms. Indeed, he was conscious of the manner in which we mark time and what this signifies for the human condition. One way in which he attempted to deal with these contingencies in an orderly manner displays the hierarchical structure of the universe. In the series of six *Trionfi,* Petrarch drew on the tradition of ancient Roman

triumphs and the medieval allegorical dream vision. These six poetic
works present the inevitable course of human events in the form of a series
of triumphal processions, beginning with the Triumph of Love (fig. 1.2).
Love is conquered by Chastity (fig. 1.3), Chastity (and every earthly crea-
ture) by Death (fig. 1.4). But Death in turn is subjugated by Fame (fig.
1.5), and Fame by Time itself (fig. 1.6). Finally, of course, Eternity con-
quers Time (fig. 1.7). In this progression we note the influence of millen-
nial/apocalyptic thinking on the man whom many critics have rightly
called the "first Humanist" or "first man of the Renaissance."

One particular representation (fig. 1.8) of the *Triumph of Death* is striking because it draws the reader into the action. The viewer unavoidably
becomes a follower of Death and becomes part of the procession, rather
than remaining a detached observer. This image suggests the Dance of
Death Ingmar Bergman draws at the end of *The Seventh Seal.* In that
film Death with scythe in hand leads all the characters—except Joseph's
family—in a dancing procession at the edge of the horizon. The photog-
raphy reduces the characters to dark, two-dimensional images against a
lighted background, suggesting the stark contrast found in famous apocalyptic woodcuts and engravings of the Renaissance. Characteristic of
works in the apocalyptic tradition, whether film, music, or literature, is
the interplay of striking visual imagery and evocative texts.

The *Liber Chronicarum,* known as the Nuremberg Chronicle, provided a
vivid example of world history from the creation to the end of the fifteenth
century. Published by Anton Koberger in Nuremberg in 1493, this chronicle, one of the most famous and beautiful products of early printing, is
illustrated with over two thousand woodcuts. The book began with full-
page woodcuts of the six days of creation (two of which are, ironically, in
the wrong order), carried the story up to the year of its publication, and
closed with a few blank pages on which the remainder of human history
might be recorded. Figure 1.9 shows the author of the Apocalypse, John
the Evangelist, seated together with his zoomorphic symbol, the eagle, and
composing his gospel. In the background we see the Virgin and Child,
representing the opening words of John's gospel, which speak of the Incarnation: "In the beginning was the Word, and the Word was with God,
and the Word was God." The image is suggestive of the "woman clothed
in the sun" in the Apocalypse. Other illustrations from the Nuremberg
Chronicle describe the Advent of the Antichrist (fig. 1.10) and the Last
Judgment (fig. 1.11). In the former we note, in particular, the Antichrist
who, inspired by a demon, preaches to the assembly and the archangel
who casts out demons from heaven. In the latter illustration we see Christ
in judgment and the souls of the elect on his right hand moving toward
heaven and those of the damned on his left hand being tormented by

1.2 The Triumph of Love, from *Li Sonetti Canzone e Trivmphi del Petrarca* . . . (Bernardino Stagnino, 1513)

IL SECONDO TRIOMPHO

DI MESSER FRANCESCO PETRARCA,
NEL QVALE SOTTO NOME DI
CASTITA, FA TRIOMPHARE
MADONNA LAVRA
D'AMORE.

TRIOMPHO DI CASTITA.

VANDO ad un gio
go & in un tem-
po quiui
Domita l'alterez=
za de gli Dei,
E de gli huomini ui
di al mendo diui;
I presi essempio de
lor stati rei,

Facendomi profitto l'altrui male
In consolar i casi & dolor miei:
Che s'io ueggio d'un'arco e d'uno strale
Phebo percosso, e'l giouane d'Abido;
L'un detto Dio, l'altr'huom puro mortale;
Et ueggio ad un lacciuol Giunone & Dido.

ABBIAMO
ueduto nel pre-
cedéte triompho
il sensitiuo appeti
to sotto nome d'a
more andar per
lo mondo de gli huomini triom-
phádo. Hora in questo, com'a prin
cipio habbiamo detto, uedremo
la ragione sotto nome di castita,
e quella sotto nome di MAdonna
LAVra d'esso appetito triomphare, E cosi, com'egli uolle le spoglie de suoi prigioni ne l'Isola di
Citherea al tempio di Venere con
sacrare, cosi uedremmo lei, che le
spoglie d'esso amore conseguire,
a Roma nel tempio di Pudicitia
consacrera. Luoghi ueramente cia

1.3 The Triumph of Chastity, from *Il Petrarca, con l'espositione d'Alessandro Vellu-tello* (Vinegia: Gabriel Giolito de Ferrari e Fratelli, 1550)

12

1.4 The Triumph of Death, from *Li Sonetti Canzone e Trivmphi del Petrarca* . . . (Bernardino Stagnino, 1513)

TRIOMPHO QVARTO DI

MESSER FRANCESCO PETRARCA,
NEL QVALE SI VEDE LA FAMA DELLE
NOSTRE OPERATIONI, MALGRADO
DELLA MORTE RESTAR NELLA
MEMORIA DE GLIHVOMINI.

DEL TRIOMPHO DI FAMA.
CAPITOLO PRIMO.

A p o r, che morte
triomphò nel uol
to,
Che di me spesso
triomphar solea;
Et fu del nostro mõ
do il suo sol tolto;
Partissi quella di=
spietata e rea

Pallida in uista, horribile e superba,
Che'l lume di beltate spento haueas;
Quando mirando intorno su per l'herba
Vidi da l'altra parte giunger quella,
Che trahe l'huom del sepolcro, e'n uita il serba.

A V E N D O
noi ueduto il sensi
tiuo appetito del
mondo, La ragio-
ne de l'appetito, Et
la morte de la ra-
gione triomphare, Hora nel pre-
sente quarto triompho, in tre cap.
distinto, uedremo, com'a principio dicemmo, la fama da infinita
moltitudine d'huomini famosi ac
compagnata, a la morte predomi-
nare, Onde'l Poeta dice, Che da-
poi che morte triomphò del bel
uolto di Madonna Laura per essa
ragione intesa, quale spesse uolte
di ui soleua triomphare, e del no-

1.5 The Triumph of Fame, from *Il Petrarca, con l'espositione d'Alessandro Vellutello* (Vinegia: Gabriel Giolito de Ferrari e Fratelli, 1550)

HAVENDO IL POETA NEL PRE-
cedente Trionfo dimoſtrato, che la fama dell'-
operationi de gli huomini, dopo la morte ancora reſta tra noi.

Hora in queſto del Tempo, moſtra quello finalmente
ogni memoria annichilare.

Il Trionfo del Tempo.

Arg. del
preſente
Trionfo.

D E L'AVREO albergo con l'aurora
inanzi
    Si ratto uſciua'l ſol cinto di raggi:
Che detto hareſti, e ſi corcò pur dianzi
Alzato un poco, come fanno i ſaggi,
Guardoſſi intorno; et a ſe ſteſſo diſſe,
Che penſi, homai connen, che piu cura haggi.
Ecco, s'un'huom famoſo in terra uiſſe,

SIamo al quinto ſtato dell'ar.-
ma peruenuti, nelquale il tem
po qui fra noi tutti i ſuoi ſucceſſi
& accidenti ultimamente ammor
za, E perche nella conſeguita fama de gli huomini piu difficultà
nien'a patire, il P. introduce'l ſo-
le, che ogni tempo partoriſce, e
termina, d'eſſi huomini, quaſi co
me di ſui emuli. dolerſi, dimoſtrà
do il ueloce corſo, che per eſſa lor
fama eſtinguere, li uide ripigliare
per

1.6 The Triumph of Time, from *Il Petrarca, con l'espositione di M. Alessandro Velvtello*
(Venetia: Gio Antonio Bertano, 1579)

1.7 The Triumph of Eternity, from *Li Sonetti Canzone e Trivmphi del Petrarca* . . . (Bernardino Stagnino, 1513)

TR IOMPHO TERZO DI MESSER

FRANCESCO PETRARCA, NELQVALE SOTTO
IL NOME DI MORTE, MOSTRA MADONNA
LAVRA CON RAGIONE ALL'APE
PETITO DOMINARE,

DEL TRIOMPHO DI MORTE,

CAPITOLO PRIMO.

VESTA leggia
dra e gloriosa don=
na;
Ch'è hoggi ignudo
spirto et poca terra
E fu gia di ualor al
ta colonna;
Tornaua con honor
da la sua guerra
Allegra, hauendo uinto il gran nemico,
Che con suo' inganni tutto'l mondo atterra,
Non con altr'arme, che col cor pudico,
E col bel uiso, e co pensieri schiui;
Col parlar saggio, e d'honestate amico.
Era miracol nouo a ueder quiui

E DVE prece-
denti triomphi
habbiamo uedu-
to prima AMO
RE del mondo,
e poi Madonna
Laura d'esso amor triomphare,
Hora nel primo Cap. diquesto uedremo il dominio de la Morte a
M Adonna LAVra predominz-
re, E nel secôdo, com'e sendo ella
nel sonno al Poe. uenuta; de l'un
con l'altro dolce ragionar insie-
me, Onde'l Poeta dice, che MA-
donna LA Vra tornaua con honor da la sua guerra conseguito
contro Amore, ilquale con suoi in
gegni e uarie persuasioni atterra

AA

1.8 The Triumph of Death, from *Il Petrarca, con l'espositione d'Alessandro Vellutello*
(Vinegia: Gabriel Giolito de Ferrari e Fratelli, 1550)

17

1.9 John the Evangelist, from Hartmann Schedel, *Liber Chronicarum* [Nuremberg Chronicle] (Nuremberg: Anton Koberger, 1493), p. 109v

demons. In the center foreground souls rise from their graves to go to the Valley of Jehosaphat for the Last Judgment.

Albrecht Dürer, the famous engraver and painter of Nuremberg, illustrated part of the Nuremberg Chronicle. Five years later, he published his magnificent series on the Apocalypse of St. John. In that series Dürer combines extraordinary technical skill, Gothic imagination, and the classical forms he'd discovered during his first trip to Italy. No image of the Apocalypse is more vivid than his "Four Horsemen," whose rushing figures became the backdrop for the conference logo (fig. 1.12). The logo attempts to capture the barely hidden turmoil of the end of time set against a title that expresses the frustration of waiting and the oxymoronic

1.10 The Advent of the Antichrist, from Hartmann Schedel, *Liber Chronicarum* [Nuremberg Chronicle] (Nuremberg: Anton Koberger, 1493), p. 262v

1.11 The Last Judgment, from Hartmann Schedel, *Liber Chronicarum* [Nuremberg Chronicle] (Nuremberg: Anton Koberger, 1493), p. 265v

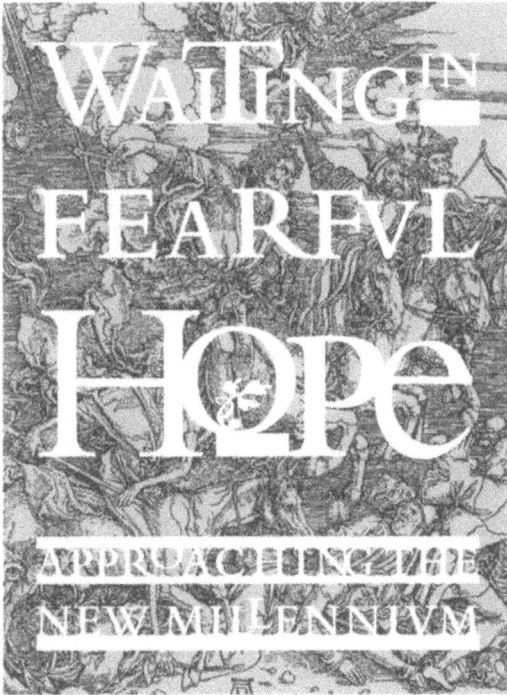

1.12 Conference logo, based on Albrecht Dürer's "The Four Horsemen of the Apocalypse," special design compliments of Lindsay, Stone and Briggs Advertising, Madison, Wisconsin

state of the human mind vacillating between hope and fear. Although the letters are jumbled, within the "O" of "Hope" a sign of new life blooms.

The end of any period of time, whether a century or a millennium, raises questions about both the past and the future. In our everpresent we set up signposts that recreate memories of the past and address present concerns for the future. The turn of the millennium is one of those artificial constructs that have no particular relation to cosmic time but have an amazingly strong resonance in Western society.

Note

1. "Arrows of Time," an exhibit presented in the Department of Special Collections in Memorial Library, contained a number of works that display a wide range of apocalyptic speculation. A selection of works by Dante and Petrarch illustrated the pervasiveness of this theme in the thirteenth and fourteenth centuries; other works in the exhibit illustrated a similar preoccupation with time and its end in the early modern period.

PART 1

APOCALYPTIC VISIONS
IN THE ANCIENT WORLD

John J. Collins

The Sense of an Ending
in Pre-Christian Judaism

The ominous message that the end is at hand was first proclaimed, to the
best of our knowledge, by the prophet Amos, outside the temple of Bethel
in northern Israel, in the eighth century B.C.E.[1] Amos did not envision the
end of the world. He spoke of the end of the kingdom of Israel, which
God was about to wipe off the face of the earth, with the assistance of the
Assyrian army. Amos conceived this destruction as divine intervention
in history—the Day of the Lord, which would be darkness and not light
(Amos 5:18–20). In the centuries that followed, other prophets used poetic
hyperbole to expand this notion into a day of cosmic judgment. An oracle
preserved in the Book of Isaiah predicts the fall of Babylon in cosmic
terms:

the day of the Lord comes, cruel, with wrath and fierce anger, to make the earth
a desolation and to destroy its sinners from it. For the stars of the heavens and
their constellations will not give their light; the sun will be dark at its rising and
the moon will not shed its light. . . . Therefore I will make the heavens tremble,
and the earth will be shaken out of its place, at the wrath of the Lord of hosts in
the day of his fierce anger. (Isa. 13:9–10, 13, RSV)

Here the prophet is still concerned with the destruction of a specific city,
Babylon, but his language evokes a catastrophe of cosmic proportions.

The notion of the end of this world has its origin in this cosmic imagery of Hebrew prophets in their oracles of destruction against specific places, including Jerusalem.

This imagery, however, underwent significant development in the period between the Babylonian exile (586–539 B.C.E.) and the rise of Christianity. In this chapter I will concentrate on two phases in this development.[2] The first is located in the latter part of the sixth and early fifth centuries B.C.E., at the time of the Jewish restoration in Jerusalem under the Persians, and is often called "proto-apocalyptic." The second occurs in the Hellenistic period and reaches its climax in the time of persecution under Antiochus IV Epiphanes (168–164 B.C.E.) and the Maccabean revolt. Further stages in the development of Jewish apocalypticism can be traced in the Dead Sea Scrolls[3] and in the apocalypses of the first century C.E., but the main characteristics of the phenomenon were already well developed in the Maccabean period.

Postexilic Prophecy

In the period that followed the Babylonian exile, we often find heightened cosmic imagery in prophetic oracles, such as Isaiah 24–27. Unfortunately, many of these are difficult to date, and we cannot be sure of the occasions that gave rise to them, or their original connotation. In the context of the canonical Hebrew scriptures, they take on the character of general eschatological predictions evoking an expectation of the end of history that may or may not be imminent. Later generations could interpret them in various ways, and could see their fulfillment in various historical circumstances.

Only in the period immediately after the exile can the emerging eschatological expectations of the later biblical period be set in historical and social context. In the year 518 B.C.E., the prophets Haggai and Zechariah were instrumental in motivating the returned exiles to complete the rebuilding of the temple. Haggai told the people that their lack of material prosperity was due to the fact that they had given higher priority to their own houses. When the building of the temple was finally undertaken, he told them to take courage: "For thus says the Lord of hosts: Once again, in a little while, I will shake the heavens and the earth and the sea and the dry land; and I will shake all the nations, so that the treasures of all nations shall come in, and I will fill this house with splendor, says the Lord of hosts" (Haggai 2:6–7). In the brief text of Haggai's oracles, there are signs that the promised transformation was delayed. Haggai is insistent: "From this day on I will bless you" (2:19). It is apparent, however, that the Jewish community did not experience a transformation of fortune such as Haggai had promised.

Haggai expected the rebuilding of the temple to be the catalyst for a new age. Not all his contemporaries shared his views. The final section of the Book of Isaiah (chaps. 56–66) preserves a skeptical view of the temple project: "Thus says the Lord: Heaven is my throne and the earth is my footstool; what is the house which you would build for me, and what is the place of my rest? All these things my hand has made, and so all these things are mine, says the Lord. But this is the man to whom I will look, he that is humble and contrite in spirit, and trembles at my word" (Isa. 66:1–2). The tremblers (ḥārēdîm) have given their name to apocalyptically oriented ultraorthodox Jews in modern Israel. They probably constituted a distinct group also in the Persian period.[4] They were no less eschatological in their outlook than the proponents of the rebuilding: "For behold, I create new heavens and a new earth" (Isa. 65:17), and "as the new heavens and the new earth, which I will make, shall remain before me, says the Lord; so shall your descendants and your name remain" (66:22).

In a seminal study published in 1975, Paul Hanson argued that Isaiah 56–66 represented the "Dawn of Apocalyptic."[5] He posited a sharp division in the postexilic community between the hierocratic party, represented by Haggai, Zechariah 1–8, and Ezekiel 40–48, whose piety focused upon the preservation of the sacred, and a visionary party, represented by Isaiah 56–66, that gave a higher priority to social and humanitarian concerns. In the categories of the sociologist Karl Mannheim, the hierocrats were ideological, while the visionaries were utopian.[6] While both sides used eschatological symbols, one side used them to shore up the existing power structures of the temple and priesthood, while the other side used them to undermine these structures. Hanson reconstructed the history of the visionary party, from the initial enthusiasm shown in Isaiah 60–62 to eventual disillusionment with history and the desperate hope for a new creation.

This ingenious reconstruction has been criticized on several grounds.[7] The twofold division of postexilic society is almost certainly too simple, and the unsympathetic portrayal of the hierocratic movement requires modification. The hierocrats must be credited with genuine religious motives, and not merely the desire to maintain the current power structures. Moreover, the "hierocratic" books of Zechariah and Ezekiel 40–48 are no less visionary than Isaiah 56–66 and may equally well be considered forerunners of apocalypticism.[8] Nonetheless, Hanson must be credited with an imaginative reconstruction of a situation where the hope for a new heaven and earth made sense: it arises from profound alienation and a sense of hopelessness in the present world. While it is certainly possible to find "millennial groups in power,"[9] we must remember that even those who wielded power in postexilic Judah experienced relative deprivation in the broader context of the Persian empire. Haggai and Zechariah may have been close to the center of power in Jerusalem, but they were very marginal figures in the broader Persian context. The significance of Hanson's work, however, lies in the light it sheds on the role of intra-community conflict in the rise of apocalypticism. Eschatological hope in the early postexilic period was not only prompted by the powerlessness of the Jewish people in the international context. It also arose from division and alienation within the Jewish community. Both factors, the international situation and internal division, continue to play a part in generating eschatological expectations throughout Jewish history.

The hope for a new heaven and a new earth (Isa. 65:17) is certainly relevant to the history of apocalypticism, but it should not be labeled "apocalyptic" without serious qualification. Formally, the last chapters of Isaiah are prophetic oracles, just like the oracles of the pre-exilic prophets. The content of the oracles also has much in common with older prophecy. The conditions of the new creation that are spelled out in Isaiah 65 are closer to the expectations of the prophets of old than to those of the later apocalyptic visionaries: "No more shall there be in it an infant that lives but a few days or an old person who does not live out a lifetime; for one who dies at a hundred years will be considered a youth, and one who falls short of a hundred will be considered accursed. They shall build houses and inhabit them; they shall plant vineyards and eat their fruit . . . for like the days of a tree shall the days of my people be" (Isa. 65:20–22). What is envisioned here is an earthly life such as we know, but longer and free of pain and care. This is a utopian hope that can properly be called eschatological. It is very different, however, from the hope that we will find in the apocalyptic literature of the Hellenistic age.

We may summarize the developments of the early postexilic period as follows. There is increased use of cosmic imagery to express the hope of a radical transformation of human affairs. In many cases, the expected judgment takes on a general character that cannot be tied specifically to any known historical events. We find eschatological hopes in various theological traditions, some oriented toward the temple cult, some critical of it. Eschatological hopes arise both to compensate for the powerlessness of Israel among the nations and to console groups that were alienated from the power structures within Jewish society. The hopes that we find in these late prophetic texts, however, are still oriented toward a restored earthly society in a way that has more in common with earlier prophets than with later visionaries.

It is not possible to show any social continuity between the visionaries of the Persian period and their Hellenistic successors.[10] The prophetic oracles were taken up into the canon of scripture, and so became part of the source material of the later visionaries, who picked up motifs like the creation of a new heaven and a new earth. The apocalypticism of the Hellenistic period, however, is a new phenomenon in many crucial respects.

The Hellenistic Period

The Books of Enoch

The oldest Jewish apocalypses are found in the *Book of Enoch,* a composite work that is fully preserved only in Ethiopic. Greek fragments of the work have long been known, and Aramaic fragments have been found among the Dead Sea Scrolls.[11] The book includes at least five distinct works: the Book of the Watchers (chaps. 1–36), the Similitudes (37–71), the Astronomical Book (72–82), the Book of Dreams (83–90), and the Epistle (91–105). Two smaller units, the Animal Apocalypse, in the Book of Dreams, and the Apocalypse of Weeks, in the Epistle, also stand out as distinct compositions. The Similitudes are not attested in the Dead Sea Scrolls and can be dated no earlier than the first century C.E. The other books, however, must be dated to the third or early second centuries B.C.E. on the basis of the paleography of the Dead Sea fragments and also on internal evidence.

While the prophets of old had spoken in their own names, and oracles such as Isaiah 24–27 probably circulated anonymously, the books of Enoch are pseudonymous, since they are ascribed to an antediluvian patriarch who cannot possibly have been their actual author. Pseudonymity henceforth is a trademark of Jewish apocalypses. Other pseudonymous authors include Daniel, Moses, Ezra, Baruch, and Abraham. There was a precedent for pseudonymity in Jewish tradition: the Book of Deuteronomy was ascribed to Moses, although it was promulgated by King Josiah in 621 B.C.E. and probably took its present form during the Babylonian exile. In the Hellenistic period the device was widespread, and it was not peculiar to oracles and apocalypses. We find new Psalms of David and Solomon, and a new wisdom book, written in Greek, also in the name of Solomon. Pseudonymity, then, was something of a literary fashion, and could serve different purposes in different contexts. In all cases, it presumably enhanced the authority of a work by giving it an aura of antiquity. While the authors of such works must have been aware of the fiction involved, their effectiveness depended on the credulity of the masses. This is not to say that the authors sought to deceive; they may have had a sophisticated understanding of their literary device. In general, the pseudonyms are appropriate to their material. Enoch is the authority on heavenly mysteries, since he had been taken up to heaven before the Flood (Gen. 5:24).

Solomon is the authority for wisdom teaching, and Moses for matters pertaining to the Law.

In the context of apocalyptic writing, pseudonymity offered some other advantages. It permitted the author to create an extended "prophecy" of history, most of which could be verified because it was written after the fact. The actual prophecy of future events was thereby rendered more credible. Such prophecies conveyed a sense that the course of history was predetermined, since events could be predicted so far in advance. They also allowed the readers to identify their own place in the unfolding drama and to see the events of their time in a cosmic perspective.

The Book of the Watchers serves as an introduction to 1 Enoch and is a work of major influence in Jewish apocalyptic tradition. There are two major themes in the Book of the Watchers: the story of the Watchers or fallen angels in 1 Enoch 6–11 and the story of Enoch's ascent to heaven and his journeys to the ends of the earth (chaps. 12–36). The story of the Watchers has its point of departure in Genesis 6, where the "sons of God" become enamored of the daughters of men and come down and beget giants. In 1 Enoch, this story is developed into an explanation of the spread of sin on earth. According to this explanation, sin results from the influence of supernatural, demonic forces on human behavior. The fallen angels impart to humanity forbidden knowledge: "and they taught them charms and spells and showed to them the cutting of roots and trees" (7:2); "and Azazel taught men to make swords and daggers and shields and breastplates, and he showed them the things after these, and the art of making them: bracelets, and ornaments and the art of making up the eyes and of beautifying the eyelids and the most precious and choice stones and all kinds of colored dyes. And the world was changed. And there was great impiety and much fornication, and they went astray, and all their ways became corrupt" (8:1–2). Later we are told that evil spirits came out of the flesh of the giants, to cause evil and sorrow on earth (15:8–16:1). This myth is developed in the Book of Jubilees, where Mastema, the chief of the spirits, gets permission from God for one-tenth of the spirits to remain on earth so that humanity can be corrupted and led astray (Jub. 10:7–11).

Paolo Sacchi has argued that the story of the Watchers is the kernel in which the essence of apocalypticism is contained and from which the whole tradition grows.[12] The underlying problem that all apocalyptic literature addresses is the problem of evil. The characteristic apocalyptic explanation lies in the appeal to supernatural, demonic forces. While we may demur from the view that this motif constitutes the essence of apocalypticism, there is no doubt that Sacchi has highlighted a very fundamental element in apocalyptic literature. The idea that evil should be traced to a supernatural source also figures prominently in the dualism of the two spirits in the Dead Sea Scrolls.

It should also be noted that the story of the Watchers very probably has an allegorical quality. The passage cited above from 1 Enoch 8 complains that "the world was changed." It is difficult not to read this passage as a loose allegory for the cultural crisis brought on by the advent of Hellenism, which entailed the spread of information and new ideas of morality that were often scandalous to traditional Jews. The story of the Watchers, then, is not only an etiology of the spread of wickedness before the Flood. It is also paradigmatic of the way the world was changed in the author's own time, the Hellenistic age.[13]

The author evidently perceived the change as negative, but his composition does not end in despair. Rather, he offers two resolutions of the crisis. First, the story of the Watchers ends with their imprisonment by the archangels; second, Enoch's tour reveals that the apparatus of judgment and retribution is already in place.

In 1 Enoch 11, the punishment of the Watchers is described. The angel Raphael is bidden:

Bind Azazel by his hands and his feet, and throw him into the darkness. And split open the desert which is in Dudael, and throw him there . . . and cover his face that he may not see light and that on the great day of judgment he may be hurled into the fire. And restore the earth, which the angels have ruined. (10:4–7)

Again, the angel Michael is told to bind *Shemihaza,* the other leader of the rebel angels, "for seventy generations under the hills of the earth until the day of their judgment and of their consummation, until the judgment which is for all eternity is accomplished" (10:12). The passage goes on to describe how the earth will be transformed and cleansed from corruption. The prospect of a final judgment provides the ultimate solution to the crisis of the Watchers. We do not, however, get the impression that this judgment is imminent. In the narrative context of the book, it is deferred for seventy generations, until the end of history.

The eschatology of the Book of the Watchers is filled out in the account of Enoch's journeys. Enoch is introduced in chapter 12 as a "scribe of righteousness" whom the Watchers ask to intercede for them. There follows an intriguing scene in which Enoch sits down "by the waters of Dan" and reads out the petition of the Watchers until he falls asleep. Then in his vision clouds call him, and the winds lift him up to heaven. We have no way of knowing whether the author was reporting his own visionary experience here, but recitation and the proximity of water are often associated with visions in many cultures. Enoch then describes his entry into the heavenly palace and the presence of God enthroned (chap. 14).[14] He is told to tell the Watchers that they should intercede for men, not the reverse, and that they should have remained spiritual and holy, living an eternal life, and not lain with women and begotten children. We see here that the fundamental antithesis in the Book of the Watchers is between heaven and earth, spirit and flesh (although the latter distinction should not be confused with the Greek distinction between body and soul). The ideal life is the holy, spiritual, eternal life in heaven, which the Watchers have forsaken. Enoch, in contrast, is a human being admitted to the heavenly court, whose elevation betokens a new possibility for human existence. The negative attitude toward sex and procreation should also be noted. A similar tendency toward asceticism is found in the Dead Sea Scrolls and in the Greek accounts of the Essene sect, some of whose members are said to have been celibate.

Enoch's actual tour begins in chapter 17 and takes him to the ends of the earth, accompanied by angelic guides. He sees the storehouses of the winds and the elements and the cornerstone of the earth and other such cosmological marvels. A major part of his revelations, however, concerns places of judgment. In chapters 18 and 19 he sees the prison of the stars and the host of heaven, where the Watchers also are kept until the great judgment day, and another form of this vision is repeated in chapter 21. In chapter 22 he sees chambers inside a mountain, where "the spirits of the souls of the dead" are kept to await judgment. This is the earliest attestation of the judgment of the dead in Jewish tradition. The following chapters go on to describe the place where God's throne will be set when he comes down to visit the earth for good (chap. 25), the tree of life whose fruit will be given to the chosen after the judgment (chap. 26), and the valley of judgment (chap. 27). In a later chapter (32) Enoch sees the tree of knowledge from which Adam and Eve ate.

The world that Enoch tours in chapters 17–36 is normally hidden from human sight, and is accessible here only by supernatural revelation. It is antithetical to the world defiled by the Watchers. The message of the book is that all is not as it seems on earth. In the hidden regions, all is in order. The places of judgment are prepared to ensure the triumph of justice, and provision has been made for retribution on an individual basis. Moreover, the holiness of the divine throne and its surroundings provides the greatest contrast to life on earth. The expectation of a future day of judgment is of basic importance in this book, but it is not the only, or even the primary, focus of the author's attention. Rather, the emphasis is on the present reality of everything that Enoch sees. While most human beings can only hope for access to the angelic world after death, the revelation of Enoch assures them that it is already there, waiting for them.

While the Book of the Watchers anticipates a day of judgment, its focus is on the contrast between the heavenly and the earthly, the hidden and the visible. Concern for chronology appears more clearly in two other apocalypses composed in the name of Enoch during the Maccabean era: the Apocalypse of Weeks and the Animal Apocalypse. The Apocalypse of Weeks divides history into ten "weeks" (presumably weeks of years), which will be followed after a new creation by "many weeks without number forever." The turning point of history comes in the seventh week, when there is an apostate generation, but at the end of the week "the chosen righteous from the eternal plant of righteous will be chosen, to whom will be given sevenfold teaching concerning his whole creation" (93:10). The eighth week will be that of the righteous, and "a sword will be given to it that the righteous judgment may be executed on those who do wrong" (93:12). If the apocalypse was written in the eighth generation, the sword would presumably be a reference to the Maccabean revolt. It is more likely that it was written in the seventh week, at the time of the emergence of the chosen righteous. It is clear, however, that this apocalypse envisages a militant role for the righteous in the last generations. In the ninth generation, the world will be written down for destruction, and in the tenth there will be an eternal judgment on the Watchers. Then the first heaven will vanish and pass away, and a new heaven will appear. The Apocalypse of Weeks is probably the first Jewish document to envision the end of the world in a literal sense.

This apocalypse is also noteworthy for literary reasons. The revelation takes the form of an extended prophecy, most of which is after the fact. The time of the author can be identified as the point of transition in the apocalypse, from the woeful present to the glorious future. The idea that history can be divided into a set number of periods is a very common idea in Jewish, and later Christian, apocalyptic literature. We find here a distinctively historically oriented apocalypse that is formally quite different from the otherworldly journeys of Enoch in the Book of the Watchers. It is closer to much of what we will find in the Book of Daniel. It conveys a sense that history is predetermined, and serves to legitimate the group called "the chosen righteous" (to which the author surely belonged) as playing a providential role in history.

The Animal Apocalypse is another extended prophecy after the fact, although the division into periods is less clearly defined. The apocalypse gets its name from its dominant literary device—the representation of human beings as animals. Adam is a white bull; the fallen angels are stars who have members like the members of horses and whose offspring are elephants and camels and asses; and so forth. In the postexilic period, Israel is subjected to the rule of seventy shepherds. The turning point of history comes when small lambs are born, and horns grow upon them, and a big horn grows on one of them. The lamb with the big horn is clearly Judas Maccabee, and the context is the Maccabean revolt. The outcome of the revolt, however, is not just described in historical terms. The Lord of the sheep comes down in anger, and a judgment scene unfolds. A big sword is given to the sheep (Israel) to kill the wild animals (Gentiles). The judgment extends not only to the seventy shepherds (the patron angels of the nations) but also to the Watchers of old. Here again the device of prophecy after the fact serves to locate the author and his group at the turning point of history. Like the Apocalypse of Weeks, this apocalypse is unabashed in its endorsement of violence as a means of executing justice. As in all of these Enochic writings, however, the final judgment is executed by God, and it affects all generations simultaneously. The sheep that had been destroyed are assembled at the judgment (90:33), which is a figurative way of giving expression to the resurrection of the dead.[15]

In the writings attributed to Enoch, then, we can trace a progression, from those that are more speculative in content to those that are more concerned with history.[16] The pseudonym of Enoch was presumably chosen because Enoch was pre-eminently qualified to disclose the mysteries of the heavenly world. Already in the Book of the Watchers, which shows no awareness of the Maccabean crisis, these mysteries include the judgment of the individual dead. There are indications in several of these apocalypses that the authors belonged to a group that considered itself to be chosen by God. In the heat of the Maccabean crisis, the interest shifts from the mysteries of the cosmos to those of history, and the sense of imminent expectation becomes greater. At least the Animal Apocalypse, and possibly the Apocalypse of Weeks, express outright support for the militant policies of the Maccabees.

The Book of Daniel

Another major witness to Jewish apocalypticism in the Hellenistic period is found in the biblical Book of Daniel. Like 1 Enoch, Daniel is a composite book.[17] Chapters 1–6 contain a collection of traditional tales, often legendary in character, about Daniel and his companions in the Babylonian exile. These tales were written down somewhere in the third or early second century B.C.E. Chapters 7–12 report the visions of Daniel, interpreted by an angel. Already in antiquity the neo-Platonist Porphyry showed that these visions did not come from the time of the Babylonian exile. They give an accurate report of history down to the time of Antiochus Epiphanes (to about 167 B.C.E.), but not beyond that point. Although Porphyry did not realize it, the account of the death of the king "between the sea and the holy mountain" (11:45) was inaccurate, and so we know that this prophecy was completed before the news of his death reached Jerusalem. (He died in Persia, late in 164 B.C.E.). The visions of Daniel are pseudonymous, just like those of Enoch.

The stories in Daniel 1–6 represent the tradition lying behind the apocalyptic visions in chapters 7–12. In the stories, Daniel is pre-eminently an interpreter of dreams and mysterious signs. Most notable for our purpose is the interpretation of Nebuchadnezzar's dream in chapter 2. The king refuses to tell his dream, so Daniel can only know it by divine revelation. The dream concerns a large statue composed of different metals: the head of gold, the chest and arms of silver, the middle and thighs of bronze, and the feet of iron mixed with clay. Daniel interprets the statue in terms of four kingdoms, in declining succession, beginning with Nebuchadnezzar as the head of gold. The use of metals to symbolize a declining sequence has a famous parallel in Hesiod's *Works and Days,* where the ages of humankind are represented as gold, silver, bronze, and iron. It is also paralleled in a Persian apocalypse, the Bahman Yasht. In Daniel 2, the end of the sequence is represented by a stone cut from a mountain that destroys the statue. The stone represents the kingdom of God, which will last forever. There is, however, no sense of imminent expectation. The coming of the kingdom of God is in the distant future from the viewpoint of Daniel and Nebuchadnezzar.[18]

The theme of four kingdoms is picked up again in Daniel's vision in chapter 7, but this time the imagery is very different. Daniel sees four beasts coming up out of the sea, one more fearsome than the other, and the fourth, which has ten horns plus an additional upstart one, is the most fearsome of all. Then he sees thrones set, and the Deity, in the form of an Ancient One, takes his seat and passes judgment on the beasts. Then "one like a son of man" (7:13) appears with an entourage of clouds and is presented before the Ancient One. He is given "dominion and glory and kingship" (7:14) that shall never be destroyed. An angel subsequently explains to Daniel that the four beasts are four kings, or kingdoms, and that "the Holy Ones of the Most High" will receive the kingdom (7:27). Finally the angel explains further that the little horn will attempt to change the times (i.e., the cultic calendar) and the law, and that "the people of the Holy Ones of the Most High" will receive the kingdom.

Chapter 7 of Daniel is arguably the most influential passage in Jewish apocalyptic literature, and it had a profound influence on the synoptic gospels, where Jesus is identified as the Son of Man. It is also a powerful vision in its own right. Like some prophetic passages such as Isaiah 24–27, it draws on the ancient imagery of the Canaanite combat myth, where Baal, rider of the clouds, triumphs over Yamm, the turbulent sea.[19] It is clear that the little horn represents Antiochus Epiphanes, and that the vision predicts his overthrow. But as Daniel sees it, the struggle is not just between Greeks and Jews. It is a re-enactment of the primordial struggle where the beasts of chaos rise from the sea in rebellion against the rightful God. The most striking aspect of the imagery is that there seem, *prima facie,* to be two divine figures. Elsewhere in the Hebrew Bible it is always YHWH, the God of Israel, who rides on the clouds; here he must be identified with the Ancient of Days.[20] This anomaly reflects the Canaanite background of the imagery. In the ancient myth, El is the Ancient One, while Baal is the rider of the clouds. In the Jewish context, the "one like a son of man" has often been taken as a symbol for Israel. He does indeed represent Israel in some sense, but such an interpretation misses the significance of the imagery. Elsewhere in Daniel, human figures in visions often represent angels (e.g., 10:5, 18; 12:5–6). "Holy Ones" nearly always represent angels both in Daniel and in the contemporary Jewish literature. In the context of Daniel, the one like a son of man is most satisfactorily identified as the archangel Michael, who is introduced as the "prince" of Israel in 10:21 and 12:1. The Holy Ones of the Most High are the angelic host, and Israel is the people of the Holy Ones. The vision predicts the exaltation of Israel, but the real conflict is between the angelic hosts and the infernal beasts.[21]

This reading of Daniel 7 is confirmed by the dialogue between Daniel and the angel Gabriel in chapter 10. There the angel explains that he is engaged in conflict with "the prince of Persia," and that shortly "the prince of Greece" will come, but he is aided in his struggle by "Michael, your prince." Conflicts between peoples on earth are understood as reflections of struggles between their patron angels. Chapter 11 continues with an extended "prophecy" of the history of the Hellenistic age. At the end Michael arises in victory (12:1), and the resurrection and judgment follow.

Much of the "prophecy" of Hellenistic history is focused on the persecution of the Jews by Antiochus Epiphanes in the Maccabean era. Unlike the Enochic apocalypses, however, Daniel evinces no support for the Maccabees. Instead, the heroes of the drama are the "wise" (*maśkîlîm*), who instruct the common people and some of whom are killed. Their instruction presumably corresponds to the understanding of events found in the Book of Daniel itself. They are not said to fight. At the resurrection, however, these wise teachers are said to shine like the brightness of the firmament and be like the stars forever and ever. Like the righteous in the Epistle of Enoch, they become companions to the host of heaven. They can afford to lose their lives in this world because they are promised a greater glory in the next. They cooperate with the angelic hosts in defeating the enemy, not by fighting but by keeping themselves pure. A very similar viewpoint is found in the Testament of Moses 9–10, where a man called

Taxo reacts to persecution by taking his sons into a cave and telling them to die rather than transgress the commandments of the Lord, "for if we do this and die, our blood will be avenged before the Lord and then shall his kingdom appear throughout all his creation . . . and God will exalt you and set you in heaven above the stars." The innocent righteous are, in effect, martyrs. By sacrificing their lives they ensure their eternal reward and hasten the coming of the kingdom of God.

Two other motifs in the Book of Daniel are especially important for the development of apocalypticism. In chapter 9, Daniel ponders Jeremiah's prophecy that Jerusalem would be desolate for seventy years (Jer. 25: 11–12; 29:10). The angel Gabriel appears to him and explains that the seventy years are really seventy weeks of years, or 490 years. This passage is important for several reasons. First, it shows the importance of biblical prophecy in apocalyptic thought. But the prophecies are not understood in their historical context. Rather, they are reinterpreted in light of the circumstances of the apocalyptic author. The logic behind this move is expressed very clearly in the commentary on Habakkuk from the Dead Sea Scrolls (column 7): "God told Habakkuk to write what was going to happen to the last generation, but he did not let him know the end of the age." Biblical prophecy is treated like the writing on the wall or Nebuchadnezzar's dream. It is a coded message, to be deciphered by the inspired interpreter. Second, Daniel 9 offers a calculation of the duration of the period from the end of the exile to the end of the persecution. The seventy weeks of years would be reinterpreted over and over again in early Christianity in an attempt to calculate the end of the world.[22]

The final motif in Daniel that influenced later apocalypticism is related to this. In chapter 12 we are told the exact number of days until the coming of "the end." This is in fact the only instance in an ancient Jewish apocalypse of an attempt to calculate the exact number of days. According to Daniel 8:14, the temple cult would be disrupted for two thousand three hundred evenings and mornings, or one thousand one hundred and fifty days. At the end of the book, however, we are given two further calculations:

From the time that the regular burnt offering is taken away and the abomination that makes desolate is set up, there shall be one thousand two hundred ninety days. Happy are those who persevere and attain the thousand three hundred thirty five days. (Dan. 12:11–12)

Two things about this latter passage are remarkable. First, we are given two different numbers side by side. Both may be regarded as approximations of three and a half years, but the fact that two different figures are given strongly suggests that the second calculation was added after the first number of days had passed. The phenomenon of recalculation is well known in later apocalyptic movements, such as the Millerite movement in nineteenth-century America.[23] Second, Daniel is not specific as to what will happen when the number of days has passed. Since the days are calculated from the time that the temple cult was disrupted, we might assume that the expected "end" is simply the restoration of that cult, and this would seem to be the implication in Daniel 8:14. But, according to 1 Maccabees 1:54 and 4:52–54, Judas purified the temple three years to the day after it had been polluted, so both numbers in chapter 12 point to a date after that restoration. At least the last date must have been added after the purification had taken place. Presumably, the author of Daniel did not think that the restoration under Judas was satisfactory. But there is probably more at stake. The numbers in Daniel 12 follow the prophecy of the victory of Michael and the resurrection of the dead. In Daniel 12:13 Daniel is told that he will rise from his rest at the end of days. The end, then, is the time when the archangel Michael intervenes and the resurrection takes place, roughly what later tradition would call the end of the world.[24]

A New Kind of Literature

One of the major modern debates about Jewish apocalypticism has concerned the origin of the phenomenon. The most influential schools of thought have seen it either as a child of prophecy (e.g., recently Hanson) or as a product of wisdom circles (Gerhard von Rad).[25] There is manifest influence of biblical prophecy in both Enoch and Daniel, especially in the crucial expectation of a day of judgment. It is also true that both Enoch and Daniel are depicted as wise men rather than as prophets. But this whole debate about the origins of apocalypticism is misplaced. In the books of Enoch and Daniel, we are dealing with a new phenomenon in the history of Judaism, which was very much a product of the way in which "the world was changed" by the impact of Hellenism on the Near East. The apocalyptic visionaries drew on materials from many sources: ancient myths, biblical prophecies, Greek and Persian traditions. But what they produced was a new kind of literature, which had its own coherence and should not be seen as a descendant or adaptation of something else.

Whether these books, and the later Jewish and Christian apocalypses, can be said to constitute a literary genre has also been debated. Von Rad argued that they were a "corpus permixtum," embracing various *Gattungen*.[26] In this he was thinking of the constituent forms that make up the apocalypses: visions, heavenly journeys, *ex eventu* (after the fact) prophecies, dialogues, and more. But on a higher level of abstraction, these books also have significant commonalities in form and content. The common elements of apocalypses are summed up in the following definition:

an apocalypse is a genre of revelatory literature with a narrative framework, in which a revelation is mediated by an otherworldly being to a human recipient, disclosing a transcendent reality which is both temporal, insofar as it envisages eschatological salvation, and spatial insofar as it involves another, supernatural world.[27]

Every individual apocalypse has some distinctive features, but this common core identifies a new macro-genre in the history of Jewish religious literature.

The definition of an apocalypse given above should be qualified in a few respects. As Sacchi especially has argued, this literature has a history and evolved over time.[28] In the early books of Enoch and Daniel, the genre is in an experimental stage. No subsequent otherworldly journey is quite like that of Enoch in the Book of the Watchers. Both the early Enoch books and Daniel incorporate material that would not be considered apocalyptic if taken on its own (e.g., the stories in Dan. 1–6). Further, it is important to recognize at least two distinct types of apocalypse: the otherworldly journey, typified by the Book of the Watchers, and the historically oriented apocalypses, such as the Apocalypse of Weeks or Daniel 7–12. The popular stereotypes of apocalypticism are dominated by the historical type, but the otherworldly journeys also have an illustrious history in mysticism and even in literature (culminating in Dante's *Divine Comedy*). Finally, while the functions of apocalypses may vary from one situation to another, one may say, on a fairly high level of abstraction, that they serve to exhort and console their addressees.[29] The books of Enoch and Daniel arise out of a cultural crisis precipitated by Hellenism and aggravated by the persecution of Antiochus Epiphanes. Regardless of their status within the Jewish community, the authors of these books surely felt relatively deprived because of the impact of foreign culture and religious persecution. The nature of the crises may vary, however, in other apocalyptic situations.

The definition given above concerns a literary genre. Implicit in that genre, however, is a world view that can also find expression in other ways.[30] The crucial elements of this world view are: (1) the prominence of supernatural beings, angels and demons, and their influence on human affairs and (2) the expectation of a final judgment not only of nations but of individual human beings. Both of these elements can be paralleled elsewhere in the Hellenistic world, but in Jewish tradition they constituted a new and distinctive world view, as can be seen if we contrast the Book of Enoch with the Deuteronomic tradition or with the roughly contemporary writings of Ben Sira or 1 Maccabees. Especially important was the belief in the judgment of the dead and the hope for a blessed immortality. Ancient Israel was exceptional in the ancient world in its reluctance to embrace such notions. In most of the Hebrew Bible, the hope of the individual was for long life, prosperity, and offspring, in the context of a prosperous nation. In the apocalyptic literature we still find hope for a glorious kingdom, but the hope of the individual is for eternal glory with the angels. Consequently the Enoch literature could look on sexual relations with women as a defiling activity, unworthy of spiritual beings, and the wise men of Daniel could let themselves be killed rather than compromise their convictions. The expectation of judgment after death brought with it a profound change of values and laid the foundation for one of the more significant shifts in spirituality in the Jewish tradition.

The Functions of Apocalyptic Literature and Ideas

Most scholars would probably agree with the view of David Hellholm that apocalypses are "intended for a group in crisis with the purpose of exhortation and/or consolation, by divine authority."[31] A few qualifications are in order, however. All the Jewish apocalypses can be said to have been written for a group in crisis, if only because the entire Jewish people can be said to have been in crisis for most of the period in question. The crises were of various kinds, ranging from the cognitive dissonance brought on by cultural change to outright persecution. Since the "group in crisis" can be either the whole Jewish people or a specific group with a specific problem, like the Qumran sect, the designation is of only limited help. The same may be said of the sociological theory of relative deprivation: almost everyone can feel deprived relative to someone or something.

Nonetheless, it is true that all the Jewish apocalypses are born out of a sense that the world is out of joint. The visionaries look to another world, either in the heavens or in the eschatological future, because this world is unsatisfactory. This sense of dissatisfaction is not necessarily an invariable aspect of apocalyptic expectations. In principle, it is possible to conceive of an apocalypticism of the powerful. Divine revelation can be used to buttress established authority, and one might look for its ultimate confirmation in the eschatological judgment. But in practice none of the Jewish apocalyptic writings of the Second Temple period reflects the viewpoint of established power. Typically, the appeal for divine intervention is necessitated because the world is believed to be in the grip of hostile powers.

Apocalypses surely were written to exhort and console. We should note, however, that exhortation and consolation are not the same thing, and that the nature of the exhortation is in no way implied in the apocalyptic form. Some of the apocalypses were militant: the Apocalypse of Weeks and the Animal Apocalypse may be understood to exhort their readers to support the Maccabean revolt. Others are quietistic: Daniel shows little enthusiasm for the Maccabees. In some apocalypses, the expectation of an "end" seems to neutralize any urge toward militant action: God will act in the proper time, the pious person should wait patiently.

The consolation of apocalyptic hope may have been considerable in the short term, but it was highly prone to disillusionment. It is in the nature of apocalyptic eschatology that it cannot be fully realized in this life. Even when the hopes could be realized in principle, they most often failed to materialize. The Jewish visionaries rarely ventured specific dates for their predictions and so avoided the pitfalls that beset such groups as the Millerites in modern times. Nonetheless the eventual rejection of the apocalypses by the rabbis bespeaks a sense of disillusionment that is readily understandable. The pathos of apocalyptic hope is nicely captured in the alleged exchange between Rabbi Akiba and R. Yoḥanan b. Torta at the time of the Bar Kochba revolt. When Akiba hailed Bar Kochba as "the king, the messiah," Yoḥanan allegedly replied: "Akiba, grass will grow between your cheekbones and he (the messiah) will not have come." Apocalyptic hope is invariably hope deferred. Nonetheless, it has persisted as a recurring feature of Western religion for over two thousand years. While it can never deliver on its promises, it continues to speak eloquently to the hearts of those who would otherwise have no hope at all.

Notes

1. See, however, Norman Cohn, *Cosmos, Chaos, and the World to Come: The Ancient Roots of Apocalyptic Faith* (New Haven: Yale University Press, 1993), who argues that the apocalyptic view of history ultimately derives from the teachings of Zoroaster, whom he dates to the second millennium B.C.E.

2. A longer form of this essay, extending the survey to the early second century C.E., can be found in "From Prophecy to Apocalypticism: The Expectation of the End," in J. J. Collins, Bernard McGinn, and Stephen J. Stein, eds., *The Encyclopedia of Apocalypticism,* vol. 1: *The Origins of Apocalypticism in Judaism and Christianity* (New York: Continuum, 1998). See also J. J. Collins, *The Apocalyptic Imagination,* (rev. ed. Grand Rapids: Eerdmans, 1998).

3. J. J. Collins, *Apocalypticism in the Dead Sea Scrolls* (London: Routledge, 1997).

4. Joseph Blenkinsopp, "A Jewish Sect of the Persian Period," *Catholic Biblical Quarterly* 52 (1990), 5–20.

5. Paul D. Hanson, *The Dawn of Apocalyptic* (Philadelphia: Fortress Press, 1975).

6. Karl Mannheim, *Ideology and Utopia* (New York: Harcourt, Brace and Co., 1936).

7. See especially Stephen L. Cook, *Prophecy and Apocalypticism: The Post-exilic Social Setting* (Minneapolis: Fortress Press, 1995).

8. Ibid.; Eibert J. C. Tigchelaar, *The Prophets of Old and the Day of the End* (Leiden: Brill, 1996).

9. Cook, *Prophecy and Apocalypticism*, 55.

10. The attempt of Otto Plöger (*Theocracy and Eschatology*, trans. Stanley Rudman [Richmond: John Knox Press, 1968]) to trace such continuity has been abandoned. See P. D. Hanson, "Apocalypticism," in *The Interpreter's Dictionary of the Bible, Supplement* (Nashville: Abingdon, 1976), 28–34.

11. J. T. Milik, *The Books of Enoch: The Aramaic Fragments of Qumran Cave 4* (Oxford: Clarendon Press, 1976).

12. Paolo Sacchi, *Jewish Apocalyptic and Its History* (Sheffield: Sheffield Academic Press, 1997); See also Gabriele Boccaccini, "Jewish Apocalyptic Tradition: The Contribution of Italian Scholarship," in J. J. Collins and J. H. Charlesworth, eds., *Mysteries and Revelations. Apocalyptic Studies since the Uppsala Colloquium* (Sheffield: Sheffield Academic Press, 1991), 33–50.

13. George W. Nickelsburg, "Apocalyptic and Myth in 1 Enoch 6–11," *Journal of Biblical Literature* 96 (1977), 383–89.

14. On Enoch's throne vision see Ithamar Gruenwald, *Apocalyptic and Merkavah Mysticism* (Leiden: Brill, 1980), 32–37; Martha Himmelfarb, *Ascent to Heaven in Jewish and Christian Apocalypses* (Oxford: Oxford University Press, 1993), 9–28.

15. On the Animal Apocalypse see further P. A. Tiller, *A Commentary on the Animal Apocalypse of 1 Enoch* (Atlanta: Scholars Press, 1993).

16. The progression within 1 Enoch is well shown by James C. VanderKam, *Enoch and the Growth of an Apocalyptic Tradition* (Washington: Catholic Biblical Association of America, 1984).

17. J. J. Collins, *Daniel*, Hermeneia (Minneapolis: Fortress, 1993), 24–38.

18. See further J. J. Collins, "Nebuchadnezzar and the Kingdom of God: Deferred Eschatology in the Jewish Diaspora," in idem, *Seers, Sibyls and Sages in Hellenistic-Roman Judaism* (Leiden: Brill, 1997), 131–37.

19. J. J. Collins, "Stirring Up the Great Sea: The Religio-Historical Background of Daniel 7," ibid., 139–55.

20. J. A. Emerton, "The Origin of the Son of Man Imagery," *Journal of Theological Studies* 9 (1958), 225–42.

21. See further Collins, *Daniel*, 274–324.

22. Ibid., 116–17.

23. Leon Festinger, Henry W. Riecken, and Stanley Schachter, *When Prophecy Fails: A Social and Psychological Study of a Modern Group That Predicted the Destruction of the World* (New York: Harper & Row, 1956), 12–23.

24. J. J. Collins, "The Meaning of the End in the Book of Daniel," in idem, *Seers, Sibyls and Sages*, 157–65.

25. Gerhard von Rad, *Theologie des Alten Testaments*, 4th ed. (Munich: Kaiser, 1965), 316–38.

26. Ibid., 330.

27. J. J. Collins, ed., *Apocalypse: The Morphology of a Genre*, Semeia 14 (Missoula: Scholars Press, 1979), 9.

28. Sacchi, *Jewish Apocalyptic and Its History.*

29. David Hellholm, "The Problem of Apocalyptic Genre and the Apocalypse of John," *Semeia* 36 (1986), 27; Adela Yarbro Collins, "Introduction: Early Christian Apocalypticism," ibid., 7.

30. J. J. Collins, "Genre, Ideology and Social Movements in Jewish Apocalyptism," in Collins and Charlesworth, *Mysteries and Revelations,* 11–32 (= Collins, *Seers, Sibyls and Sages,* 25–38).

31. Hellholm, "The Problem of Apocalyptic Genre," 27.

3 *Henry Chadwick*

Hope for the Millennium
in the Early Church
Expectation for This World?

As we all know, the millennium into which we shall soon be entering is the third period of a thousand years since the approximate year of the birth of Jesus of Nazareth. That is an occasion for contemplating the role of the Christians in transmitting what his name and authority have represented in our culture, imposing an indelible stamp upon our Western understanding of human nature and destiny. This is a related but of course distinct sense of the word *millennium* from that given to the idea in early Christian writings. It would be sad if our celebration were like the pagan commemoration in 248 C.E. of the millennium of the city of Rome, which was marked by bloody gladiatorial entertainments.

Our imminent millennium derives its reckoning from an era first proposed for convenient dating in the mid-sixth century during the reign of the emperor Justinian by a learned monk and canonist, Denys the Tiny, Dionysius Exiguus. Denys came from the Danube delta, a region where people then spoke both Greek and Latin. He settled in Rome, and, to promote friendly relations between Greek and Latin churches, he produced a Latin edition of Greek canon law with some Western rulings to form a single body of church rules. He later added rulings from bishops of Rome addressed to Western provinces. A man with a tidy mind, he wanted everyone to celebrate Easter on the same day, which incidentally entailed getting everyone to agree on the date of the spring equinox in

44

March, which was more difficult than you might think. In the preface to a table of dates for Easter, he remarked that he felt it wrong to use dating based on the era of Diocletian, the pagan persecuting emperor. He preferred to reckon dates from the date of Christ's incarnation. Probably he was four or five years out in his calculations, and contemporary critics thought his reckoning inaccurate. Debate continued in medieval times. Nevertheless, Denys' system had a great virtue in that it was not at all bad for reckoning dates Before Christ, B.C., as we may say. Denys did not foresee what would become of his new system, but in the next century we have an African chronicler who thought it good, and in the early 700s the learned Bede in Northumbria took Denys up and made the system popular and general in the West.

When people in the West realized that on Denys' system a millennium had passed since the birth of Christ, there was some measure of excited speculation about the end of the world. A famous paper by an eminent Byzantinist, Professor Alexander Vasiliev of the University of Wisconsin, expressed grave skepticism.[1] He was right as far as the Greek East is concerned, but not about the Latin West.

Denys' system was derived from ancient calculations of the age of the world. A number of ancient people supposed that the world—if not eternal, as some Platonic philosophers liked to claim—had been created by divine agency between five and six thousand years before their time. One can also meet the opinion that the world is of incalculable antiquity, but that human beings are more recent than the world they inhabit and began to make a mess of things about five or six thousand years previously. That was the view of John Chrysostom about 400 C.E.

A widespread belief coming into the Mediterranean world from Babylonia and Persia about the time of Alexander the Great declared that the course of things on this earth was under the deterministic control of seven planets—Sun, Moon, Mars, Jupiter, Mercury, Venus, Saturn—who gave their names to the days of the week. Were there seven ages to correspond to the number of planets?

In the Greek world the notion of successive ages of the world was well known from Hesiod's *Works and Days,* which associated the ages with metals: gold, silver, bronze, and iron. The golden age saw humanity free of toil, unaffected by old age, enjoying the effortless growth of fruits of the earth. In Hesiod human beings behave worse in each successive period, but between bronze and iron he inserted a heroic age. The stress on metals is reminiscent of Nebuchadnezzar's dream in the Book of Daniel of a statue with head of gold, breast and arms of silver, belly and thighs of brass, legs of iron, and feet of iron and clay mixed (Dan. 2:31–33.). These parts symbolize five successive world kingdoms. Ancient people also liked to distinguish stages of development as human beings pass from infancy to childhood, adolescence, youth, middle age (regarded in antiquity as a period of decline), and *senectitude.*

The analogy drawn by the apostle Paul in 1 Corinthians 13 between a child's apprehension in contrast with a grown-up understanding together with the concept of spiritual growth could suggest adapting the notion of six or seven succeeding ages to advances in the spiritual life. Augustine liked to trace seven stages in the human development of a grasp of divine realities.[2]

The first chapter of Genesis has creation in seven days, the seventh having no evening, being the eternal rest of God. The psalmist has a famous, indeed momentous, text: "A thousand years in thy sight are but as yesterday" (90:4, RSV). These words sparked off a great deal of what was to follow. In the second century before the Christian era, an orthodox Jew, alarmed by the pressures for assimilation in the Greek world and perturbed by lax observance of the Mosaic law, wrote a version of Genesis which decorated it with numerous more exact details. The name of his work was the Book of Jubilees; the calendar was of special concern to him. At one point (Jub. 4:29–30), he emphasizes the statement in Genesis that Adam died at the age of 930, and thereby fell short by seventy of the thousand years. So he fulfilled the saying, "In the day you eat of the tree of life you shall die." How so if he lived so long? The answer is in the Psalm: a day with God is a thousand years, and therefore his life fell significantly short of a full day of divine length.

So in the second epistle of Peter (3:8), where the author answers Christians disillusioned about the expectation of Christ's return and asking, "Where is the promise of his coming? Ever since the fathers fell asleep, all things have continued as they were from the beginning of creation," the author finds the reply in the same Psalm text notably expanded: "With the Lord one day is as a thousand years, and a thousand years as one day."

In 2 Thessalonians 3 the delay in the end of the world is explained by the operation of a mysterious unidentified power, which some early Christians interpreted (in the light perhaps of Rom. 13) to be the Roman empire. For the empire's magistrates and courts acted as a restraint on the total lawlessness which Antichrist or the man of sin was already trying to bring about. The final end is not to be expected before the man of sin in his opposition to all worship goes to the length of installing himself in the temple of God and proclaiming himself to be God. Here we notice a theme that will be recurrent in our story—namely, the central role of the temple at Jerusalem in the apocalyptic expectation. In fact, for the comprehension of ancient millennial hopes, the city of Jerusalem is far more important than the period of a thousand years.

The first generations of believers were, in the main, Jews who naturally shared in the excited expectations held by numerous devout Jews of the time. The Jewish historian Josephus knew of ancient traditions that inspired men had foretold the fall of the holy city;[3] according to an admittedly ambiguous oracle in the Hebrew scriptures, a person would emerge from Judaea to become ruler of all the inhabited world.[4] Among the people of the land, the hope of divine intervention in time and space took the form of urgent longing for political independence. Naturally there was disagreement whether the correct course was to make things easier for the messianic military commander by using force—in short, by making war on the Romans in occupation. The Zealots were men of violence determined to bring in a restored kingdom of God and Jewish independence.

The gospels suggest that Jesus himself put a distance between his cause and this political aspiration unrealizable without bloodshed. He did not identify himself with the Zealots, perhaps to their disappointment and disillusion. In the temptations in the dry, waterless Judean desert (Matt. 3:8–10; Luke 4:5–8), the earthly sovereignty associated with popular nationalistic hopes of world rule is explicitly set aside. This record in Matthew and Luke anticipates the saying in John's gospel (18:36), "My kingdom is not of this world," a declaration one would not expect to find in nationalistic texts about the messiah. Mark's gospel (12:35–37) has a dialogue in which Jesus seems to put a distance between himself and the title "son of David." From John (7:41–42) we hear of disputers arguing that, since ancient scripture prophesies a messiah coming from Bethlehem, someone coming from Galilee cannot be the expected leader.

Nevertheless, gospel texts presuppose an intimate link between the city of Jerusalem and the hope of the coming Anointed figure. Luke 19:11 tells us how, as on his journeyings Jesus came near the city, some of the disciples supposed the kingdom of God imminent. Evidently to their expectation the holy city was central. But among the words of Jesus about Jerusalem there are some of the darkest foreboding and gloom, such as the great lament "O Jerusalem, Jerusalem, . . . your house is forsaken" (Luke 13: 34–35). No less doom and gloom appears in the later Luke 19:41–44: "As Jesus came near the city, he wept over it. Would that even at this day you could recognize what makes for your peace. Your enemies will come and dash you to the ground. They will not leave one stone upon another, because you failed to discern the time of God's visitation and appraisal." The Christians were detached from the armed struggle.

Such utterances, however, are strikingly similar to language found in Josephus, who was utterly opposed to the Zealots and thought the war with Rome an act of extreme folly. In his account of the Jewish war, the judgment is repeatedly made that God condemned Jerusalem because of the pollutions in the city,[5] including sexual perversions[6] and mockery of prophets.[7] Transgressions blinded the minds of the city's defenders,[8] and God himself raised up the Romans to correct impiety.[9] Before the final torching of the temple, portents were seen—a comet, a star hanging over the city (an evident analogy to Matthew's infancy narrative), a cow giving birth to a lamb, and above all a voice declaring, "We are departing hence."

The sack and pollution of Jerusalem by Antiochus Epiphanes moved the author of the Book of Daniel to his famous chapter 9, with a long prayer of humility and penitence, beseeching the Lord to grant restoration to the holy city:

I prayed to the Lord my God and made confession, saying, "O Lord, the great and terrible God, who keepest covenant and steadfast love with those who love him and keep his commandments, we have sinned and done wrong and acted wickedly and rebelled, turning aside from thy commandments and ordinances. . . . O Lord, according to all thy righteous acts, let thy anger and thy wrath turn away from thy city Jerusalem, thy holy hill; because for our sins, and for the iniquities of our fathers, Jerusalem and thy people have become a byword among all who are round about us. Now therefore, O our God, hearken to the prayer of thy servant and to his supplications, and for thy own sake, O Lord, cause thy face to shine upon thy sanctuary, which is desolate. O my God, incline thy ear and hear; open thy eyes and behold our desolations, and the city which is called by thy name." (Dan. 9:4–5,16–18)

The angel Gabriel answers, that after a purgation of seventy weeks of years to put an end to sin, and to anoint a most holy place, there is to be a period of seven weeks between the promise to rebuild the city and the coming of an anointed prince. Then for sixty-two weeks it shall be built again. Yet after sixty-two weeks the anointed one is to be cut off:

While I was speaking and praying, confessing my sin and the sin of my people Israel, and presenting my supplication before the Lord my God for the holy hill of my God; while I was speaking in prayer, the man Gabriel, whom I had seen in the vision at the first, came to me in swift flight at the time of the evening sacrifice. He came and he said to me, "O Daniel, I have now come out to give you wisdom and understanding. At the beginning of your supplications a word went forth, and I have come to tell it to you, for you are greatly beloved; therefore consider the word and understand the vision.

Seventy weeks of years are decreed concerning your people and your holy city, to finish the transgression, to put an end to sin, and to atone for iniquity, to bring in everlasting righteousness, to seal both vision and prophet, and to anoint a most holy place. Know therefore and understand that from the going forth of the word to restore and build Jerusalem to the coming of an anointed one, a prince, there shall be seven weeks. Then for sixty-two weeks it shall be built again with squares and moat, but in a troubled time. And after the sixty-two weeks, an anointed one shall be cut off, and shall have nothing; and the people of the prince who is to come shall destroy the city and the sanctuary." (Dan. 9:20–26)

A Christian writer in the name of Barnabas wrote a little treatise in the form of a letter on the proper interpretation of the Hebrew scriptures in the community of the Church of Jesus the messiah. He wrote probably about the end of the first century of our era or in the first thirty years of the second. He was aware of Jews building on the prophecy of Daniel to affirm that the holy city was going to be restored and the temple rebuilt. It seems clear that Barnabas was writing before the Jewish revolt led by one entitled the Son of a Star, Bar Kochba, in 135 in the reign of the emperor Hadrian, a revolt with catastrophic consequences for the city and its inhabitants. Hadrian rebuilt the city in a different form, with a pagan name (Aelia Capitolina) and pagan temples. And no circumcised person might set foot inside it. (Perhaps by chance, Hadrian brought Golgotha inside the new city.)

Barnabas has an ambivalent reference to an earthly millennium. He declares that the world will last for six thousand years, for with the Lord one thousand years are one day. After that time the Son of God will abolish the time of the Lawless One, who is evidently Antichrist, a figure already current in Jewish apocalyptic. The Son of God is to judge the ungodly as prelude to a seventh millennium which belongs to this world of time and space. Beyond that there will be an eighth period of a thousand years; but that means another world than this. It is in view of the eighth age that Christians observe the eighth day in commemoration of Jesus' resurrection and ascension to heaven.[10]

In the letter to the churches of Galatia, Paul contrasts the Jerusalem which now is, in slavery with her children subject to the Law, with a Jerusalem which is above in heaven. The epistle to the Hebrews likewise speaks of the community of believers as citizens of a celestial city which belongs to the unseen world of the spirit. The epistle sees the nomadic life of the patriarchs as being that of exiles on this earth, seeking their true homeland in a heavenly country: "God prepared for them a city" (11:13–16). And now the community of authentic believers has come to Mount Zion and to the city of the living God, the heavenly Jerusalem: "Here we have no lasting city but seek one to come" (13:14).

So the apostolic generation was engaged in transmuting the traditional expectation into a vision of God's kingdom beyond time and space. Some biblical texts reinforced a spiritualizing interpretation of temple, ritual, circumcision, sabbath, and other themes characteristic of Judaism. The idea of a circumcision of the heart is already in Deuteronomy (30:6) and twice in the prophet Jeremiah (4:4; 9:25–26). Paul tells the Corinthians that for the believer the body is God's temple.[11] In Hebrews 6:20 the sacrifice to sum up all sacrifices is the self-offering of Jesus whereby as eternal high priest he has entered the celestial holy of holies. The house of God now is the community of the church (3:6), and the destiny of the wander-

ing people of God is a sabbath rest analogous to God's rest on the seventh
day of creation (4:9–10).

The Revelation granted to John in exile on the dry and beautiful island
of Patmos ends with an exalted vision of a new Jerusalem coming down
from heaven (21). The twelve gates of this city are inscribed with the
names of the twelve tribes of Israel, like Aaron's high priestly vestment in
Exodus (28:21; 39:14). The twelve foundations of the city wall carry the
names of the twelve apostles of the Lamb. Echoing the prophecy of Isaiah
54 about the rebuilt Jerusalem after the exile in Babylon, the city will be
adorned with precious stones. As in Isaiah 60 the gates of this city will
never be shut, and the wealth of Gentile peoples shall pour into it; moreover, as in Isaiah 60:17, light will come from God himself, not from sun
and moon.

One could hardly wish for a stronger affirmation of continuity between
new covenant and old. Nevertheless, this new Jerusalem of the Apocalypse
has no temple: the temple is the Lord God almighty and the Lamb. Those
with rights of citizenship are those whose names are written in the Lamb's
book of life, who have washed their robes and have free access to quench
their thirst from the water of life, a stream flowing from the throne of God
and of the Lamb.

The Apocalypse of John of Patmos restates in transformed language the
traditional Jewish hope of a restored Jerusalem, to which the messiah and
the twelve apostles are as central as the twelve tribes of Israel. Moreover,
before the new city descends from heaven, Satan is to be bound for a
thousand years and flung into a sealed pit. The martyrs are restored to
reign with Christ for a thousand years, sharing in his priestly and royal
authority. After the incarceration Satan's release sharply ends the interme-
diate age.

One of the major threats in ancient society was famine. Food shortages
were not at all uncommon. So among the dreams in apocalyptic hopes
was plentiful food and drink, with crops flowering without toil. At Hierapolis in Asia Minor in the mid-second century, Papias was an enthusiast
for an earthly millennium where and when feasting was effortless. Stress
on the fulfilling of ancient prophecy was naturally likely to encourage literalism in expectation of a restored Jerusalem, the hopes expressed in Isaiah
and Daniel being foundation texts. The second-century church also had
severe critics within its own ranks, and some on the edge of the community
thought the apostle Paul had intended a cleaner break with the Judaic
past. Among these was Marcion, for whom appeals to Old Testament
prophecy were irrelevant. Expectations of a rebuilt Jerusalem or some
celestial wonder city descending to this earth seemed too Judaic to be
congenial or acceptable to Gentile believers like himself. There were also

questions about the concept of resurrection. In antiquity it was a general axiom that individuality resides in the body rather than in the soul or spirit. Therefore, to believe in individual responsibility and in an individual's continuing life after death was easier on the assumption that hereafter the soul would be granted a physical, even if ethereal, vehicle for self-expression. Although Platonic philosophers like Celsus and Porphyry in the second and third centuries could be very scornful about Jewish and Christian belief in resurrection of the body, Porphyry allowed that the soul hereafter would not be wholly disembodied but needed a vehicle for itself.

In the middle years of the second century, Justin came from Samaritan territory at Nablus, moved probably through Asia Minor or Corinth, where he learned his way about Greek philosophy, and finally settled in Rome. On his travels he had been converted to Christianity during a seaside conversation with an old man who expounded the Hebrew prophets and with Aristotelian arguments destroyed his confidence in Plato. At Rome he became a free-lance lecturer on the Christian philosophy. On his way to Rome he met a well-instructed orthodox Jew called Trypho soon after the disastrous war led by Bar Kochba. He wrote up the discussion in a dialogue, most of which survives for us to read. Various traditions had come to him about the soul's destiny, but one of them was millennialist. He delights Trypho by affirming that in his view, shared by many other if not all Christians, Jerusalem would be rebuilt in fulfillment of prophecies in Ezekiel, Isaiah, and others.[12] He grants that there are orthodox believers who dissent from this as well as a number of heretics. A characteristic belief of gnostic followers of Valentine said that, at death, elect souls are immediately admitted to heaven and to the presence of God. Justin's new Jerusalem was not, however, to include only Jews. The redeemed people of God are drawn from many nations.[13] Justin knew the revelation given to John of Patmos, but never tells us just what he thought about it. His authority for a rebuilt Jerusalem is located in Old Testament prophecy.

A similar emphasis on earthly restoration is found in Irenaeus, bishop of Lyon in the Rhône valley about 180. Like many settlers in that river valley, he had come from Asia Minor and embodied the traditions of the churches there, notably Polycarp of Smyrna and Papias among others called "elders." For Irenaeus the essence of redemption is a restoration of what was God's will for Adam and Eve before the Fall which resulted from their youthful inexperience. Since the martyrs have suffered in this world, it should be in this world of time and space that their vindication takes place.[14] The Lord said, "Blessed are the meek for they shall inherit the earth" (Matt. 5:4). He also said: "I shall not drink of the fruit of the vine until that day when I drink it new with you in my Father's kingdom" (Matt. 26:29). Annual commemorations of the anniversaries of martyrdoms were usually marked by the consumption of large quantities of food and especially drink—to the considerable anxiety of bishops—but probably the celebrating people were sharing in the feast of the millennium to which the martyrs had already been admitted.

Both Justin and Irenaeus found a literal earthly millennium a very useful anti-gnostic assertion. In both, the thousand years are secondary to the restoration of the holy city in the holy land. Already in the second century believers were going to sacred places where the gospel history had been acted out. Pilgrimage and millennial hopes have often been akin in Christian history. One of the evidences for a Western concern soon after 1000 C.E. according to Tiny Denys' calendar is that a particularly massive party of Western pilgrims made their way to the holy land to commemorate the millennium of the Lord's passion and resurrection.

Montanist charismatic prophecy was millennialist in some forms, but strong regional patriotism led them to hold that the New Jerusalem consisted of their community in Phrygia. The North African Tertullian about 200 had faith in Montanist prophecies. But he understood prophecies about a restored Jerusalem to be an allegory of Christ and his church, yet not entirely beyond this world. Before we get to heaven, we may hope for a Jerusalem coming from heaven which will be the life of the church now. The "millennium" is a training period making the ordinary believer fit for heaven.

Frontal attack on literalism in millennial belief first comes with Origen in the third century. He thought materialist interpretation too close to Judaism. Could the savior of the world have intended to promise the disciples a kingdom feast of delicious wine? To Origen's deeply ascetic mind, a dream of earthly pleasures seemed altogether lacking in true religious aspiration. Moreover, whereas in heaven the saints neither marry nor are given in marriage, it is presumably the case that the literalists have to reckon with the reproductive process continuing during the earthly millennium. Origen thought that unfitting.

In the background of the debate lay an argument with learned rabbis out to prove that Jesus could not be the messiah of ancient prophecy, on the ground that the prophets predicted an earthly felicity which had not come either for or from Jesus. The expected signs of a messianic age seemed strikingly absent. Lions were not seen lying down with lambs, and above all the temple at Jerusalem remained a ruin. In Deuteronomy (15:6; 28:11–12), Moses looks forward to the Jews becoming rich and powerful, spreading over all the earth, and liquidating their enemies. Jesus had not brought this about, and the second- and third-century situation of the Jewish people, excluded from the holy city, is appalling. Origen insisted in reply that the inner meaning of scripture is spiritual, not material.[15] The authority of the apostle Paul (Gal. 4:24) suffices to vindicate allegory as a method; and in contrast to literal interpretation of the Law in which the inner meaning is veiled, believers are taught the meaning by the Holy Spirit (2 Cor. 3).

A hostile reaction to Origen was led in Egypt by a bishop named Nepos, who called his own book a refutation of allegorizers.[16] Although Nepos was highly respected as a church leader and a careful Bible student who wrote popular hymns, his book produced faction, secessions, and schisms. Pamphlets had appeared attacking the Old Testament as valueless, or indeed dismissing all written texts including the gospels and epistles. The bishop of Alexandria, Dionysius or Denys, visited the local church, courteously refuting the literalists, and going so far as to deny that the Apocalypse came from the same author as the Johannine gospel and epistles. He even mentioned past Christian commentators who had rejected the Revelation from their New Testament, declaring it to be so unintelligible as to make its title false.[17]

Millennial literalism did not die in the Greek East but remained the hope of isolated individuals rather than of the community as a whole. In the Latin West it lasted longer. But Jerome wrote his commentary on Daniel partly to scotch remnants of it, and rewrote a commentary on the Book of Revelation by a late third-century bishop of Pettau, Victorinus, which advocated a literal exegesis: "Let the fable of a thousand years die."[18]

In North Africa about 370 a schismatic Donatist theologian named Tyconius wrote a commentary (lost) on the Apocalypse of John, and an extant handbook of "Rules" for interpreting scripture which Augustine of Hippo found congenial. Tyconius, and Augustine after him, treat the six days of creation as the six thousand years of world history. But both authors understand the millennium to refer in the language of poetry and symbol to the life of the Spirit in the church now. For both writers numbers in scripture are regularly symbolic, and a thousand signifies a state of perfection.

A famous passage in Augustine's *City of God* (20.7)[19] tells us that, at one time in his life, he had held that the millennium would be terrestrial, but mature consideration convinced him that it must be purely spiritual. The millennium of John's Revelation is now when the signs of God's kingdom are present through word and sacrament, through healings and other divine gifts.

Augustine's final position remained hugely influential, at least on bookish Christians. His letter to a bishop of Salona (by Split in Dalmatia) deplored all endeavors to calculate when the end of the world might come. But we may surely take it for granted that many people after the bishop of Salona wondered if the obscurities of the Book of Revelation concealed clues to the consummation of history. Speculation about the time and identity of Antichrist was never likely to die easily. Formidable Arab attacks on Sicily and southern Italy in the ninth century provided apocalyptic writers with fertile soil. Avar attacks on Constantinople (which could be regarded in the Greek East as indeed the new Jerusalem) could stimulate similar apprehensions. Were not Gog and Magog the Huns? Or were they the Russians from the steppes?

On 29 May 1453 Constantinople fell to the Turks. A learned ecumenical patriarch interpreted the disaster as heralding the end of history. An American audience may like to know that by his calculation the world was going to end in the significant year 1492.[20]

Notes

1. Alexander A. Vasiliev, "Medieval Ideas of the End of the World: West and East," *Byzantion* 16 (1943), 462–502.

2. E.g., *De vera religione* 48–50.

3. *Bellum Judaicum* 4.388: ἦν γὰρ δή τις παλαιὸς λόγος ἀνδρῶν ἐνθέων τότε τὴν πόλιν ἁλώσεσθαι καὶ καταφλέξεσθαι τὸ ἁγιώτατον νόμῳ πολέμου. [For there was an ancient saying of inspired men that the city would be taken and the sanctuary burnt to the ground by right of war.]

4. Ibid., 6.311.

5. Ibid., 4.323.

6. Ibid., 4.562.

7. Ibid., 4.386.

8. Ibid., 5.343.

9. Ibid., 5.395 and 401 ff.

10. *The Epistle of Barnabas,* in *The Apostolic Fathers,* ed. and trans. Kirsopp Lake, (London: Heinemann, 1912; New York: Macmillan), vol. 1, 15.8,9.

11. 1 Cor. 3:16 even says that the church as such is the temple: οὐκ οἴδατε ὅτι ναὸς Θεοῦ ἐστε καὶ τὸ πνεῦμα τοῦ Θεοῦ οἰκεῖ ἐν ὑμῖν? [Do you not know that you are God's temple and that God's Spirit dwells within you?]

12. *Dialogue with Trypho* 80.5.

13. Ibid., 119.5.

14. *Adversus Haereses* 5.32.1.

15. *Contra Celsum* 7.18 ff.

16. Eusebius, *Historia Ecclesiastica* 7.24.

17. Ibid., 7.25.1.

18. "Cesset ergo mille annorum fabula" (*Patrologia Latina* 25.534a).

19. "Quae opinio esset utcumque tolerabilis, si aliquae deliciae spirituales in illo sabbato adfuturae sanctis per Domini praesentiam crederentur. Nam etiam nos hoc opinati fuimus aliquando. Sed cum eos qui tunc resurrexerint dicant inmoderatissimis carnalibus epulis vacaturos, in quibus cibus sit tantus ac potus ut non solum nullam modestiam teneant sed modum quoque ipsius incredulitatis excedant, nullo modo ista possunt nisi a carnalibus credi. Hi autem qui spirituales

sunt istos ista credentes chiliastas appellant Graeco vocabulo, quos verbum e verbo exprimentes nos possemus miliarios noncupare." [Now this opinion would be tolerable up to a certain point, if it were believed that in that sabbath some few spiritual delights were to fall to the lot of the saints through the presence of the Lord; I, too, was once of this opinion. But since they say that those who are to rise again will enjoy a holiday of most immoderate carnal feasts, in which food and drink will be so plentiful that not only will they observe no limits of moderation but will also exceed all bounds even of incredulity, all this can be believed only by the carnally minded. Those who are spiritually minded call those who believe these things, in Greek, chiliasts, and we may in Latin translate the term literally as "millenarians." *The City of God,* Loeb Classical Library, tr. William M. Green.]

20. Scholarios 4.511.

PART 2
THE APOCALYPTIC TRADITION FROM THE MIDDLE AGES TO THE TWENTIETH CENTURY

"To the Scandal of Men, Women Are Prophesying"
Female Seers of the High Middle Ages

In the Berlin fragment of Hildegard of Bingen's *Physica,* the learned abbess gives a brief survey of seven ages of world history in which she identifies her own time with the fifth age of "womanish lightness" begun with Emperor Henry IV. Because of this *muliebris levitas,* Hildegard goes on to say, "And therefore now women are prophesying to the scandal of men, and it will go on like this until the time when justice will arise after the destruction of some of the churches."[1] This was a true prophecy. Men were indeed scandalized at women prophesying, and women have continued to predict the last days from Hildegard's time until our own, if only because the era of justice still seems so far off. In what follows I would like to examine the origins of this unusual prophetic role for women in the Middle Ages through an investigation of the first two major apocalyptic prophetesses of the Middle Ages, Hildegard and Mechthild of Magdeburg.[2]

When we think of the origins of apocalyptic traditions in Judaism and Christianity, we call to mind a long line of male visionaries, writing under the aliases of renowned masculine archetypes, as in the apocalypses ascribed to Daniel, Enoch, and Ezra in the Hebrew Bible and Jewish apocrypha, or the apocalypses said to have been written by Peter, Paul, and Elijah among Christian writings. John the wandering prophet of early Christian Asia Minor, of course, wrote his own apocalypse; to this same John, by now confused with the evangelist, other apocalypses were also later assigned. The apocalyptic writers of early Christianity, scriptural commentators, poets, and theologians, were also all male. The same gender monotony pervades the history of apocalypticism in the Middle Ages up to the twelfth century. Visions of the end circulated under the names of Fathers of the church (such as Methodius, Ephrem, and Epiphanius), while sermons, treatises, and commentaries dealing with the last things were penned by male monastics like Beatus of Liébana, Ælfric of Eynsham, and Adso of Montier-en-Der.

Two major exceptions to this male dominance can be identified. The first is Jewish and Christian adoption of the Sibyl, the mysterious female seer of the Greco-Roman world. From as early as the second century B.C.E., Jews had produced sibylline verses containing an apologetic form of apocalypticism designed to demonstrate the superiority of their religion, often by predicting divine judgment to come against the practitioners of polytheistic perversity.[3] With its interest in political prophesy, especially hopes for world transformation under a coming divinely sent ruler, the sibylline literature spoke to both the positive and the negative side of apocalypticism. Early Christians soon began to revise these Jewish texts and produce verses of their own to highlight the seer's status as a pre-Christian member of the "City of God" through her predictions of Christ's coming and redemptive death. The Sibyl's reputation remained strong in the Middle Ages and Renaissance. A number of politico-apocalyptic prose sibylline texts, the most noted being the *Tiburtine Sibyl* and the *Erythraean Sibyl,* were popular in medieval Europe.[4] We must remember, however, that this literature, to the best of our knowledge, was written by men, albeit pseudonymously promulgated under the aegis of the female seer.

The other exception is the evidence regarding female prophetism in early Christianity. The revival of prophecy among the first Christians is a phenomenon that has recently received attention.[5] Given the way in which Christianity, initially at least, challenged traditional gender roles, it is not surprising that some women seem to have been recognized as prophetesses, though the subsequent tradition tended to erase their name and message.[6] The most significant, perhaps because they became test cases of the triumph of institutional over charismatic power, were the female seers, Maximilla and Priscilla, of the movement of the "New Prophecy," or Montanism.[7]

After the defeat of Montanism and its female prophets,[8] women's contribution to the history of apocalypticism virtually disappears for a millennium. There are, to be sure, occasional references to women among heretical or prophetic movements between c. 200 and 1150 C.E. The most notable example is that of the wandering prophetess named Thiota who received public chastisement in Mainz in 847 for predicting that the world would end that very year.[9] But these women were marginal and quickly suppressed. It is only in the twelfth century that women again began to take on the role of messengers of both millennial hopes for a better age to come and apocalyptic fears of approaching doom. Surprisingly, this new initiative was more successful than early Christian female prophetism, not only because it left extensive literary remains, but also because it was the beginning of a phenomenon that has continued down to the present day. No century since the twelfth has lacked for female seers of the end.

The significance of female apocalyptic prophecy in medieval and post-medieval Christianity deserves more attention than it has thus far received. Here we will examine only some aspects of its origins as portrayed in the lives and writings of Hildegard of Bingen and Mechthild of Magdeburg. Tempting as it is to consider later examples, such as the fourteenth-century Birgitta of Sweden,[10] as well fifteenth-century seers like Marie Robine and Joan of Arc,[11] Hildegard and Mechthild are the most interesting medieval examples of women prophets, not only for their initiating role, but also for the originality of their apocalypticism.

The sudden emergence of women as apocalyptic seers, or "live" sibyls, was part of the wider phenomenon of the medieval *Frauenbewegung*, the movement by which women took on a new series of roles in late medieval religious life. It was also tied to a crisis in reform that allowed women as the "weaker instrument" to be used by God to take up the work of moral and institutional *reformatio ecclesiae* in which men had failed. Finally, it was based upon a revival of the visionary authorization that had been claimed by the Jewish and Christian biblical apocalypticists.

Women writers were not unknown in ancient Christianity or in the early Middle Ages,[12] but it was only after 1200 that women began to play a major part in the production of the vernacular theology of the later Middle Ages.[13] The growing literacy of women, as well as female initiatives in the creation of new forms of religious life, were important factors in this process, but the dramatic increase in writing by religious women remains one of the most surprising aspects of the period.

Hildegard of Bingen represents a somewhat different case, since her theology is different from that of most of the thirteenth-and fourteenth-century women. In its Latin expression and salvation-historical emphasis, it can be seen as a variant of medieval monastic theology, one in which Hildegard's visions serve as the base text, a new visionary scripture, for her theological exegesis.[14] From the perspective of the history of apocalypticism, however, the act of writing, whether by a woman herself or by a male scribe recording her message, was dependent on the public role these women adopted as preachers of reform in the shadow of the Second Coming. In this respect Hildegard was the prototype of the female seers of the later Middle Ages.

Medieval apocalypticism has sometimes been seen as a countercultural phenomenon in which rootless prophets from the lower ranks of the clergy sought to overthrow the established powers of church and state in the name of a radical earthly utopia.[15] Though there were some of these, research over the past forty years has demonstrated that medieval apocalypticism was a much more complex phenomenon and that predictions about the imminent last times were more often used for institutional support than for subversive critique. Both *sacerdotium* and *imperium* employed apocalyptic rhetoric to encourage their supporters in the face of crisis, internal as well as external. Apocalypticism served more often as an ideology for the support of the threatened status quo, or else for correction and reform in the light of the approaching end, than as a call to revolution.

A number of leaders of the movement for church reform of the late eleventh and twelfth centuries employed traditional apocalyptic concepts in presenting their message. The papally directed movement to restore moral purity to the clergy and right order to the church that began in the last half of the eleventh century had a definite apocalyptic element. Pope Gregory VII, like his namesake Gregory the Great, argued that pious clerics needed to struggle more intensely for personal and institutional *reformatio* in the light of an end whose imminence was not less real for being primarily psychological rather than chronological.[16] Those who resisted his efforts for establishing true *libertas ecclesiae* by that very fact marked themselves out as agents and forerunners of Antichrist. As Gregory put it in one letter:

I have labored with all my power that Holy Church . . . might come again into her own splendor and might remain free, pure, and catholic. But because this was not pleasing to our ancient enemy, he stirred up his members against us to bring us to nought. . . . And no wonder! For the nearer the day of Antichrist approaches, the harder he fights to crush out the Christian faith.[17]

The pope's message was provided with a more detailed apocalyptic agenda by his twelfth-century followers, such as Rupert of Deutz and Gerhoh of Reichersberg.

The links between reform programs and beliefs about the end containing both optimistic and pessimistic elements were many throughout the later Middle Ages. This is not the place to try to survey them or to suggest ways to group the various strands.[18] What is clear, however, is that the failure of the Gregorian reform to bring about a truly purified church and holy clergy created possibilities for other ways of thinking about the relation between *reformatio* and the last days. It also opened up doors for new kinds of apocalyptic propagandists, including women.

In the Christian understanding of history, the last events, conceived of both as a possible period of earthly peace and perfection before the end (the prototype of which is the millennium of Revelation 20) and as the dreaded Doomsday, are always the work of God, not of humans. Efforts for reform, while they necessarily involve human cooperation, cannot be brought to fulfillment without divine grace. If popes, cardinals, bishops, and other clergy failed to effect lasting reform, perhaps it was time for God to step in and subdue human pride by showing that reform was his alone to accomplish, with other kinds of instruments. St. Paul himself had said, "God chose the lowly and despised of the world, and those who count for nothing, to reduce to nothing those who are something, so that no human being might boast before God" (1 Cor. 1:28–29, New American Bible).[19] This kind of failure of "those who are something" was increasingly evident from the middle of the twelfth century on, though it waxed and waned with the hopes and discouragements of each decade. Such disappointments had an important impact in making possible the new role of women as apocalyptic propagandists. The time was ripe for the "weaker sex" to take up the task of proclaiming the message of reform in the light of the approaching end-times. Both Hildegard and Mechthild, as well as most other female seers, appealed to this familiar topos of reversal of values to defend their status as prophets of things to come.[20]

It was not enough, however, for a woman to claim that God had chosen her weakness in which to reveal his divine strength. She also needed some form of authorization—a sign from heaven. This is why all late medieval female seers appealed to visions to confirm the truth of their message. Many male apocalyptic propagandists were also visionaries, though often, as in the case of Joachim of Fiore, these credentials were secondary to their claim of possession of *intelligentia spiritualis,* the charism that enabled them to interpret in more detailed and specific fashion the meaning of biblical prophecies about the end.[21]

The Bible, both the Old and the New Testaments, is filled with visions, and medieval Christians were convinced that such manifestations from God had not ceased with the apostolic church. In the Middle Ages, as C. J. Holdsworth once put it, "visions were one aspect of the continuing revelation of God."[22] The most common form of vision in the early Middle Ages was a one-time journey to the other world, a type of manifestation rarely given to women. In the twelfth century, however, a new type of vision began to appear, as Peter Dinzelbacher has shown.[23] These showings were characterized by repeatable manifestations of the supernatural realm, often through an encounter with a heavenly being, but also in the form of allegorical visualizations of complex scenes and dramas, as is the case with Hildegard and Mechthild. In the new type of vision, women took on an equal role with men from the start and within a century even surpassed them. By the fourteenth and fifteenth centuries, the majority of visionaries were women.[24] This new category of vision included a host of varieties, many of a private or personal nature directed toward achieving loving union with Christ. Others concerned revelations about the moral life and the fate of individuals. But there were also visions dealing with the last events, manifestations of "what must soon take place," as John's Apocalypse put it (Rev. 1:1). An investigation of the apocalypticism of Hildegard and Mechthild will show how each woman made use of visionary authority to guarantee the truth of her distinctive message about the end.

Hildegard of Bingen

Hildegard of Bingen's astonishing career as an apocalyptic prophetess has received considerable attention in recent years,[25] not only due to the carefully constructed *persona* that appears in her writings, but also because of the public preaching role she undertook. Not only was Hildegard a visionary, a prophet, and an apocalyptic reformer, but she also consciously reflected on each of these roles in her writings. It is impossible to separate the three, but a successive examination of her visionology, prophetology, and eschatology will reveal much about this first female apocalypticist.

Although Hildegard's visions fit within the broad typology mentioned above (at least to the extent that they are frequent and varied), their individuality challenges all standard categories. The abbess's visions were unusual with regard to both their mode of reception and the scope of their content. Most medieval descriptions of visions are consciously patterned on the three kinds of visions (corporeal, spiritual or imagistic, and intellectual) that Augustine laid out in book 12 of his *Literal Commentary on Genesis.*[26] Hildegard, however, emphasizes a psychological presentation of two ways in which she received showings from God—one *"in* the *umbra* [i.e., shadow, or reflection] of the living light," and the other *"of* the living light" itself. Her accounts of the former type, comprising the visions that formed the basis for her main trilogy of works,[27] as well as many of the manifestations recounted in her letters (some 390 of which survive),[28] are remarkable among medieval visionary recitals and have prompted modern speculation about whether or not Hildegard suffered from some form of epilepsy, though the abbess claimed this visionary state was constant, and I know of no medical account of someone who was continuously epileptic for over seventy years. This is how she described it in her famous letter to Guibert of Gembloux:

The brightness that I see is not spatial, yet it is far, far more lucent than a cloud that envelops the sun. I cannot contemplate height or length or breadth in it; and I call it "the reflection of the living brightness." As the sun, moon, and stars appear mirrored in water, so scripture, discourses, virtues, and works of humans are reflected radiant in this brightness.

This kind of manifestation, which Hildegard insisted she "always" saw, was explicitly nonecstatic—that is, it co-existed with her ordinary modes of consciousness. She clearly distinguished it from the infrequent experiences of another kind, of a more ecstatic nature, which she characterized as follows:

And in that same brightness I sometimes, not often, see another light, which I call the "living light" (*lux vivens*). When and how I see it, I cannot express; and at the time I do see it, all sadness and anguish are taken from me, so that I have the air of an innocent young girl and not of a little old woman.[29]

Hildegard claims to have received experiences of the former kind from the age of five. She does not say here when the second type, whose content is never imagistic or pictorial, began; but it seems to be associated with the influx of divine light and fire she received in 1141, described in the preface to the *Scivias*. This marked the turning point in her career from private visionary to public seer.

The second remarkable aspect of Hildegard's accounts of her visions is the variety of their content. Most of Hildegard's visions are not mystical, at least in the sense found in so many late medieval female mystics, whose personal, often erotic, contact with Jesus was the heart of their narratives. The showings contained in Hildegard's visionary trilogy of the *Scivias,* the *Liber Vite Meritorum* [*The Book of the Rewards of Life*], and the *Liber Divinorum Operum* [*Book of Divine Works*] can be described as primarily didactic and theological, in the sense that they are centered on the mysteries of the inner life of the Trinity and its manifestation in creation and salvation history. In these showings Hildegard sees images within her mind appearing in, or projected onto, the shadow, or reflection, of the living light, like a kind of inner movie screen. She often also hears a divine voice explaining the meaning of the image so that she can grasp it—*vidi–audivi–percepi* are essential terms describing this process.[30] Along with these general didactic visions, at least two other forms of visionary communication are found in her works. Fully a third of the abbess's letters contain references to visions.[31] While these are often of the didactic form, others are individually tailored to the needs of her correspondents—private revelations of approval or judgment, such as will later characterize Birgitta of Sweden's famous *Revelations*. Finally, a few accounts of truly mystical visions of the "living light" itself are presented, apparently because they play such an important role in the authorization of her message. Among these are the description of the "fiery light of exceeding brilliance" that penetrated her brain and heart, as mentioned in the preface to the *Scivias* and noted above.[32] An autobiographical passage preserved in the *Vita* written about her also reflects the claim that such visions guaranteed that Hildegard's message proceeded from the depths of divine inspiration, like that given to John the Theologian:

> Afterwards I saw a mystic and wondrous vision, such that all my womb was convulsed and my body's sensory powers were extinguished, because my knowledge was transmuted into another mode, as if I no longer knew myself. And from God's inspiration as it were drops of gentle rain splashed into the knowledge of my mind, just as the Holy Spirit permeated John the Evangelist when he sucked supremely deep revelation from the breast of Jesus. There his understanding was touched in such a way by holy divinity that he revealed hidden mysteries and works, when he said, "In the beginning was the Word." (John 1:1)[33]

Hildegard's bold claim that she speaks from within God himself, not from external study of the biblical text, was repeated in other places. In her *Explanatio Symboli S. Athanasii,* for example, she advises "the magistrates and doctors of the people" not to despise her "feminine form" for writing a comment on a sacred text precisely because she sees it and hears it, "not with the eyes and ears of the exterior person, but only in the interior knowledge of her soul."[34] Also, as Gillian Ahlgren points out, in her letters Hildegard often speaks in what can be called a "representative" mode—one in which she addresses her audience not merely as a reporter or instrument of God, but in the very voice of God, the *lux vivens* itself, as in Letter 52r: "These words do not come from a human being but from the Living Light. Let the one who hears see and believe where these words come from."[35]

Hildegard's unusual visions are rooted in a sophisticated theology of prophecy.[36] According to the abbess, prophecy has existed in one form or another throughout the whole course of salvation history. As she says in the *Liber Divinorum Operum:*

> Prophecy began in God's first work, that is, in Adam. It has shone from generation to generation through the different ages of humanity like a light through darkness and it will not cease its sound until the end of the world, sending forth voices of manifold meanings, imbued in divine mysteries with the Holy Spirit's inspiration.[37]

After Adam lost his natural gift of prophecy, or knowledge of the divine world, through the Fall, God continued to send prophets into the world as a reminder of the first man's original state and as a sign of the coming of the Son of God made man who "illustrates prophecy through himself."[38] The Blessed Virgin Mary and the apostles were all prophets, and the new prophecy of the time after the Incarnation, superior to the old prophecy in its spiritual character,[39] will never cease until the end of time. All prophets, like Hildegard herself, have a special connection with *umbra viventis lucis,*—that is, the Holy Spirit who "overshadowed" the Virgin at the Incarnation (Luke 1:35). In the *Liber Divinorum Operum,* Hildegard says that her *Scivias* "proceeded from this *umbra* through a woman's form."[40]

Hildegard thus presents herself as one of a long line of prophets, but there is one biblical seer she identifies with more than any other: John the Evangelist and author of the Apocalypse. John is Hildegard's model for both forms of her visions—namely, those seen in the *umbra viventis lucis,* and those which involve direct contract with the *lux vivens.* John the Evangelist, who sucked the depths of wisdom from the breast of Christ, proclaimed that God is imageless light (see John 1:9). Hildegard's identification of God as *lux vivens* is based on this text from the Johannine prologue, as well as on passages from Job, both prophets who were models of direct and inexpressible contact with God.[41] John the *theologus,* however, was also John the *propheta,* that is, the apocalypticist who received imaginative representations of heavenly mysteries and visions of the last days. The preface to the *Scivias,* as well as other texts in the abbess's trilogy, demonstrates that she saw her visionary accounts not so much as a commentary on John's Apocalypse (as would be the case for a male apocalyptic author), but rather as a *re-creation* of the Apocalypse—that is, a new divine revelation concerning what was soon to come to pass. All three of her major works contain warnings based on one of the final verses of the Apocalypse (Rev. 22:19) against tampering with the words of the book.[42]

Finally, we need to examine, if only briefly, Hildegard's message about the end, based on such an unusual mode of vision and theory of prophecy. The German nun's apocalypticism is distinctive and not easy to summarize, not only because of the symbolic form of her presentations, but also because of the development that seems to have taken place in her thought.[43] The major apocalyptic visions, especially *Scivias* 3.11 and *Liber Divinorum Operum* 3.5, lay out an original theory of the last days based on the scheme of five final ages or kingdoms symbolized by a fiery hound, a tawny lion, a pale horse, a black pig, and a gray wolf. Her own age, that of the fiery hound, is described as the *tempus muliebre,* the era of "womanish" weakness and clerical corruption that began with the evil ruler Henry IV.[44] It is precisely because the church has become "woman-ish" that God has chosen a woman to take up the task of prophet of the last days, as the abbess states in the passage from the *Physica* cited at the outset and as she implies throughout her letters.[45]

Like most male apocalyptic authorities, Hildegard proclaimed both hope and fear to her contemporaries in the light of the last days. While it is not always easy to correlate her epistolary warnings with the fivefold scenario of the end-time,[46] it is clear, as Kathryn Kerby-Fulton has shown, that Hildegard should be seen as a prophet of both clerical chastisement and clerical restoration.[47] The sins of the clergy during the *tempus mulie-bre,* especially simony, avarice, and incontinence, as well as the ominous growth of heresy, are signs of imminent woes to be unleashed upon clerics and the entire Christian world. Priests and religious will be attacked, dis-possessed, and cast out into the world to wander homeless. But this chas-tisement will bear the seeds of restoration, leading to a new form of the eremitical life and a revival of prophecy during the *tempus virile* of the lion.[48] The stinging rebuke to the clergy of Cologne written in the early 1160s, Hildegard's most popular prophecy in later centuries, is typical in also containing a promise of better things to come: "Then the dawn of justice will arise and your last days will be better than those before, and on account of your past trials, you will be devout, and you will shine like pure gold, and thus you will remain through long ages."[49]

During the time of the pale horse, however, the church will once again suffer from inner pollution and heathen attacks. Hildegard broke with the Gregorian concept of apocalyptic reform by claiming that both empire and papacy would wither away during this time,[50] though, paradoxically, in this era, too, troubles will eventually lead to restitution of the church's pristine discipline. The time of the black pig, therefore, will begin well, with justice flourishing and a renewal of prophecy,[51] but will soon decline as the growth of heresy presages the advent of Antichrist in the era of the wolf. The abbess's striking theology of Antichrist has been treated else-where and cannot be taken up here,[52] but it is important to note that she was also convinced that there would be a final post-Antichrist period of peace and justice for the church on earth before Christ's Second Coming.[53]

Hildegard of Bingen's prophetic apocalypticism was amazingly success-ful. The growing fame of the ancient Sibyl in the twelfth and thirteenth centuries, the crisis of male-dominated reform programs, and the new roles for women in medieval Christianity provide us with hints, but scarcely a complete explanation, regarding Hildegard's achievement: be-coming the first live *sibylla* in Christian history. In 1146 Bernard of Clairvaux expressed guarded encouragement for her revelations, and in 1148 his former pupil Pope Eugene III approved the abbess's publication of her visionary message at the Council of Trier. This allowed the abbess the opportunity to launch four unprecedented preaching campaigns in Germany between 1158 and 1170.[54] The basic thrust of this public preaching, as we can see from her letters, was the necessity for reform of clergy and church in the shadow of the Second Coming. While Hildegard's preaching made her some enemies, her message had great appeal for many. The Cistercians of Amorbach, for example, writing about 1160, adopt her own theology of the *lux vivens,* begging the abbess as the messenger of the Divine Light not to leave the world in darkness: "And so even though almost the whole world is overwhelmed by the darkness of error, that ray of ancient grace has shone in you, lest all the people perish."[55] It was Hildegard the prophet of the end, not Hildegard the theologian, poet, and musician, who was the object of reverence during her lifetime. In her, apocalyptic prophecy had come back to life in female form. This was to remain the case in the later Middle Ages, when the abbess's own rich writings faded from view, while the anthology of her apocalyptic texts put together by the Cistercian Gebeno of Eberbach under the title *Pentachronon* became widely popular.[56]

Mechthild of Madgeburg

Mechthild was born about thirty years after Hildegard's death and lived into the 1280s. Unlike the powerful abbess, Mechthild was a beguine, an adherent of the new urban style of the poor *vita apostolica.* She was less literate than Hildegard; she did not know Latin, and her book, *The Flowing Light of the Godhead,* was written down with the help of the Dominican Henry of Halle.[57] She was also less famous, though there is no doubt that the beguine was considered a public teacher both among her original circle of followers and by some of the mystical "Friends of God" in the fourteenth century. Mechthild is best known as a mystic. Her visions witness to the erotic mysticism associated with many of the female visionaries of the late Middle Ages. This is perhaps why the prophetic and apocalyptic aspects of her teaching have been rather neglected.[58] Although only a handful of the chapters in *The Flowing Light* deal with the last times, they express an apocalyptic vision that is among the most remarkable of the entire Middle Ages.[59]

Mechthild's descriptions illustrate the typical mode of vision found in most late medieval female mystics, featuring frequent transports to heaven and personal encounters with Christ, the Blessed Virgin, saints, and angels. Some of her showings, like Hildegard's, are elaborate scenarios that are given an allegorical and didactic interpretation. It is not so much in her visionary style, however, as in her self-presentation as a divine emissary whose book is of a quasi-scriptural weight that she reminds us of the abbess of Bingen.[60] She also uses the topos of the weak and lowly woman chosen by God to confound the mighty and proud clerics who have failed in their task of reforming the church. In the prologue to *The Flowing Light,* God himself announces the importance of the book:

One should receive this book eagerly, for it is God himself who speaks the words. This book I hereby send as a messenger to all religious people, both the bad and the good, for if the pillars fall [i.e., the prelates; see Gal. 2:9], the building cannot remain standing; and it signifies me alone and proclaims in praiseworthy fashion my inner life.[61]

Mechthild conceives of herself as conveying God's message, often quite a critical one, to the clergy.[62] In defending her teaching in *Flowing Light* 2.26, Mechthild notes that Divine Goodness of its very nature is diffusive, so it must flow down to the depths—that is, to the humble and lowly beguine. It is precisely because Mechthild is triply disadvantaged—she says, "Ah, Lord, if I were a *learned religious man"*—that God chose her as his instrument. God tells her that many a wise master of scripture is really a fool in his eyes and declares that "the unlearned mouth (*ungelehrte munt*) teaches the learned tongue through my Holy Spirit."[63] In *Flowing Light* 3.20 Mechthild claims that five prophetic figures of the Bible—Moses, David, Solomon, Jeremiah, and Daniel—illumine her book, but (as is true of Hildegard) among the biblical prophetic books it is the Apocalypse of John that the *Flowing Light* most resembles, not only because of its visions of the heavenly liturgy and dialogues with Christ and other celestial figures, but also because of its warnings about the imminent end.

Mechthild's apocalypticism, like Hildegard's, is part of a complex theology of salvation history, though she does not express this in terms of a doctrine of world ages. The beguine brings together in a new way the mystical and apocalyptic dimensions of Christianity. Her visionary contact with the heavenly world, as well as her growing identification with her precreated self in the eternal Trinity,[64] gave her a unique sense of participation in Christ's redemptive suffering and a perception of her own presentiality to the whole of the church's history down to the last times, as Hans Urs von Balthasar noted.[65] Like Hildegard, Mechthild is a reformist in the sense that she continually cries out against the evils of church and clergy in the light of the approaching end. Though she does have an optimistic outlook for the immediate future, she is far more pessimistic than Hildegard about the time before the end.

Mechthild's apocalypticism has been described as Joachite,[66] but this is true only in one sense: her expectation for a coming order of *viri spiritu-*

ales. The beguine was untouched by Joachim's teaching about an age of the Holy Spirit, or by his distinctive treatment of Antichrist. Essentially, there are three components to Mechthild's prophecy. The first act in her apocalyptic agenda is the appearance of the *viri spirituales,* or "spiritual men," who will reform the church through their preaching and penance. In this hope she taps into the tradition of Joachim, though her picture has rich details found nowhere else. The second act is the coming of Antichrist and his conflict with Enoch and Elijah. Here Mechthild retrieves a rich lode of apocryphal lore in a highly dramatic fashion. Finally, the third act is the resurrection of the body and the Last Judgment itself. Echoing through all three acts is the beguine's original sense of the sufferings of the last days as a form of second crucifixion of Christ, in which she desires to take a full share.[67] Since the Latin version of *The Flowing Light* combines these three aspects into a single treatise, I will present them in that fashion here.

Mechthild's apocalypticism was triggered by an event that many interpreted in apocalyptic terms, the "Scandal of the Eternal Gospel" of 1254–1257. The Franciscan Gerardo of Borgo San Donnino's *Introductorius in Aeternum Evangelium* (1254), announced the arrival of a Franciscan third age of the Holy Spirit in 1260. Its publication called forth attacks of the Paris Masters upon the friars as emissaries of Antichrist, as well as papal condemnation of the book and its author. Though the Franciscans were especially noted for their appropriation of Joachim's hopes for new orders of *viri spirituales,* the Dominicans were not immune to this form of apocalyptic expectation, as is shown by the joint Franciscan-Dominican encyclical of 1255.[68] Concern over these events is evident in Mechthild's note that it was the attack of "false masters" (*valschen meistern*) on her beloved Dominicans that prompted her to ask God if the friars would last until the end of the world. God assured her that this was indeed the case, but he went on to reveal the coming of even more important "men of a new religious life."[69]

The beguine's account of the appearance, dress, and lifestyle of this new order of "last brothers" (*jungesten bruodere*) is more explicit than any other description of the *viri spirituales* to be found in the thirteenth century. The details need not delay us here, but it is important to note that the coming order is devoted to poverty, preaching, and a wandering life— like a more potent form of the existing friars. Mechthild makes some startling claims for them, as when she says, "Their power is very great, for no bishop is their equal."[70] But the new religious order comes to reform the church, not to supersede it. Their mysterious "first master," described as "the son of the King of Rome; his name before God in German is 'Alleliua,'" receives his power and rule of life directly from the pope.[71] The order is described as illuminating and instructing the church for thirty years before the coming of Antichrist.

A second, shorter, and later treatment of these *viri spirituales* is far more critical of the present clergy and closer to the tone of Hildegard's attacks on priestly perfidy. It begins by bewailing how "the Crown of Christianity"—that is, the clergy in general—has become a scandal, and goes on to condemn the "Crown of Holy Priesthood," presumably the bishops, in even stronger terms. In a manner that foreshadows the tone and form of address to be used by Birgitta of Sweden a century later, Mechthild reports Christ's address to the pope himself:

> I shall touch the pope of Rome in his heart with great misery, and in this misery I shall tell him reproachfully that my shepherds of Jerusalem have become murderers and wolves. . . . He who does not know the path to hell, let him look at the corrupt clergy. . . . This is why it is necessary that the last brothers come.
> For when the cloak is old,
> So it is also cold.[72]

What is more, Christ warns the pope that the reason his predecessors did not enjoy long lives is that they did not bring about the secret intentions of his will by giving his Bride, *heligen cristanheit,* a new cloak.[73]

After thirty years of the reformation of the church through the preaching of the new order, however, the pessimistic second stage of Mechthild's apocalyptic scenario begins as Antichrist is revealed to the world. Unlike traditional accounts, Mechthild's says nothing about Antichrist's birth and upbringing, though she does echo Adso of Montier-en-Der and others in her references to the Last Enemy's appeal to both the worldly powers and the clergy.[74] Like Joachim of Fiore, she views the *viri spirituales* as the first line of defense against Antichrist's lies, bribes, and deceptions. Through their prayer and example, "many Jews and some wise heathens shall receive holy baptism," and many Christians will resist Antichrist unto martyrdom.[75] Enraged at this, Antichrist will seize the "Holy Preacher" (presumably the master of the new order) and have him impaled on a iron stake to suffer for all the world to see.

Mechthild's account of Antichrist focuses on detailed descriptions of the tortures and slaughters he will inflict on the faithful, both the *viri spirituales* and all those who will be empowered by their example to resist him. This is reminiscent of a popular theme in German apocalypticism, as evidenced by the illustrations of Antichrist's persecutions found in Herrad of Landsberg's version of Adso's *Epistola de Antichristo* from the *Hortus Deliciarum.*[76] As the *viri spirituales* falter in the face of Antichrist's attack, God will call in the second line of defense, Enoch and Elijah, to succor the faithful.

The identification of Enoch and Elijah with the "Two Witnesses" of Revelation 11:3–13 was ancient, going back to the second century.[77] A rich variety of apocryphal literature, both patristic and medieval, testifies to their importance in the history of Christian apocalypticism.[78] It is difficult to know how much of this material may have been available to Mechthild, but her presentation of the Two Witnesses has details found nowhere else.[79] According to the beguine, these two Old Testament friends of God, who had never died, live in the earthly paradise somewhere in India,[80] feeding on the food meant for Adam (with the exception of the fruit of the forbidden tree).[81] When asked to return to the world, they are at first fearful, but an angel accompanies them and they are restored to "earthly appearance" (*irdenschen schin*) to become fully mortal again.[82] The Two Witnesses first come to the aid of the *viri spirituales,* leading them out of their refuge in the woods to preach against Antichrist and convert "noble men and beautiful women" who were misled by the great deceiver. But since Antichrist "has been given supreme power on earth," he summons those who have abandoned him, slaughtering all who reject him with gruesome public tortures. The "last brothers" are hung up in trees by their uncut "Nazarite" hair and left to expire.[83] Even Enoch and Elijah, the final line of defense, cannot stand before Antichrist's power.

Some early traditions, like that found in the Old High German poem *Muspilli,* as well as those from Slavic lands, had emphasized the role of Elijah in the final struggle with Antichrist. Mechthild, however, gives pride of place to Enoch as "the last person to cultivate the spiritual life." First, Elijah is crucified because "he constantly spoke of the cross," hanging in pain for three days and nights until God the Father receives his soul. Antichrist keeps Enoch alive for a time, hoping to convert him and profit from his heavenly wisdom; but so many are being turned away from Antichrist by this last just man that he finally attacks Enoch "with fierce words." Mechthild's account contains four speeches in the form of dramas resembling the twelfth-century *Ludus de Antichristo* and later Last Judgment plays.[84] Enoch's first speech proclaims Antichrist as the "scourge of the world"; Antichrist responds by commanding the prophet to be silenced by having burning pitch poured down his throat and then killed. Enoch makes an internal speech "in his pure heart," praising God and praying for the remaining faithful.[85] The drama closes with God's response praising Enoch, which Mechthild says she "read as it is written in the Holy Trinity."[86]

It is peculiar that there is no description of Antichrist's destruction, but

the Latin version's attempt to give a full picture of Mechthild's apocalypticism then moves on to its final act, a vision of Christ on "the last day"
with the scales of judgment in his hand.[87] On the right pan of the scales
Mechthild sees all Christ's "holy toil and innocent suffering," as well as all
human suffering for the love of Christ, including the various kinds of innocent blood that will be counted along with Christ's blood against the
weight of sin on the other side of the scales. This description is followed
by a dialogue between the beguine and Christ that at first glance may
seem out of place, but that actually reflects the most personal aspect of
Mechthild's apocalyptic theology. Mechthild prays to "Mighty Divine
Love" that she might live until the last day to continue to suffer for Jesus
and to praise him.[88] In other words, she desires to join with Christ as far
as possible in the suffering that will overcome the weight of sin on the last
day.[89] In a remarkable speech Christ assures her that because her "desire"
(*gerunge*) is eternal, she will remain until (or perhaps better, really now *is*)
at the end of time:

Your longing shall live. It cannot die because it is eternal. If it keeps striving for
my sake until the last day, then soul and body shall be reunited. When I put them
together again, she shall praise me without end. Also, she has served me since the
very beginning, for you wanted to exist from the time of Adam until now for love
of me, just as you wanted to experience all human suffering and serve in all human
labor for love of me. I say further: Your being shall remain until the end of
humanity.[90]

Mechthild's vision of the history of salvation fittingly closes with one of
the most beautiful passages in *The Flowing Light,* the address of the soul
welcoming back the body in which it participated in redemption through
suffering.[91]

It is remarkable that women like Hildegard of Bingen and Mechthild of
Magdeburg were able to take such public roles as apocalyptic prophetesses
in the twelfth and thirteenth centuries. More remarkable still is the originality of their message. Perhaps it was precisely because they were not
official interpreters of scripture that they could employ their visionary
contact with scripture's divine source to present their messages about the
need to reform in light of the approaching end.[92] With the exception of
Joachim of Fiore, it is difficult to think of any other late medieval apocalypticist who created such striking visions of the end. This fact alone deserves the attention of all who await the new millennium, whether in literal
or spiritual fashion.

Notes

1. Heinrich Schipperges, "Ein unveröffentliches Hildegard-Fragment (Codex Berlin. Lat. Qu. 674)," *Sudhoffs Archiv für Geschichte der Medizin und der Naturwissenschaften* 40 (1956), 71: "et ideo nunc ad scandalum virorum mulieres prophetant, quod ita procedet usque ad tempus illud, cum post destructionem quarumdam ecclesiarum iusticia exsurget." There is a similar passage in Hildegard's *Scivias* 3.11.18. The ages, as given here, seem to be the abbess's own enumeration: (1) from Adam until the generation of the giants; (2) from thence to the Flood; (3) to Abraham's circumcision; (4) from Moses to Christ; (5) from Christ to the "womanish time"; (6) from then to the overthrow of Antichrist; and (7) the rest in heaven already enjoyed by Christ and the saints. *Scivias* 3.11.23–24 implies a different sevenfold enumeration.

2. A case could be made that Hildegard's younger contemporary, Elisabeth of Schönau, should also be considered to be a female prophet, especially given her controversial prediction (c. 1154) that the world would end in a year when Good Friday coincided with the Feast of the Annunciation (which did happen in 1155). The public criticism that Elisabeth received for this vision, as well as the subsequent arrival of her brother Ekbert to manage her public *persona* in 1155, seems to have moved her away from forms of prophecy that included an apocalyptic scenario. On Elisabeth as prophet, see Anne L. Clark, *Elisabeth of Schönau. A Twelfth-Century Visionary* (Philadelphia: University of Pennsylvania Press, 1992), 14–15, 69–74, 91–100, 132–34. For Elisabeth's apocalyptic prediction, see F. W. E. Roth, "Aus einer Handschrift der Schriften der heiligen Elisabeth von Schönau," *Neues Archiv der Gesellschaft für ältere deutsche Geschichtskunde* 36 (1911), 220.

3. On the pagan sibyls, see H. W. Parke, *Sibyls and Sibylline Prophecy in Classical Antiquity,* edited by B. C. McGing (London: Routledge, 1988). For the Jewish sibyls, see J. J. Collins, *The Sibylline Oracles of Egyptian Judaism* (Missoula: Scholars Press, 1972). For a translation of the Jewish and Christian *sibyllina,* see J. J. Collins, "Sibylline Oracles (Second Century B.C.–Seventh Century A.D.)," in James H. Charlesworth, ed., *The Old Testament Pseudepigrapha. Apocalyptic Literature and Testaments* (Garden City: Doubleday, 1983), 317–472.

4. See Bernard McGinn, *"Teste David cum Sibylla:* The Significance of the Sibylline Tradition in the Middle Ages," in Julius Kirshner and Suzanne F. Wemple, eds., *Women of the Medieval World: Essays in Honor of John H. Mundy* (Oxford: Blackwell, 1985), 7–35.

5. See David Aune, *Prophecy in Early Christianity and the Ancient Mediterranean World* (Grand Rapids: Eerdmans, 1983).

6. Anna is described as a "prophetess" (*prophêtis*) in Luke 2:36. Eusebius, *Historia Ecclesiastica* 3:31 records the tradition that the apostle Philip and his four prophetess daughters were buried at Hierapolis in Asia Minor.

7. The basic source is *Historia Ecclesiastica* 5:14–19. The most recent treatment is Christine Trevett, *Montanism, Gender, Authority, and the New Prophecy* (Cambridge: Cambridge University Press, 1996).

8. See James L. Ash, Jr., "The Decline of Ecstatic Prophecy in the Early Church," *Theological Studies* 37 (1976), 227–52.

9. See the *Annales Fuldenses* in Monumenta Germanie Historica: Scriptores 1:365, [hereafter MGH.SS], as well as Jeffrey Burton Russell, *Dissent and Reform in the Early Middle Ages* (Berkeley: University of California Press, 1965), 107–8.

10. See the recent study of Claire L. Sahlin, "Gender and Prophetic Authority in Birgitta of Sweden's *Revelations*," in Jane Chance, ed., *Gender and Text in the Later Middle Ages* (Gainesville: University Press of Florida, 1996), 69–95.

11. There are useful remarks on these female prophets in André Vauchez, *The Laity in the Middle Ages: Religious Beliefs and Devotional Practices* (Notre Dame: University of Notre Dame Press, 1993), 219–29, 255–64. For a recent comparison of Hildegard and Joan of Arc, see Anita Obermeier and Rebecca Kennison, "The Privileging of *Visio* over *Vox* in the Mystical Experiences of Hildegard of Bingen and Joan of Arc," *Mystics Quarterly* 23 (1997), 137–67.

12. For a bibliographical survey, see Andrew Kodel, *Matrology: A Bibliography of Writings by Christian Women from the First to the Fifteenth Centuries* (New York: Continuum, 1995). Sensitive studies of such early medieval authors as Dhuoda and Hrotswitha, as well as an important treatment of Hildegard, can be found in Peter Dronke, *Women Writers of the Middle Ages. A Critical Study of Texts from Perpetua (d. 203) to Marguerite Porete (d. 1310)* (Cambridge: Cambridge University Press, 1984).

13. On the notion of vernacular theology, see Bernard McGinn, "Introduction. Meister Eckhart and the Beguines in the Context of Vernacular Theology," in Bernard McGinn, ed., *Meister Eckhart and the Beguine Mystics* (New York: Continuum, 1994), 1–14.

14. This is not to say that Hildegard did not also claim a miraculous insight into the meaning of the Bible.

15. The most noted presentation of this view is Norman Cohn, *The Pursuit of the Millennium: Revolutionary Millenarians and Mystical Anarchists of the Middle Ages* (New York: Oxford University Press, 1970).

16. On the notion of the "psychological" imminence of the end, see Bernard McGinn, "The End of the World and the Beginning of Christendom," in Malcolm Bull, ed., *Apocalypse Theory and the End of the World* (Oxford: Blackwell, 1995), 58–89.

17. Gregory VII, *Epistolae Collectae* 46, as translated by Ephraim Emerton, *The Collected Letters of Pope Gregory VII* (New York: Norton, 1969), 195.

18. See Kathryn Kerby-Fulton, *Reformist Apocalypticism and 'Piers Plowman',* Cambridge Studies in Medieval Literature, vol. 7 (Cambridge: Cambridge University Press, 1990); Bernard McGinn, "Apocalypticism and Church Reform (1100–1500)," in *The Encyclopedia of Apocalypticism,* vol. 2 (New York: Continuum, 1998), 74–109.

19. Pauline authority for the role of women prophets was also found in 2 Cor. 12:5–10, where the apostle glories in his infirmities because in being weak for Christ he is made strong.

20. The notion of prophecy in the Middle Ages was a broad one and should not be restricted to the ability to foretell the future. The medieval *propheta* kept much of the original sense of the Hebrew *nabi'*, a special messenger from God.

Prophecy was often connected with unusual insight into the interpretation of scripture and its proclamation in preaching. For an overview of the development of
medieval views of prophecy, see the papers in G. L. Potestà and Roberto Rusconi,
eds., *Lo statuto della profezia nel Medioevo, Cristianesimo nella Storia* 17.2 (June
1996). On the scholastic debates over the nature of prophecy, see also Jean-Pierre
Torrell, *Théorie de la prophétie et philosophie de la connaissance aux environs de
1230* (Louvain: Spicilegium Sacrum Lovaniense, 1977); and idem., *Recherches sur
la théorie de la prophétie au moyen âge, XIIe–XIVe siècles. Études et textes* (Fribourg: Éditions Universitaires Fribourg Suisse, 1992).

21.   G. L. Potestà considers Joachim's attitude toward *prophetia* in his article,
"Progresso della coscienza teologica e critica del profetismo in Gioacchino da Fiore," in Potestà and Rusconi, *Lo statuto della profezia,* 305–34. Actually, Joachim
might well have called himself a prophet, since in the early Middle Ages *propheta*
was often applied to the inspired exegete; see Bernard McGinn, "Prophetic Power
in Early Medieval Christianity," ibid., 251–69.

22.   C. J. Holdsworth, "Visions and Visionaries in the Middle Ages," *History*
48 (1963), 144.

23.   Peter Dinzelbacher, *Vision und Visionsliteratur im Mittelalter* (Stuttgart:
Hiersemann, 1981), especially chaps. 10–17. See also his *Visiones,* Typologie des
sources du Moyen Age Occidental, fasc. 57 (Turnhout: Brepols, 1991).

24.   Dinzelbacher, *Vision,* 226–27.

25.   Two recent books in English highlight this: Barbara Newman, *Sister of
Wisdom: St. Hildegard's Theology of the Feminine* (Berkeley: University of California Press, 1987), and Sabina Flanagan, *Hildegard of Bingen 1098–1179. A Visionary
Life* (London and New York: Routledge, 1989). For Hildegard's visionary authority and apocalyptic message, see also Peter Dronke, "Hildegard of Bingen," in
Women Writers of the Middle Ages, 144–201; Barbara Newman, "Hildegard of
Bingen: Visions and Validations," *Church History* 54 (1985), 163–75, Barbara Newman, "Divine Power Made Perfect in Weakness: St. Hildegard on the Frail Sex,"
in John A. Nichols and Lilian Thomas Shank, eds., in *Peaceweavers* (Kalamazoo:
Cistercian Publications, 1986), 103–22 (vol. 2 of *Medieval Religious Women*); Kathryn Kerby-Fulton, "A Return to 'The First Dawn of Justice': Hildegard's Visions
of Clerical Reform and the Eremitical Life," *American Benedictine Review* 40
(1989), 383–407, and Kathryn Kerby-Fulton, "The Visionary Prophecy of Hildegard of Bingen in Relation to *Piers Plowman,*" in *Reformist Apocalypticism,* 26–75;
Gillian T. W. Ahlgren, "Visions and Rhetorical Strategy in the Letters of Hildegard of Bingen," in Karen Cherewatuk and Ulrike Wiethaus, eds., *Dear Sister:
Medieval Women and the Epistolary Genre* (Philadelphia: University of Pennsylvania Press, 1993), 46–63; Christel Meier, "Prophetentum als literarische Existenz:
Hildegard von Bingen," in Gisela Brinker-Gabler, ed., *Deutsche Literatur von
Frauen,* 2 vols. (Munich: Beck, 1988), 1:76–87, and in expanded form as "Ildegarde
di Bingen. Profezia ed esistenza letteraria," in Potestà and Rusconi, *Lo statuto
della profezia,* 271–303. See also Kerby-Fulton, "Prophet and Reformer: 'Smoke
in the Vineyard,'" in Barbara Newman, ed., *Voice of the Living Light: Hildegard
of Bingen and Her World* (Berkeley: University of California Press, 1998), 70–90,
213–18.

26. This is true even of the late medieval visions of women, which tend to fuse the three types.

27. Hildegard's trilogy consists of the *Scivias* (1142–1151), based on twenty-six visions; the *Liber Vite Meritorum* (1158–1163), recounting six visions; and the *Liber Divinorum Operum* (1163–1173), based on ten visions. All these works have received recent critical editions in the Corpus Christianorum Continuatio Mediaevalis [CCCM]: *Hildegardis Scivias,* edited by Adelgundis Führkötter and Angela Carlevaris, 2 vols., CCCM 43–43A (Turnhout: Brepols, 1978). *Hildegardis Liber Vite Meritorum,* edited by Angela Carlevaris, CCCM 90 (Turnhout: Brepols, 1995); *Hildegardis Bingensis Liber Divinorum Operum,* edited by Albert Derolez and Peter Dronke, CCCM 92 (Turnhout: Brepols, 1996).

28. Two volumes of the critical edition of Hildegard's letters have been published: *Hildegardis Bingensis Epistolarium,* edited by Lieven Van Acker, CCCM 91–91A (Turnhout: Brepols, 1991, 1993). Vol. 1 contains Epp. 1–90 and vol. 2 contains Epp. 91–250r. There is an English translation of the first volume: *The Letters of Hildegard of Bingen: Volume I,* tr. Joseph L. Baird and Radd K. Ehrman (New York and Oxford: Oxford University Press, 1994). For a study, see Joan Ferrante, "Correspondent: 'Blessed Is the Speech of Your Mouth,'" in Newman, *Voice of the Living Light,* 91–109, 219–23.

29. See Ep. 103r (2:261–62): "Lumen igitur quod uideo, locale non est, sed nube que solem portat multo lucidius, nec altitudinem nec longitudinem nec latitudinem in eo considerare ualeo, illudque umbra uiuentis luminis mihi nominatur, atque ut sol, luna et stelle in aqua apparent, ita scripture, sermones, uirtutes et quedam opera hominum formata in illo mihi resplendent. . . . Et in eodem lumine aliam lucem, que lux uiuens mihi nominata est, interdum et non frequenter aspicio, quam nimirum quomodo uideam multo minus quam priorem proferre sufficio, atque interim dum illam intueor, omnis mihi tristitia omnisque dolor de memoria aufertur, ita ut tunc mores simplicis puelle, et non uetule mulieris habeam." Here I make use of the felicitous translation of Dronke, *Women Writers,* 168–69, with a few minor changes.

30. On this formula, see Anne Clark Bartlett, "Miraculous Literacy and Textual Communities in Hildegard of Bingen's *Scivias,*" *Mystics Quarterly* 18 (1992), 49–50.

31. These are the figures arrived at by Ahlgren, "Visions and Rhetorical Strategy," 50, on the basis of her analysis of vol. 1 of the letters.

32. *Scivias,* Protestificatio (CCCM 43:4). This is described as giving her a total knowledge of the Bible.

33. This is the seventh and culminating vision of those described in the autobiographical fragment constituting book 2 of the *Vita S. Hildegardis.* See *Vita Sanctae Hildegardis,* edited by Monica Klaes, CCCM 126 (Turnhout: Brepols, 1993), bk. 2.16 (p. 43): "Subsequenti demum tempore mysticam et mirificam uisionem uidi, ita quod omnia uiscera mea concussa sunt et sensualitas corporis mei extincta est, quoniam scientia mea in alium modum conuersa est, quasi me nescirem. Et de Dei inspiratione in scientiam anime mee quasi gutte suauis pluuie spargebantur, quia et Spiritus sanctus Iohannem euangelistam imbuit, cum de *pectore Iesu* profundissimam reuelationem *suxit,* ubi sensus ipsius sancta diuinitate

ita tactus est, quod absconsa mysteria et opera aperuit '*In principio* inquiens *erat uerbum*' et cetera."

34. *Explanatio Symboli S. Athanasii* (Patrologia Latina 197:1078C): "quae scripturam hanc oculis et auribus exterioris hominis non vidit nec audivit, sed quae tantum in interiori scientia animae suae eam vidit et audivit."

35. See Ep. 52r (CCCM 91:130): "Hec dicta sunt a uiuente lumine et non ab homine. Qui audit, uideat, et credat unde sint." See also Epp. 2, 20r, 24, and 36 (CCCM 91:7, 57, 67, 94–95). On this form of address, see Ahlgren, "Visions and Rhetorical Strategy," 52–54.

36. See especially the studies of Meier, as well as Kerby-Fulton, "Prophet and Reformer," and Constant J. Mews, "Hildegard of Bingen: The Virgin, the Apocalypse, and the Exegetical Tradition," in Audrey Ekdahl Davidson, ed., *Wisdom Which Encircles Circles: Papers on Hildegard of Bingen* (Kalamazoo: Medieval Institute Publications, 1996), 27–42.

37. *Liber Divinorum Operum* 3.2.2 (CCCM 92:355): "prophecia in primo opere Dei, uidelicet in Adam, incepit. Que ita a generatione in generationem per diuersas etates hominum ut lumen per tenebras lucebat, nec a sono suo usque ad terminum mundi cessabit uoces multimodarum significationum proferendo, cum inspiratione Spiritus Sancti diuersis misteriis imbuitur." The second vision of book 3 (CCCM 92:353–78) forms a treatise on prophecy.

38. *Liber Divinorum Operum* 3.2.12 (CCCM 92:371): "Scientia quoque in Adam uelut prophecia fuit, et hec usque ad filium Dei hominem factum perdurauit; ita quod ipse illam per se illustraret, quemadmodum sol totam terram illuminat, et quod omnia que predicta sunt, scilicet que ante legem et sub lege facta dinoscuntur, spiritaliter in se compleuit, cum se totum superno patri obtulit." For the role of prophecy in history, see Meier, "Ildegarde di Bingen," 281–88.

39. *Liber Divinorum Operum* 3.5.6 (CCCM 92:414).

40. *Liber Divinorum Operum* 3.3.2 (CCCM 92:380): "De umbra autem hac scriptura Sciuias processit per formam mulieris, que uelut umbra fortitudinis et sanitatis erat, quoniam uires iste in ea non operabantur."

41. The phrase *lux vivens,* not found as such before Hildegard (see Constant Mews, "Religious Thinker: 'A Frail Human Being' on Fiery Life," in Newman, *Voice of the Living Light,* 52–69, 209–13), has its roots in John 1:9 and Job 33:28–30.

42. This has been noted by Newman, "Visions and Validation," 171. See *Scivias* 3.13.16 (CCCM 43A:635–36); *Liber Vite Meritorum* 6.45 (CCCM 90:292); *Liber Divinorum Operum* 3.5.38 (CCCM 92:462–63). For more on Hildegard's relation to John's Apocalypse, see Mews, "Hildegard of Bingen: The Virgin, the Apocalypse, and the Exegetical Tradition."

43. The apocalyptic scenario in the *Liber Divinorum Operum* is more detailed and somewhat different from that found in the *Scivias.* In addition, Meier, "Ildegarde di Bingen," 292–94, stresses the abbess's attempts to create a more systematic relation between cosmology and eschatology in her final work.

44. For sketches of the five ages, see *Scivias* 3.11.1–6 (CCCM 43A:578–81), and *Liber Divinorum Operum* 3.5.15–37 (CCCM 92:432–61).

45. See, e.g., Ep. 26r (CCCM 91:74–75), as well as the reforming letters to the

Trier clergy (Ep. 44), to the Cologne clergy (Ep. 48), to Werner of Kircheim (Ep. 149r), and to the bishop of Trier (Ep. 223).

46.   For summaries of Hildegard's apocalyptic scenario, see Kerby-Fulton, *Reformist Apocalypticism*, 49–50; and Sylvain Gouguenheim, *La sibylle du Rhin. Hildegarde de Bingen, abbesse et prophétesse rhénane* (Paris: Publications de la Sorbonne, 1996), 122–24.

47.   See Kerby-Fulton, "A Return to 'The First Dawn of Justice,'" esp. 390–93; "Prophet and Reformer."

48.   On the revival of prophecy, see *Liber Divinorum Operum* 3.5.17, 20 (CCCM 92:437, 439–40).

49.   Ep. 15r (CCCM 91:43; trans. 60): "Tunc aurora iustitie exsurget, et nouissima uestra meliora prioribus erunt, ac de omnibus preteritis timorati eritis, et quasi purissimum aurum fulgebitis et sic per longa tempora permanebitis." Some manuscripts at this point add a promise of a coming "spiritual people" (*viri spirituales*), a hope later central to the apocalypticism of Joachim of Fiore and found in Mechthild, as we will see below.

50.   *Liber Divinorum Operum* 3.5.25 (CCCM 92:446). Hildegard also differed from her Gregorian predecessors in giving secular rulers a positive role to play in her apocalyptic scenario through their chastisement of unworthy clergy (see Epp. 15r, 149r, 223r).

51.   For this renewal of prophecy, see *Liber Divinorum Operum* 3.5.26 (CCCM 92:447).

52.   For a summary of Hildegard's teaching on Antichrist, see Bernard McGinn, *Antichrist. Two Thousand Years of the Human Fascination with Evil* (San Francisco: Harper San Francisco, 1994), 128–32. See also Horst Dieter Rauh, *Das Bild des Antichrist im Mittelalter: Von Tyconius zum deutschen Symbolismus* (Münster: Aschendorff, 1973), chap. 7.

53.   See *Liber Divinorum Operum* 3.5.17 (CCCM 92:437), as well as *Scivias* 3.11.40 (CCCM 43A:600). For a survey of post-Antichrist melioristic hopes, see Robert M. Lerner, "Refreshment of the Saints: The Time after Antichrist as a Station for Earthly Progress in Medieval Thought," *Traditio* 32 (1976), 97–144.

54.   These four campaigns were: (1) 1158–1159, along the Main River to Würzburg and Bamberg; (2) 1160, south into Lorraine with important stops at Trier and Metz; (3) 1161–1163, down the Rhine to Andernach, Bonn, Cologne, and Werden; and (4) 1170, a land journey into Swabia, visiting Speyer, Hirsau, Kircheim, and Zwiefalten. The unprecedented character of this public preaching can be seen from the experience in the ninth century of Thiota, who was condemned to public whipping precisely because of her public preaching of the end: "Quapropter synodali iudicio publicis caesa flagellis, ministerium praedicationis, quod inrationabiliter arripuit et sibi contra morem ecclesiasticum vindicare praesumpsit, cum dedecore amisit, suisque vaticiniis tandem confusa finem imposuit" (MGH.SS. 1:365).

55.   Ep. 51 (CCCM 91:124; trans. 125): "quamuis totus iam pene orbis tenebris erroris inuolutus sit, radius quidam antique gratie, ne tota gens pereat, in uobis resplenduit."

56.   Gebeno's *Speculum Futurorum Temporum sive Pentachronon* was partly ed-

ited by Johannes Baptista Pitra in his *Analecta Sanctae Hildegardis Opera* in the *Analecta Sacra* (Montecassino, 1882), vol. 8:483–88. Gebeno saw Hildegard as the fulfillment of the eagle crying a triple woe in Rev. 8:13 (cf. pp. 487–88).

57.   Hildegard, of course, had also used amanuenses, but she appears to be more of an "author" in the modern sense at least. The first five books of Mechthild's work were composed c. 1250–1260, and the sixth book in the 1260s prior to her entrance into the Cistercian convent of Helfta c. 1272. The seventh book was written during her last years at Helfta. The original Middle Low German version does not survive, but all seven books were translated into Middle High German in the early fourteenth century and have recently been critically edited by Hans Neumann, *Mechthild von Magdeburg. "Das fliessende Licht der Gottheit,"* 2 vols. (Munich: Artemis, 1990, 1993) [hereafter *FL*]. Antedating this (c. 1290) is a somewhat different Latin version of books 1–6, the *Lux Divinitatis*, edited by the monks of Solesmes (Louis Paquelin) in vol. 2 of the *Revelationes Gertrudianae et Mechtildianae* (Paris-Poitiers: Oudin, 1875, 1877), 423–643 [hereafter *LD*]. For a survey of the scholarship on Mechthild, see Frank Tobin, *Mechthild von Magdeburg: A Medieval Mystic in Modern Eyes* (Columbia, SC: Camden House, 1995). For the translations from the Middle High German version I use those in *Mechthild of Magdeburg. The Flowing Light of the Godhead,* trans. Frank Tobin (New York: Paulist Press, 1998), with occasional minor adaptations.

58.   Two older treatments of Mechthild touch on her apocalyptic prophecy: Wilhelm Preger, *Geschichte der deutschen Mystik im Mittelalter,* 3 vols. (Leipzig: Dörffling and Franke, 1874–1877) 1:91–112; Jeanne Ancelet-Hustache, *Mechthilde de Magdebourg (1207–1282): Étude de psychologie religieuse* (Paris: Champion, 1924), 272–99. More recently, her view of the last events was brilliantly discussed by Hans Urs von Balthasar, "Mechthilds kirchlicher Auftrag," in *Das fliessender Licht der Gottheit,* trans. Margot Schmidt (Einsiedeln-Zürich: Benziger, 1955), 19–45. There are also some useful comments in Nigel Palmer, "Das Buch als Bedeutungsträger bei Mechthild von Magdeburg," in Wolfgang Harms and Klaus Speckenbach, eds., *Bildhafte Rede in Mittelalter und früher Neuzeit: Probleme ihrer Legitimation und Funktion* (Tübingen: Niemeyer, 1992), 217–35. A detailed, but not penetrating, treatment of her eschatology can be found in Marianne Heimbach, *Der "ungelehrte Mund" als Autorität. Mystische Erfahrung als Quelle kirchlich-prophetischer Rede im Werk Mechthilds von Magdeburg* (Stuttgart–Bad Cannstatt: frommann-holzboog, 1989). It is indicative of this lack of attention that the beguine's name appears just once in Marjorie Reeves's exhaustive study of Joachim of Fiore's posterity, *The Influence of Prophecy in the Later Middle Ages. A Study in Joachimism,* 2d ed. (Notre Dame: University of Notre Dame Press, 1993).

59.   The apocalyptic chapters in *FL* consist of three long texts (4.27, 6.15, 6.21) and three shorter treatments (5.3, 6.26, 6.35)—about 425 lines of text. The *LD* version rearranges this material, grouping most of it into an apocalyptic treatise at the end of the third book, *LD* 3.12–16. The comparisons are as follows: (1) *LD* 3.12 = *FL* 4.27; (2) *LD* 3.13 = the second part of *FL* 6.15; (3) *LD* 3.14 = *FL* 5.3; (4) *LD* 3.15 = the first part of *FL* 6.15, and (5) *LD* 3.16 = *FL* 6.35. Of the apocalyptic texts, the only one not contained in the treatise is *FL* 6.21, which forms *LD* 3.7. In addition, *FL* 5.34 (= *LD* 2.12) is important for Mechthild's sense of the

crisis of her times in its account of six messengers sent to condemn the evils of the day (Elizabeth of Thuringia, Dominic, Francis, Peter Martyr, Jutta of Sangershausen, and the *Flowing Light* itself). This chapter also speaks of the three forms of blood that Christ sheds throughout history—his own blood, the blood of the Father, and "the third blood which shall be shed in Christian faith before the last day is the blood of the Holy Spirit" (ed. 195.49–50).

60.   On Mechthild's appeal to divine authority, see Frank Tobin, "Audience, Authorship and Authority in Mechthild of Magdeburg's *Flowing Light of the Godhead,*" *Mystics Quarterly* 23 (1997), 8–17.

61.   *FL* 1. prol. (4–5): "*Dis buoch sol man gerne enpfan, wan got sprichet selber dú wort.* Dis buoch das sende ich nu ze botten allen geistlichen lúten beidú boesen und guoten, wand wenne die súle vallent, so mag das werk nút gestan, und ez bezeichent alleine mich und meldet loblich mine heimlichkeit."

62.   For Mechthild's criticism of the clergy, see Heimbach, *Der "ungelehrte Mund" als Autorität,* 139–61.

63.   *FL* 2.26 (ed., 69.32–33): "das der ungelerte munt die gelerte zungen von minem heligen geiste leret."

64.   On this aspect of Mechthild's thought, see *FL* 1.22, 2.22, 4.14, and 7.16 (ed., 18, 55, 128–29, 268).

65.   Von Balthasar, "Mechthilds kirchliche Auftrag," 28–38.

66.   E.g., Preger, *Geschichte der deutschen Mystik,* 1:98–103; Ancelet-Hustache, *Mechthilde de Magdebourg,* 279–82.

67.   Mechthild would have appreciated Pascal's *Pensées* 920, "The Mystery of Jesus": "Jesus will be in agony until the end of the world. There must be no sleeping during that time." Blaise Palscal, *Pensées,* trans. with an introduction by A. J. Krailsheimer (Harmondsworth: Penguin, 1966), 313. There is a parallel to this sense of Christ's suffering at the end of time in Hildegard in the speech Christ addresses to the Father during Antichrist's persecution, showing his wounds and begging for his people to be spared; see *Liber Divinorum Operum* 3.5.34 (CCCM 92:457–58).

68.   For an overview of the development of the ideology of the *viri spirituales* in the thirteenth century, see Bernard McGinn, "Apocalyptic Traditions and Spiritual Identity in Thirteenth-Century Religious Life," in *Apocalypticism in the Western Tradition* (Aldershot: Variorum, 1994), essay 7. There is a rich collection of materials on the history of the motif in Reeves, *The Influence of Prophecy,* part 2. The encyclical of 1255 is translated in Bernard McGinn, *Visions of the End. Apocalyptic Traditions in the Middle Ages,* 2d ed. (New York: Columbia University Press, 1998), 164–65.

69.   I follow the more explicit Latin here—"homines novae religionis" (ed., 529) as compared with the MHG "einer hande lúte." The description of the new order takes up 82 lines (*FL* 4.27; ed., 143.8–145.90) in the MHG and three pages in *LD* 3.12 (ed., 529–31).

70.   *FL* 4.27 (ed., 145.67–68): "Ir gewalt ist vil gros, wan kein bischof ist ir genos." *LD* 3.12 (ed., 531): "Est autem magna eorum auctoritas, quibus nullus Pontificum comparatur."

71.   *FL* 4.21 (ed., 144.57–59): "Der erste meister, der dis leben sol erheben, das

sol des kúnges sun von Rome wesen. Sin namme sprichet vor gotte ze túte Alle-luia." See also *LD* 3.12 (ed., 530): "Primus ordinis hujus auctor erit filius regis Romanorum. Nomen ejus [teutonicum] interpretatur coram Deo: Alleluia."

It is surprising that this interesting prophecy has received so little attention. Ancelet-Hustache, *Mechthilde de Magdebourg,* 286–92, took it as evidence of Mechthild's German sympathies for the Hohenstaufen dynasty, hoping for a rap-prochement between the papacy and the descendants of Frederick II. She argued that the prince's name was not "Alleluia" (seeing this as an exclamation), but "vor gotte" (Latin *coram Deo*), an anagram of Conradin, the ill-fated grandson of Frederick.

72. *FL* 6.21 (ed., 231.13–16;–242.20–23): "Ich wil dem babest von Rome sin herze rueren mit grossem jamere, und in dem jamere wil ich ime zuosprechen und im klagen, das minú schafhirten von Jerusalem *mordere* und wolve sint wor-den, ... Swer den helleweg nit weis, der *sehe* an die verboesete pfafheit, . . . So ist des not, das die jungesten bruoder kommen; wan swenne der mantel ist alt, so ist er ovch kalt." Compare *LD* 3.7 (ed., 524), which is less direct in making the connection between corruption and the coming of the new order.

73. *FL* 6.21 (ed., 232.23–29). This might indicate that the pope in question is the Franciscan Nicholas III (1277–1280), because his three predecessors (Innocent V, Hadrian V, and John XXI) all had very brief reigns. This would put the proph-ecy during Mechthild's years at Helfta, however, and it is usually held that only book 7 of *The Flowing Light* was composed there.

74. The tenth-century abbot Adso was the author of the standard Western account of Antichrist, *Adso Dervensis. De Ortu et Tempore Antichristi,* ed. Daniel Verhelst, CCCM 45 (Turnhout: Brepols, 1976).

75. Hildegard also looked forward to the two mass conversions of heathens, the first in her messianic time of the lion, the second after the defeat of the pagans in the time of the horse; see *Liber Divinorum Operum* 3.5.20, 24 (CCCM 92:440–41, 445).

76. See *Herrad of Hohenbourg: Hortus Deliciarum,* ed. Rosalie Green et al., 2 vols. (Leiden: Brill, 1979), facsimile vol., fols. 241v–242v, for seven scenes of tor-ture based on Adso's *Epistola de Antichristo.*

77. Elijah was already foretold as returning before Judgment Day in Mal. 3:23, a prediction also found in the second century in such texts as *Oracula Sibyllina* 2:196–213, and Justin, *Dialogue with Trypho* 43. The earliest surviving reference to the identification of Enoch and Elijah with the Two Witnesses occurs c. 200 in Hippolytus, *De Antichristo,* chap. 43, but the identification is probably earlier. On the history of the theme, see Wilhelm Bousset, *The Antichrist Legend* (London: Hutchinson, 1896), 203–11. On the importance of Hippolytus in the formation of the Antichrist legend, see McGinn, *Antichrist,* 60–63.

78. One of the most important Christian apocrypha, the *Apocalypse of Elijah,* probably written in Egypt in the third century c.e., describes an epic conflict be-tween the Two Witnesses and Antichrist in 4:7–19 and their eventual return to kill the Final Enemy in 5:32–34. See David Frankfurter, *Elijah in Upper Egypt. The Apocalypse of Elijah and Early Egyptian Christianity* (Minneapolis: Fortress, 1993). Enoch and Elijah were popular in many medieval accounts. From the sixth century

we have the fragment, *De Enoc et Helia* (MGH, Auctorum Antiquissimorum 9:493), which may reflect the teaching of Cassiodorus: see Fabio Troncarelli, "Il Consolato dell'Anticristo," *Studi Medievali,* 3d ser. 30 (1989), 589–92. Another popular account is found in the apocryphal *Evangelium Nicodemi* 25–26. Two of the most unusual descriptions occur in early medieval vernacular texts. The first is the Old Irish "Two Sorrows of the Kingdom of Heaven," which in its present form dates from the eleventh century. See Martin McNamara, *The Apocrypha of the Irish Church* (Dublin: Dublin Institute for Advanced Studies, 1975), 24–27, and, for a translation into English, *Irish Biblical Apocrypha: Selected Texts in Translation,* ed. Mairé Herbert and Martin McNamara (Edinburgh: T&T Clark, 1989), 19–21. The second is the Old High German "Muspilli" from c. 850, which witnesses to Elijah alone as opponent of Antichrist and sees his shed blood as inaugurating the world conflagration (see the translation and comments in McGinn, *Visions of the End,* 80–81). There are representations of Elijah battling Antichrist in the mid-sixteenth-century Apocalypse cycle in the Annunciation Cathedral of the Kremlin. See I. Ya. Kachalova, N. A. Mayasova, and L. A. Shchennikova, *The Annunciation Cathedral of the Moscow Kremlin* (Moscow: Iskusstvo, 1990), plate 62.

79. In what follows I am conflating the two accounts (*FL* 4.27 and 6.15 = *LD* 3.13). Hildegard also discusses the Two Witnesses at length; see *Scivias* 3.11.10, 16, 33–36, and 42 (CCCM 43A:582, 584–85, 596–97, 603), and *Liber Divinorum Operum* 3.5.33–35 (CCCM 92:455–59).

80. See *FL* 6.15 (ed., 146.29). It is admittedly difficult to say whether Mechthild considered the paradise to be a terrestrial or a celestial one.

81. Mechthild says she has seen the fruit and gives a description of it in *FL* 4.27 (ed., 147.131–36).

82. *FL* 4.27 (ed., 148.164–70) describes this transformation and their subsequent diet of prophetic "honey, figs and water mixed with wine." *FL* 6.15 (ed., 222.29–223.30) describes their journey from "India to the sea."

83. These scenes with their descriptions of tortures and dramatic speeches (see *FL* 4.27 [ed., 148.148–63]) have no precedent in earlier accounts of the Two Witnesses. For the "last brothers" see *FL* 6.15 (ed., 222.22–29).

84. On the Antichrist dramas of the Middle Ages and Reformation, see Klaus Aichele, *Das Antichristdrama des Mittelalters, der Reformation und Gegenreformation* (The Hague: Nijhoff, 1974). The argument between Enoch and Antichrist here bears some resemblance to the "flyting" between the Two Witnesses and the Final Enemy in the late medieval Chester "Play of Antichrist." See Richard K. Emmerson, "'Nowe ys common this daye': Enoch and Elias, Antichrist, and the Structure of the Chester Cycle," in David Bevington, ed., *Homo, Memento Finis: The Iconography of Just Judgment in Medieval Art and Drama* (Kalamazoo: Medieval Institute Publications, 1985), 89–120.

85. In the apocryphal collection of apocalyptic texts known as 1 Enoch, parts of which were available in the Middle Ages, Enoch also prays for a remnant to be saved (1 Enoch 84:5–6).

86. The four speeches are found in *FL* 6.15 (ed., 224.55–225.88) and *LD* 3.13 (ed., 534–35).

87. *LD* 3.14 (ed., 536) = *FL* 5.3 (ed., 155). The two versions are rather different.

88. *LD* 3.15 (ed., 536–37) = *FL* 6.15 (ed., 222.1–21). Here the German and Latin are quite close.

89. On Mechthild's desire to be crucified with Christ, see especially *FL* 3.10 (ed., 90). There are also a number of comparable passages in the last book of *The Flowing Light:* e.g., 7.18, 21, and 27.

90. *FL* 6.15 (ed., 222.11–17): "Din gerunge sol leben, wan si mag nit sterben, dur das si ewig ist. Erbeitet si alsus dur mich untz in die jungesten zit, so kumt wider zesamme sel und lip; da setze ich si denne wider in, so lobet si mich ane ende. Und si hat mir gedienet sit dem ersten beginne, wan du woltest mit Adame untz har dur mine liebi gewesen sin, alsust woltestu aller menschen kumber und aller menschen dienest vollebringen dur mich; ich spriche me: Din wesen sol stan untz an den jungesten menschen." There is a comparable passage about Mechthild's *gerunge* for suffering stretching from the time of the martyrs to the last day in *FL* 6.26 (ed., 234–35), thus matching Christ's declaration in *FL* 5.34 (ed., 195) that his blood shall be shed again in the last times. It is interesting to note that Mechthild of Hackeborn, nun of Helfta and therefore a companion of Mechthild's last days, also expresses the desire to live in pain until the Last Judgment in order to help atone for sins; see her *Liber Specialis Gratiae* 3.8 (*Revelationes Gertrudianae et Mechtildianae* 1:207).

91. *LD* 3.16 (ed., 537) = *FL* 6.35 (ed., 243.44).

92. At the end of the *Liber Divinorum Operum* Hildegard explicitly denies having the knowledge to interpret scripture (3.5.38 [CCCM 92:461–62), though this does not prevent her from acting as an exegete at times, even with regard to apocalyptic texts, as can be seen from her interpretation of the noted Pauline passage on Antichrist (2 Thess. 2:2–4) in *Liber Divinorum Operum* 3.5.29 (CCCM 92:449–51). To compare the abbess's reading of the passage with other interpretations, see Kevin L. Hughes, *The Apostle and the Adversary: Paul and Antichrist in the Early Medieval Exegesis of 2 Thessalonians* (Ph.D. diss., University of Chicago, 1997).

5 *Richard K. Emmerson*

Beyond the Apocalypse
The Human Antichrist in Late Medieval
Illustrated Manuscripts

This chapter goes "beyond the Apocalypse" to examine the depiction of a human Antichrist in late medieval manuscripts that are not illustrated Apocalypses.[1] These representations have, to date, received little attention, probably because they are not found in Apocalypses, which have been the focus of most art-historical research.[2] Our examination has three goals: first, to show how widespread Antichrist is in a variety of late medieval manuscripts, thus adding to our knowledge of the genres that represent a human Antichrist; second, to show how these representations are based on traditional orthodox and popular eschatology, rather than on the polemical and radical apocalypticism usually emphasized by modern historians; and, third, to understand better the ways in which Antichrist was received in the later Middle Ages by studying the relationships between word and image in these manuscripts.

In *Reading "Rembrandt": Beyond the Word–Image Opposition,* Mieke Bal describes three relationships to be considered when studying a work of art from the past.[3] The first is the relationship between the visual representation and its pre-text—that is, its inherited textual and iconographic tradition; for manuscript illustrations of Antichrist, this has, to a large extent, been the primary focus of previous scholarship, evident in the art-historical emphasis on illustrated Apocalypses. The second relationship is between the image and its context or the historical "background" of the image being foregrounded.[4] The relationship between text and historical context is complicated. It is clearly important to situate each manuscript within its interpretive community, but it is not possible to pursue this approach here other than to provide some basic information about date and provenance. The third is the relationship between an image and its co-text—for our purposes the miniature's manuscript environment composed of verbal and other visual texts. Since the six manuscripts to be studied are not well known, this chapter focuses particularly on examining the co-texts.

We will begin with the pre-text of the six manuscripts—that is, with the representation of Antichrist in illustrated Apocalypses. The long tradition of interpreting the apocalyptic creatures as symbolizing an anthropomorphic Antichrist is based on exegesis of Revelation 11, which describes Two Witnesses who are attacked by the Beast that rises from the abyss.[5] This interpretation is visualized as early as the tenth century in the Mozarabic Beatus Apocalypse now in the Pierpont Morgan Library.[6] I will not trace this tradition here; instead, I will summarize it to establish the apocalyptic pre-text of later non-Apocalypse depictions of Antichrist. A handy summary is available in a fifteenth-century German Apocalypse now in the Wellcome Museum, London.[7] Its account of the Two Witnesses (fol. 9v) begins by identifying them as Enoch and Elijah, and the Beast as a regal Antichrist who is pictured enthroned and holding a huge sword. The biblical text states that the beast will kill the Two Witnesses, a scene portrayed in the top register of the following folio (fol. 10; fig. 5.1), where Antichrist directs his henchmen to decapitate Enoch and Elijah. Chapter 11 continues to describe the Two Witnesses as lying in the streets of Sodom or Egypt and then, after three and a half days, as being resurrected and taken to heaven, while an earthquake destroys a tenth of the city. These events are depicted in the lower register of this folio.

This is the kernel of the legend of Antichrist as it was developed over a thousand years by exegetes interpreting the Book of Revelation. By the high Middle Ages the legend had become so popular that mini illustrated *vitae Antichristi* were sometimes inserted within the biblical text between illustrations of chapters 11 and 12. These were influenced by the *Libellus de Antichristo,* a brief compendium of eschatological lore written in 954 by Abbot Adso for the French Queen Gerberga.[8] Its popularity was based on Adso's ingenious transformation of the genre of the saint's legend, so that the *Libellus* in form and subject matter resembles an anti–saint's life.[9] Translated into several vernaculars, the *Libellus* had a great influence on theological, literary, and visual texts.

5.1 Antichrist Orders the Execution of Enoch and Elijah, from the *Wellcome Apocalypse* (Wellcome Library MS 49), fol. 10. Published by permission of the Wellcome Institute for the History of Medicine Library, London

The influence of Adso and the short *vitae Antichristi* often found in later theological compendia is evident in the sixteen scenes, three to a folio page (fols. 10v–13), that form the illustrated legendary life of Antichrist included in the *Wellcome Apocalypse* after its portrayal of the death and resurrection of Enoch and Elijah (fig. 5.1). For example, folio 10v portrays various deeds that Antichrist will perform in the last days to overcome the opposition of the faithful.[10] Its upper register thus shows Antichrist burning books and rebuilding the temple in Jerusalem. He was also expected to stage several strange marvels, which are portrayed in the middle register, where he makes water flow upward, the roots of upside-down trees blossom, and a man emerge from an egg.[11] But far more disturbing, Antichrist was also expected to resurrect the dead and stage a false Pentecost. This expectation, represented in the lower register, is based on exegetical identifications of the two-horned ram-like Beast of Revelation 13 as the prophet of Antichrist, which the *Wellcome Apocalypse* depicts on folio 16v, in its regular illustration of the biblical text. One of the supernatural powers of the ram-like Beast is to bring fire down from heaven upon the followers of the seven-headed Beast that rises from the sea—that is, Antichrist.[12] The tradition holds that as a result of such marvels, Antichrist will convert

5.2 Conception of Antichrist, from *Jour du Jugement* (Bibliothèque Municipale de Besançon MS 579), fol. 6v. ©Photographie J.-Paul Tupin. Published by permission of the Bibliothèque Municipale de Besançon

many Jews as well as Christians to his false doctrine, signing them with the Mark of the Beast, which the *Wellcome Apocalypse* illustrates on folio 11. Here again Antichrist is linked to the two-horned Beast of Revelation 13, who marks the foreheads of those he converts, who then become known by the mysterious number 666, a scene also depicted on folio 16v. The *Wellcome* cycle also portrays the many who join Antichrist, as well as the support he receives from the forces of Gog and Magog.[13] They are depicted in the lower register of folio 11, emerging from behind a greenish mountain. The visual *vita Antichristi* inserted after Revelation 11 thus conflates several passages from Revelation (chaps. 11, 13, and 20), Adso's *Libellus,* and later theological compendia.

On its next three folios, the *Wellcome vita Antichristi* portrays the other means by which Antichrist gains control of the world in the last days: by bribery and by gruesome tortures in which the faithful are sawed in half, chopped to pieces, boiled in oil, whipped and flayed, shredded by spikes, and fed to wild beasts. Ultimately, however, Antichrist goes too far. As portrayed in the top register of folio 13, he travels to the Mount of Olives and attempts to rise into heaven to imitate Christ's Ascension.[14] At this point he is struck down by Michael, although some exegetes, interpreting 2 Thessalonians 2:8, state that he will be destroyed by the "spirit of Christ's mouth."[15] The remainder of folio 13 then portrays events subsequent to Antichrist's death. The middle register shows Enoch and Elijah returning to warn those who were deceived by Antichrist, since they remain unprepared for Doomsday, like those in the days of Noah. Then begin the Fifteen Signs of Doomsday, which are depicted in the lower register.[16] The close connection between the death of Antichrist and the Fifteen Signs, one of the most popular medieval additions to traditional eschatological lore, confirms that the *Wellcome Apocalypse,* like the vast majority of medieval art portraying Antichrist, understands him to be the final figure of evil to appear shortly before the Last Judgment—that is, to be the Antichrist of orthodox, not radical or heretical, eschatology.

This brief summary of the apocalyptic "pre-text" allows us to track what is traditional and innovative about the six non-Apocalypse manuscripts that are the subject of this essay. The first and earliest is Besançon, Bibliothèque Municipale 579, a mid-fourteenth-century manuscript from northeastern France that is the unique witness to the *Jour du Jugement,* an elaborate early fourteenth-century French play.[17] With a cast of ninety-three characters, it stages the cosmic events of the last days, ranging from a demonic parliament in hell, where devils hatch their plan to conceive Antichrist, to Christ's return from heaven in judgment. The manuscript includes, in addition, eighty-nine remarkable and well-executed miniatures. One is a full-page frontispiece representing the Last Judgment, but the others are painted within the columns of the play's text. Of these eighty-eight column miniatures, fifty-four represent the play's dramatization of Antichrist's life, from his birth to his deception of the Jews and ten kings and his persecution of the pope.

These fifty-four miniatures are, to my knowledge, the largest and most developed cycle of Antichrist images in art—in any medium and from any period. That they are not even mentioned in Rosemary Muir Wright's recent *Art and Antichrist in Medieval Europe* only shows the extent to which art-historical research has focused on deluxe Apocalypses and ignored other manuscript genres. The manuscript follows the basic outline of the apocalyptic pre-text, detailing, for example, the well-known account of Enoch and Elijah, from their angelic summons while awaiting Antichrist

in the earthly paradise to their death at the hands of Antichrist's henchmen. But it also includes many scenes not previously represented, such as
the conception of Antichrist by the devil Engignart, who has been transformed into a handsome young man, and a Jewish prostitute living in
Babylon (fig. 5.2). They are shown in bed, discreetly covered. This is the
first example of what would become an essential image in the fifteenth-
century block books that illustrate the life of Antichrist.[18]

The textual source of this new imagery is the dramatic co-text of the
miniatures, the *Jour du Jugement.* As evident on folio 8 (fig. 5.3), the miniatures are placed within the columns of the play's text, often at crucial
points in the dramatic action and always at breaks in the dialogue. Thus
the rubrics inscribed after the miniatures are not captions for the illustrations but speaker headings introducing the dialogue that follows, and the
miniatures usually represent the action of the play suggested by the preceding lines, although they may also link the preceding and following lines
into one dramatic scene. Thus the miniature in the upper left column of
folio 8 depicts Antichrist's mother moaning about her difficult pregnancy,
concluding: "I truly believe I will die from this" (line 411). The mother's maid responds in the lines following the miniature: "Lady, don't be
frightened, for Mohammed will help you and deliver you very soon" (lines
412–14). The miniature (see fig. 5.3) links this dialogue by portraying the
mother's grimace while rubbing her belly and the girl's attentive concern.
The scene suggests a close relationship between word and image, a relationship in which the miniatures are essentially illustrative of the play's
text, visualizing the dramatic action for the reader.

The word–image relationship in this manuscript, however, is much more
complicated, since the images often provide much more information than
does the dramatic text. For example, the play's text says nothing about the
actual birth of Antichrist. Instead, after the girl's encouraging comments,
the mother responds with four lines in which she places her hope in Mohammed, and then in another four lines the devil Agrappart announces
the birth of Antichrist to his hellish companions. Following these eight
lines, inscribed in the upper right column of folio 8 (fig. 5.3), a miniature
placed in the middle right column shows Agrappart bringing the demonic
good news to the other devils in hell. The play's text, in other words, makes
no mention of Antichrist's birth. This gap in the action is, however, filled
by the miniature in the lower left column, in which the girl, now playing
the role of midwife, hands the baby Antichrist to his mother, who lies in
bed. From a narratological perspective, the miniature fills a gap in the
literary text. In "The Literary Work as a System of Gaps," Meir Sternberg
notes that "from the viewpoint of what is directly given in the language,

5.3 Pregnancy of Antichrist's Mother; Antichrist's Birth; the News Delivered to Hell, from *Jour du Jugement* (Bibliothèque Municipale de Besançon MS 579), fol. 8. ©Photographie J.-Paul Tupin. Published by permission of the Bibliothèque Municipale de Besançon the literary work consists of bits and fragments to be linked and pieced together in the process of reading: it establishes a system of gaps that must be filled in."[19] In this manuscript the miniature becomes an alternative, visual text that fills the gap and aids the reading process.

Similarly, the text (fol. 6v) is silent about the conception of Antichrist, moving from Engignart's seductive praise of the prostitute's beauty and his boast that he will beget a powerful son with her to the mother's response: "You truly deserve to be loved by me, for I have learned with utmost certainty that I have conceived a child by you" (lines 322–24). Between the devil's boast and the prostitute's response the manuscript places the conception miniature (fig. 5.2), depicting the lovers in bed. In addition to illustrating the literary text, the miniatures once again fill a gap in the dramatic narrative.

What is not clear, of course, is the source of this gap filling. Has the artist imagined the conception, placing the handsome devil and Babylonian prostitute in bed, simply extending the trajectory of seduction? Or is the artist illustrating another text not inscribed in the manuscript? This deluxe manuscript is clearly not an acting script; in his typology of French play manuscripts, Graham A. Runnalls classifies Besançon 579 as belonging to Type G, manuscripts that "were written in order to keep a record of a performed text, and were often used as gifts to patrons. They therefore follow a performance, rather than precede it."[20] Thus the miniatures may include visual traces of a theatrical production that staged a bed scene. Significantly, the miniatures also depict characters who are crucial to individual dramatic scenes, even though the playtext does not record their presence. Is this visualization of the action due to the artist's remarkable interpretive abilities, based on a sophisticated sense of dramatic conventions? Or does the artist remember a production of the play, painting settings and characters seen on stage, even though they are not specified by the play's text? Whatever the answer, it seems reasonable to consider this manuscript as including two simultaneous co-texts, one verbal and one visual, that represent the play's action in two distinct, yet clearly related, ways.

In comparison with the elaborate Antichrist cycle in the *Jour du Jugement* manuscript, the representation of Antichrist in British Library Royal 6.E.vi seems simple. The miniatures illustrate the *Omne Bonum,* a huge encyclopedia of almost 1,100 folios that includes more than 1,350 alphabetically arranged articles. As Lucy Sandler has argued in her impressive two-volume study and catalogue of the manuscript's miniatures, the *Omne Bonum* was compiled during the third quarter of the fourteenth century by the manuscript's scribe, James le Palmer, a clerk of the Exchequer.[21] The entry on Antichrist begins on folio 100v (fig. 5.4) and runs to folio

5.4 Opening of the Antichrist Entry, from *Omne Bonum* (British Library MS Royal 6.E.vi), fol. 100v. Published by permission of The British Library

104; it is divided into four major sections, two of which are signaled by two smaller portraits of Antichrist (fols. 102, 103). Unlike the pictures in the French play, these portraits are not narrative renderings, nor are they linked closely to their co-texts in the Antichrist entry, a selection of passages drawn from several thirteenth- and fourteenth-century commentaries and handbooks and the Pseudo-Methodius *Revelationes*.[22] In addition to the texts listed by Sandler, the entry also includes passages based on Adso's *Libellus de Antichristo,* which is the ultimate source of much of the detail on the life and deeds of Antichrist, even when the passages are taken from later texts such as Hugh of Strassburg's *Compendium Theologicae Veritatis*.[23]

Iconographically, the portrait of Antichrist is unusual, since the Apocalypse pre-text provides no model for the large lozenge-shaped mark on his forehead. Sandler identifies it as a third eye and notes its resemblance to an eye in the picture depicting the Harrowing of Hell, one of the 109 biblical scenes that open the *Omne Bonum*.[24] Why Antichrist should have a third eye is unclear, although Sandler points to a line in the text that reads: "And it is said by Daniel that his eyes will be enlarged and his mouth large to speak great things, and by his words he is raised beyond men, and he will be of great strength."[25] This sentence, inscribed in the lower right column of folio 102, may provide a solution to this mystery. In any case, whether or not the oblong mark is a third eye, it most likely is the artist's interpretation of the traditional Mark of the Beast, which the Two-horned Beast of Revelation 13 uses to signify Antichrist's followers.[26] The mark, a regular feature in Apocalypse pictures, is interpreted in a wide variety of ways, sometimes by the number 666 and sometimes by abbreviations of Antichrist's name. It is also interpreted figuratively, as, for example, in the *Jour du Jugement,* where Antichrist has his image stamped on coins and orders that these coins be honored by all and used to identify his followers. If the oblong mark is the artist's depiction of the Mark of the Beast, it explains why Antichrist's attendants also display the mark, and suggests that it may be applied upon conversion to the forehead and is not an anatomical feature.

Antichrist's position on the rainbow that forms the cross-line for the initial *A* is also unusual, although it calls to mind a similarly haughty Antichrist with a protruding right elbow seated on Leviathan's tail in the *Liber Floridus*.[27] A mini-life of Antichrist based on Pseudo-Methodius is inscribed within the loop of the tail and is pointed to by its subject. The exegetical linking of Antichrist to Leviathan was established by Gregory's *Moralia* on Job 41, the biblical passage that is written below the image. In this manuscript, however, Leviathan illustrates one of several encyclopedia entries based on the *Physiologus.*

It is best, though, to look to the other 750 miniatures that decorate the *Omne Bonum* for an analogue. As Sandler notes, the closest parallel for Antichrist's portrait is the image of the Second Coming introducing the entry "Adventus Domini secundus" (fig. 5.5). The parallels—including the rainbow and the two angels that flank Christ—are striking, although the true Christ and his angels are shown with nimbuses, their own distinguishing marks. As the marginal annotations state, this entry details the various signs of Christ's return, including, as noted in the upper right margin, the Fifteen Signs of Doomsday, which are ascribed to Jerome. Beginning on folio 57, it comes much earlier in the *Omne Bonum,* but it is clear that both the artist and James le Palmer wished to link the two entries.[28] Not only are they introduced by iconographically related initials, but in the lower right column the text discusses Antichrist as one of the signs of the end. Parallel to this discussion is drawn in reddish ink a human signpost that both emphasizes the text it brackets here and points forward to the Antichrist entry more than forty folios away. It is inscribed: "Nota hic de antechristo et eius potestate et miraculis" [Here take note of Antichrist and his power and wonders]. Its function resembles that of the historiated initials that introduce and designate major sections of the entries. Both facilitate the reading process by providing memorable finding guides, while drawing visual connections between the true and false Christs. As the deceiver who is expected to come in the last days and claim, "Ego sum Christus" [I am the Christ] (Matt. 24:5), Antichrist needs to be both linked to and distinguished from the true Christ, a function accomplished effectively by the marginal signpost and parallel portraits.

The third manuscript, Bodleian Library Douce 104, includes only one depiction of Antichrist. Its co-text is the C-version of the late fourteenth-century visionary poem usually attributed to William Langland, *Piers Plowman.*[29] This small Anglo-Irish manuscript, copied in 1427, includes seventy-three unframed marginal pictures, the only cycle of illustrations in the more than fifty manuscripts of the poem. Derek Pearsall has commented on "the precision with which illustrations follow the detail of the text" in this manuscript.[30] It draws the head of Antichrist in the right margin of folio 107 (fig. 5.6) in the three-line space between the alliterative long lines of passus 23.51–55. He is depicted as a relatively young bearded man with yellowish brown curly hair. The drawing may well be intended to function as a mnemonic device, as Mary Carruthers has suggested for some of the other images in Douce 104.[31] But the manuscript's depiction of an apparently innocent and harmless Antichrist—unmarked by any sign of the unnatural, whether physiognomic or demonic—is a significant interpretation in its own right. The poem states that Antichrist comes "in mans forme" (23.52), a phrase inscribed in the manuscript just to the left

5.5 Opening of the Second Coming Entry, from *Omne Bonum* (British Library MS Royal 6.E.vi), fol. 57. Published by permission of The British Library

5.6 Head of Antichrist, from *Piers Plowman* (Bodleian Library MS Douce 104), fol 107. Published by permission of The Bodleian Library, University of Oxford of Antichrist's head, which appears to look upward at these crucial words. The significance of this phrase, furthermore, is emphasized by the annotator's words placed immediately to its right and above the drawing, stating "Nota de antichryst" [Take note of Antichrist]. The beginning of the following line (23.53) then names Antichrist.

The artist clearly understands Antichrist to be the final human and Christ-like deceiver of the church who is expected to appear in the last days. This interpretation goes to the heart of the poem's apocalypticism, showing that it is traditional and orthodox, not, as Kathryn Kerby-Fulton has argued, Joachimist or Hildegardian.[32] The artist's Antichrist, and Langland's Antichrist,[33] is very different from Hildegard's, which is a composite figure of evil, a demonic figure arising within Ecclesia.[34] The illustration accompanying Hildegard's *Scivias* 3.11 shows, in its lower register, the radiant figure of Ecclesia being transformed by what Hildegard describes as "a black and monstrous head" with "fiery eyes, and ears like an ass', and nostrils and mouth like a lion's,"[35] a representation exemplifying Hildegard's visionary originality. It differs remarkably from the Apocalypse pre-text as well as from Langland's view that Antichrist comes "in mans forme." Unlike the historiated initials in the *Omne Bonum,* which are an integral part of the manuscript's sophisticated *ordinatio,*[36] and unlike the framed miniatures in the *Jour du Jugement,* which provide an extensive visual co-text for the dramatic text, the Antichrist drawing in Douce 104 is strongly interpretive: it is designed to emphasize a particular exegetical understanding of Antichrist as the Christ-like deceiver who comes in the form of a man to deceive the church in the last days.

The fourth manuscript takes us from Ireland to Yorkshire forty years or so later in the fifteenth century. British Library MS Additional 37049 is a miscellany of historical, spiritual, and eschatological texts probably copied at the Carthusian priory of Mount Grace around 1460–1470.[37] It includes seventy-one devotional, allegorical, historical, and eschatological texts, most illustrated with line drawings, perhaps by the manuscript's scribe, as evident in its two-page allegory of salvation (fol. 72v–73). It links the sacraments to the side wound of the crucified Christ and places the allegory within the full scope of salvation history. It moves from the expulsion of Adam and Eve to the punishment of the damned, including the foolish virgins, who are shown entering a hell's mouth that also opens to receive the evil angels whom Michael expels from heaven above.[38] Of particular interest is the image of the Whore of Babylon of Revelation 17, portrayed in the lower left corner of the opening. Surrounded by admirers, she is identified as the "meretrix magna" [great whore] (fol. 72v) and symbolizes the false church. The allegory typifies the ecclesiological and moral understanding of the Apocalypse; these modes, along with the historical and prophetic, are the four ways in which the last book of the Bible was interpreted in the Middle Ages.[39]

The *Carthusian Miscellany* also includes a prophetic understanding of the Apocalypse in its illustrations of the career of Antichrist, but their prophetic co-text is the Middle English version of Pseudo-Methodius *Revelationes,* which in its Latin version accompanied the Antichrist initials in the *Omne Bonum.*[40] As explained by the Pseudo-Methodius text written below the illustrations, after Islam is defeated "men sal be in þos dayes as it was in þe dayes of Noe, etyng & drynkyng & weddyng" (folio 15v). This prophecy, pictured on the left above the text, is, as we have seen, part of the Apocalypse pre-text.[41] Then the barbarous peoples of Gog and Magog will attack Christendom. In the upper right scene of folio 15v, they are depicted both as nude monsters and armored soldiers escaping from behind the Caucasus, where they were, according to legend, enclosed by Alexander the Great.[42] As in many popular accounts of the last days, Gog and Magog set the stage for the appearance of Antichrist, who comes after the destruction of his barbaric forerunners, as shown on folio 16 (fig. 5.7). In this manuscript Antichrist is the great persecutor rather than the deceiver of the Church in the last days, a violent tyrant rather than a pseudo-Christ. Thus on the next folio (fig. 5.8) he is shown in the upper left scene ordering the deaths of Enoch and Elijah. Interestingly, the artist has borrowed the iconography of the Apocalypse pre-text, as illustrated in the *Wellcome Apocalypse* (see fig. 5.1). Although the Carthusian drawing is much more crowded, its composition is clearly based on a two-hundred-year-old iconography. This should not be surprising, since there is no tradition of illustrating this text with a picture cycle.[43]

Finally, Antichrist is killed by the breath of Christ's mouth, an interpretation of 2 Thessalonians 2:8 that is shown in the upper right of folio 16v (fig. 5.8), where fire falls from Christ above. The iconography of this scene is also influenced by the widely known pre-text.[44] The *Carthusian Miscellany* here juxtaposes the deaths of Enoch and Elijah with the death of Antichrist and replaces the devils of the pre-text with Michael, which makes its visual narrative resemble the conclusion of the contemporary Middle English "Coming of Antichrist" from the Chester Mystery Plays.[45] In the Chester cycle the Doomsday play follows the death of Antichrist, as it does in the *Carthusian Miscellany.* The text of Pseudo-Methodius concludes at the bottom of this folio, noting that with the death of Antichrist, "þe endyng of þe warld sal be & þe dome" (fol. 16v). It is followed by a solemn meditation on the Last Judgment, which is illustrated by a large Doomsday on the facing folio (fol. 17).

Throughout this narrative sequence, as throughout the entire *Carthu-*

5.7 Destruction of Gog and Magog; Antichrist's Tyranny, from the *Carthusian Miscellany* (British Library MS Additional 37049), fol. 16. Published by permission of The British Library

5.8 Death of Enoch and Elijah; Death of Antichrist, from the *Carthusian Miscellany* (British Library MS Additional 37049), fol. 16v. Published by permission of The British Library

101

sian Miscellany, the connection between word and image seems close, but once again the illustrations do differ from the Pseudo-Methodius co-text in some significant ways. Although the text details the birth and life of Antichrist, including his rebuilding of the temple in Jerusalem, his miracles, and his attempt to imitate the life of Christ, the drawings focus only on his tyrannical nature. This focus seems designed to emphasize the embattled position of the faithful in the last days, which is stressed throughout the *Carthusian Miscellany.* The illustrations also seem hyper-orthodox. For example, the text explains that before the appearance of Antichrist, a Last World Emperor, described as "þe kyng of Romaynes & of Greke" (fol. 16), would first defeat Gog and Magog and then rule in Jerusalem for seven years.[46] The illustration on folio 16 (fig. 5.7), however, does not picture the Last World Emperor. Instead Christ is credited with the victory over the barbaric peoples, who are destroyed by fire falling from Christ in a cloud. The visual eliding of the human emperor and the emphasis on Christ's supernatural intervention indicates the artist's concern to avoid the potential heretical misuse of the legend of the Last World Emperor. It sometimes fed later medieval millenarian expectations that imagined the defeat of the enemies of the church and its reform by human action, leading to a period of peace and righteousness before Christ's Second Coming.[47] As has often been noted, the Carthusians were a bulwark of English orthodoxy during the fifteenth century, and the artist of this miscellany took pains to ensure that the prophecies of the last days fit the orthodox ideologies of his Carthusian interpretive community.[48]

The fifth manuscript representing a human Antichrist—Bodleian Library Douce 134, dated 1450–1470—is a unique copy of the *Livre de la Vigne notre Seigneur,* an intriguing handbook of eschatological lore covering 166 folios, which are decorated by seventy-five miniatures.[49] This deluxe French manuscript discloses a fascination with the demonic, as seen in its portrait of Satan, who is accompanied by four devils holding fleshhooks (fol. 98).[50] Breaking the frame of the miniature, Satan is depicted with seven heads and ten horns, a representation no doubt based on the seven-headed Dragon of Revelation 12. In contrast, the opening portrait of Antichrist on folio 4 is fully framed and given a human and worldly setting, although his demonic inspiration is stressed by a devil's mask placed on his head.[51] This is the artist's interpretation of the text's assurance that, although some people say Antichrist will be born of a holy nun, he has normal parentage but is possessed by the devil. The argument is an expanded version of Adso's *Libellus de Antichristo* and is filled with details concerning Antichrist's birthplace in Babylon, the invasions of Gog and Magog, and the conversion of many kings and Jews to become follow-

ers of Antichrist. The next miniature representing Antichrist (fol. 6) replaces the devil's mask with a three-part hat, which leads Wright to identify him as the pope.[52] The text, however, makes no such identification,
but notes that the armies of Gog and Magog will support Antichrist and
that he will enter Jerusalem and be accepted by the Jews. This miniature
thus portrays both the armies of Gog and Magog in the upper left background as they emerge from the Caucasus and a triumphant Antichrist
welcomed at the city gates in the near foreground.

Although the text of the *Vigne* describes how Antichrist will be challenged by Enoch and Elijah, the Two Witnesses are not pictured, which is
surprising given the centrality of this event for the pre-text. Instead, the
next miniature (fol. 30; fig. 5.9) emphasizes several horrendous tortures
that Antichrist orders to be inflicted on the faithful, a scene exemplifying
the medieval fascination with the specifics of the persecutor's cruelty.[53]
The miniature's co-text takes nine full folios to detail at length the suffering of those who oppose the persecutor and to explain why God allows
such suffering. The last miniature portraying Antichrist (fol. 36) is then
placed after the *Livre* explains that he will try to imitate the Ascension by
going to the Mount of Olives but will there be struck down by the spirit
of Christ's mouth.[54] The spectacle is set in a mountainous landscape.
Christ is in a cloud painted in the upper right corner. Flames fall di-
agonally down across the landscape onto Antichrist and his followers,
including a bishop. The soul of the pseudo-Christ is immediately captured
by a hovering devil, who in this full-page miniature replaces the devil's
mask worn by Antichrist in his introductory portrait (fol. 4).

This eschatological compendium is orthodox in identifying Antichrist
as the last deceiver of the church, not as one of many opponents preceding
its reformation and the establishment of a society of peace and righteousness. After the death of Antichrist, therefore, the manuscript depicts the
Fifteen Signs of Doomsday. The general resurrection and the Last Judgment then follow, along with descriptions of the rewards of the righteous
and the punishment of the damned. Throughout, the miniatures highlight
key events of the last days—the life of Antichrist, the signs of the end,
Doomsday, heaven, and hell—stressing their awesomeness. The relationship between word and image is close, particularly in the section on the
Fifteen Signs, where each short textual description of a sign is illustrated
by a miniature, so that fifteen somewhat smaller miniatures are compactly
painted within only eleven folios. In contrast, the Antichrist miniatures
are much larger, three of the four taking up full folios (see fig. 5.9). But
since thirty-six folios are devoted to the birth, persecutions, deceits, and
death of Antichrist, the visual text is here much more selective in its choice

5.9 Antichrist's Persecutions, from *Livre de la Vigne Notre Seigneur* (Bodleian Library MS Douce 134), fol. 30. Published by permission of The Bodleian Library, University of Oxford of details. It emphasizes Antichrist's demonic connections in his origin and death and the tyrannical power and cruelty of his military procession to Jerusalem and his persecution of the faithful.

The last manuscript illustrating the human Antichrist—Fitzwilliam Museum MS 22—is a deluxe book produced probably in northern France around 1500.[55] It includes yet another co-text, the *Légende dorée*.[56] Like Douce 134 this beautiful manuscript illustrates the Fifteen Signs of Doomsday. The last three signs are painted on page 15 (fig. 5.10) in the left and upper right columns; the three miniatures depict the death of all living beings, the consumation of the heavens and earth by fire, and the general resurrection. A brief account of Antichrist then follows. It is introduced in the lower right column of page 15 by a miniature portraying an orientalized Antichrist preaching his false doctrine, presumably based on the book placed open before his pulpit. This is the first of the four methods by which the tradition warns he will gain control of the world in the last days.[57] These four methods are the sole focus of the manuscript's co-text, which discusses the other three methods in its following two pages. The second method is the performance of deceptive miracles (p. 16), which the manuscript illustrates by showing Antichrist raising the dead. The third and fourth methods are portrayed in the left column of the facing page (p. 17, fig. 5.11), where Antichrist bribes his followers with gold and persecutes the faithful. Although not including other elements of the popular Antichrist tradition, the sequence of four Antichrist miniatures is contextualized within traditional eschatology, so that Christ's Second Advent follows, as depicted in the bottom right column of page 17. This entire sequence leads to a long discussion of the Last Judgment, which is introduced by a much larger two-column miniature (p. 18).

Although iconographically less adventurous than the other two French manuscripts we have studied, Fitzwilliam 22 develops a close relationship between image and word and uses the miniatures to visualize its *ordinatio*. Each column-width miniature, for example, introduces a subsection of text. As seen on page 15 (see fig. 5.10), each miniature depicting the last three of the Fifteen Signs of Doomsday is followed by a discussion of the sign. The Fifteen Signs, furthermore, along with the signs of the end described by Luke, make up what the *Légende dorée* describes as the first major event to precede the Last Judgment. The second major event, as explained in the lower right corner of page 15, involves Antichrist's four methods of controlling the world, each of which is introduced by a miniature. The third major event is the great fire that accompanies Christ's Second Coming (fig. 5.11), which is also depicted in a one-column miniature. This discussion of the three major events preceding Doomsday is then brought to completion by the two-column miniature on page 18, a visual

5.10 Signs of Doomsday; Antichrist Preaches False Doctrine, from *Légende dorée* (Fitzwilliam Museum MS 22), p. 15. Published by permission of the Syndics of the Fitzwilliam Museum, Cambridge

Accptis iuita Diiabit. et terra
fuo arererut Diider quos eni
fuo rarore fubiugare no poteru
auaricia fubuigabit ▓ An
tecrift acculp qul aura Xecu
moult fera X Done et alee Jfca
ples Diiufera la terre. Et cculp
qui par terreur ne pourra fai
re alui fubgets par auarer les
fourmoiitera a oberr alui ..

fea Dont Dauid Dit Dameliē
Vuȷ̃ capitulo. ▓ Supra qȝ are
Ji voteti vuiuerfa Vaftabit ꝛc
Qui ne croivoit comment il
Diffupia et tourmentera cculp
qui en lui croive neVouldroir
voiir les attraire par force ..
Et faint gregoire De lui Dit
▓ K obuftos quiupx inter
ficiet eos qui mente inuiceti
fiiit. corporaliter Viicer ꝯ
Les graiis et les fors il ochira
quaiit ceulp qui de coeur ne
de Voulente ne pourra Vaiit
cre il les Vaiicra par touruiēs
▓ Certaiii qucȝ precȝder.
iudieiuiii erit igiiis. Vehemē
tia . qui precȝder faciem iii
Dcie. isttini euiiii feptiem ..
Deus euiitter ..
▓ A tierce chose qui Xiiāt
le iugement aura . Dera

A auarie maiiere po
les Xcpuoir fera par
tourmeiis qiii leur·

feu iuquelximent lequel pa
Deuaiit la face Du fuge et Deu
ciuopera ce feu po'qiiatre aaifes

5.11 Antichrist Bribes His Followers and Persecutes the Faithful; Christ's Second Advent,
from *Légende dorée* (Fitzwilliam Museum MS 22), p. 17. Published by permission of the
Syndics of the Fitzwilliam Museum, Cambridge

punctuation mark for the text that fills the upper part of both columns. It introduces the next major textual section, the discussion of the Last Judgment itself, which is inscribed below the miniature.

The miniatures thus function like the large and small historiated initials in the *Omne Bonum* (figs. 5.4, 5.5). In fact, in *purpose* the *Légende's* text resembles the *Omne Bonum* entry on Christ's Second Avent more than it resembles the encyclopedia's entry on Antichrist himself (fig. 5.4). The annotation in the upper right margin of the "Adventus Domini secundus" entry (fig. 5.5) introduces a discussion of the Fifteen Signs, which are then followed by an explanation of Antichrist and a marginal signpost pointing the reader to the later and much fuller discussion under the heading "Antichristus." Although Sandler simply identifies the text here as a theological compilation, it is, in fact, closely related to the Latin *Legenda Aurea*.[58] Both here and in the French *Légende dorée* (fig. 5.10), in other words, Antichrist is introduced as part of a larger discussion of the signs of the end. The details of Antichrist's birth and death are not discussed; instead the emphasis is on warning readers about the four means that Antichrist will use to control the world in the last days. This textual locus also explains why the miniatures portraying Antichrist are placed near the beginning of the *Légende dorée*, because the final deceiver is subsumed within its discussion of the season of Advent. Here the cyclical liturgical calendar takes precedence over the linear structure of salvation history, since the *Légende* is arranged in liturgical order, and the Second Advent, discussed as part of the season of Advent, comes before the First Advent of Christ, celebrated at Christmas.

This chapter has focused on six manuscripts representing the human Antichrist. All go beyond the Apocalypse in that none is an illustrated Apocalypse, such as the Wellcome manuscript (fig. 5.1) we examined to establish the pre-text. Their co-texts range from a Latin encyclopedia with a rigorous *ordinatio* (figs. 5.4, 5.5) to a freewheeling Middle English miscellany (figs. 5.7, 5.8); from an elaborate French play (figs. 5.2, 5.3) and English visionary poem (fig. 5.6) to deluxe copies of an eschatological compendium (fig. 5.9) and a liturgical collection of saints legends (figs. 5.10, 5.11). Despite this variety, though, in all six manuscripts Antichrist is the traditional human figure expected in the future to deceive and persecute the church in the last days, the Antichrist of orthodox eschatology, not the symbol of contemporary evil manipulated to demonize one's opponents in radical and heretical apocalypticism. It is vital to recognize this consistent orthodoxy, especially given the tendency of scholars to emphasize the radical and heretical characteristics of late medieval apocalypticism.

Finally, the miniatures depicting Antichrist vary significantly in their relationships to their co-texts. They sometimes function less to illustrate than to aid readers of alphabetically or liturgically arranged texts; they sometimes illustrate the co-text but also recast it in a more orthodox fashion; they sometimes stress particular themes or highlight a crucial interpretation of the text; and in one manuscript they provide a visual text filling in the gaps of its dramatic co-text. They all suggest that in the late Middle Ages Antichrist was alive and well and available to readers in a wide variety of illustrated manuscripts, each fascinating in its own right.

Notes

1. For earlier, more general, studies of Antichrist in medieval art, see Richard Kenneth Emmerson, *Antichrist in the Middle Ages: A Study of Medieval Apocalypticism, Art, and Literature* (Seattle: University of Washington Press, 1981), 108–45; Bernard McGinn, "Portraying Antichrist in the Middle Ages," in Werner Verbeke et al., eds., *The Use and Abuse of Eschatology in the Middle Ages,* Mediaevalia Lovaniensia, series 1, studia 15 (Leuven: Leuven University Press, 1988), 1–48; Rosemary Muir Wright, *Art and Antichrist in Medieval Europe* (Manchester: Manchester University Press, 1995).

2. For a theoretically sophisticated example of recent work on illustrated Apocalypses, see Suzanne Lewis, *Reading Images: Narrative Discourse and Reception in the Thirteenth-Century Illuminated Apocalypse* (Cambridge: Cambridge University Press, 1995). For the full range of art based on the Apocalypse see also Richard K. Emmerson and Bernard McGinn, eds., *The Apocalypse in the Middle Ages* (Ithaca: Cornell University Press, 1992), part 2, 103–289.

3. Mieke Bal, *Reading "Rembrandt": Beyond the Word–Image Opposition* (Cambridge: Cambridge University Press, 1991), 189.

4. For the difficult relationship between art and historical context, see Norman Bryson, "Art in Context," in Ralph Cohen, ed., *Studies in Historical Change* (Charlottesville: University Press of Virginia, 1992), 18–42.

5. For Enoch and Elijah see Emmerson, *Antichrist in the Middle Ages,* 41, 95–101.

6. New York, Pierpont Morgan Library M.644. For a facsimile see John Williams and Barbara Shailor, *A Spanish Apocalypse: The Morgan Beatus Manuscript* (New York: George Braziller, 1991). For the Beatus Apocalypses see John Williams, *The Illustrated Beatus: A Corpus of the Illustrations of the Commentary on the Apocalypse,* 5 vols. (London: Harvey Miller, 1994–); Wright, *Art and Antichrist,* 31–59. See also the illustration from the *Saint-Sever Apocalypse* in Emmerson, *Antichrist in the Middle Ages,* illus. 7.

7. London, Wellcome Institute for the History of Medicine MS 49. For this manuscript see Suzanne Lewis and Richard Kenneth Emmerson, "Census and Bibliography of Medieval Manuscripts Containing Apocalypse Illustrations, ca.

800–1500," *Traditio* 42 (1986), 448, no. 128; Emmerson, *Antichrist in the Middle Ages,* 126–44 passim and illus. 11; Wright, *Art and Antichrist,* 171, 174, illus. 49, 50.

8. The standard edition is *Adso Dervensis: De Ortu et Tempore Antichristi,* ed. Daniel Verhelst, Corpus Christianorum Continuatio Mediaevalis [CCCM] 45 (Turnhout: Brepols, 1976); the best translation is Bernard McGinn, ed., *Apocalyptic Spirituality,* Classics of Western Spirituality (New York: Paulist Press, 1979), 81–96.

9. See Richard Kenneth Emmerson, "Antichrist as Anti-Saint: The Significance of Abbot Adso's *Libellus de Antichristo,*" *American Benedictine Review* 30 (1979), 175–90.

10. See Wright, *Art and Antichrist,* illus. 49.

11. On Antichrist's marvels see Emmerson, *Antichrist in the Middle Ages,* 90–94 and illus. 4.

12. On the beast of Rev. 13 and Antichrist's pseudo-Pentecost, see Emmerson, *Antichrist in the Middle Ages,* 39–41, 92, and illus. 2 and 9.

13. According to exegesis of Rev. 20:8, Gog and Magog are to be his military supporters; see Emmerson, *Antichrist in the Middle Ages,* 42, 84–88.

14. See Wright, *Art and Antichrist,* illus. 50; for a detail of Antichrist's death, see Emmerson, *Antichrist in the Middle Ages,* illus. 11.

15. This scene is represented, for example, in the thirteenth-century French Apocalypse in Bibliothèque Nationale, fr. 403; see Emmerson, *Antichrist in the Middle Ages,* illus. 10.

16. For the Fifteen Signs see William Heist, *The Fifteen Signs before Doomsday* (East Lansing: Michigan State College Press, 1952); Emmerson, *Antichrist in the Middle Ages,* 83–84.

17. See Richard K. Emmerson and David Hult, *Antichrist and Judgment Day: The Middle French Jour du Jugement,* Early European Drama in Translation (Asheville, N.C.: Pegasus, 1998); all quotations will be from this translation. The original is edited by Emile Roy, *Jour du Jugement: Mystère français sur le Grand Schisme,* Ètudes sur le théatre français au xive siècle (Paris: Emile Bouillon, 1902).

18. For an illustration see Emmerson, *Antichrist in the Middle Ages,* illus. 9. For the block-book *vitae Antichristi,* see Kurt Pfister, *Das Puch von dem Entkrist* (Leipzig: Insel Verlag, 1925); H. Th. Musper, *Der Antichrist und die fünfzehn Zeichen,* 2 vols. (Munich: Prestel-Verlag, 1970); Karin Boveland, Christoph Peter Burger, and Ruth Steffen, *Der Antichrist und die Fünfzehn Zeichen vor dem Jüngsten Gericht,* 2 vols. (Hamburg: Friedrich Wittig, 1979). For an early English version printed by Wynkyn de Worde, see Richard K. Emmerson, "Wynkyn de Worde's *Byrthe and Lyfe of Antechryst* and Popular Eschatology on the Eve of the English Reformation," *Mediaevalia* 14 (1991, for 1988), 281–311.

19. Meir Sternberg, "The Literary Work as a System of Gaps," in *The Poetics of Biblical Narrative: Ideological Literature and the Drama of Reading* (Bloomington: Indiana University Press, 1985), 186.

20. Graham A. Runnalls, "Towards a Typology of Medieval French Play Manuscripts," in Philip E. Bennett and Graham A. Runnalls, eds., *The Editor and the Text* (Edinburgh: Edinburgh University Press, 1990), 107.

21.   Lucy Freeman Sandler, *Omne Bonum: A Fourteenth-Century Encyclopedia of Universal Knowledge*, 2 vols. (London: Harvey Miller, 1996); see also Lucy Free-man Sandler, *Gothic Manuscripts, 1285–1385*, 2 vols., Survey of Manuscripts Illu-minated in the British Isles, vol. 5 (London: Harvey Miller, 1986), 2:136–38, no. 124; and Lucy Freeman Sandler, "Notes for the Illuminator: The Case of the *Omne Bonum*," *Art Bulletin* 71 (1989), 551–64.

22.   This apocalyptically charged history of the world and prophecy of the last things is falsely attributed to the fourth-century bishop Methodius. For extant manuscripts see Marc Laureys and Daniel Verhelst, "Pseudo-Methodius, *Revelati-ones*, Textgeschichte und kritische Edition. Ein Leuven-Groninger Forschungs-projekt," in Verbeke et al., *Use and Abuse of Eschatology*, 112–36.

23.   On Hugh see Emmerson, *Antichrist in the Middle Ages*, 77–78 and passim; on Adso see n. 8 above.

24.   Sandler, *Omne Bonum*, 102–3.

25.   Ibid., 103; for the Latin see 165, n. 117.

26.   On this point, see Emmerson, *Antichrist in the Middle Ages*, 134–36, 285 n. 58.

27.   This twelfth-century spiritual encyclopedia was compiled by Lambert of Saint-Omer. For Leviathan's image see *Lamberti S. Audomari Canonici, Liber Flor-idus*, ed. Albert Derolez (Ghent: Story-Scientia, 1968), fol. 62v. The image is repro-duced in Emmerson, *Antichrist in the Middle Ages*, illus. 1; McGinn, "Portraying Antichrist," illus. 4; and Wright, *Art and Antichrist*, illus. 13. For a study see Jesse Poesch, "The Beasts from Job in the *Liber Floridus* Manuscripts," *Journal of the Warburg and Courtauld Institutes* 33 (1970), 41–51.

28.   Both historiated initials were painted by Artist A; see Sandler, *Omne Bo-num*, 77–79, 183, app. 3.

29.   For an edition of the C-text see *Piers Plowman by William Langland: An Edition of the C-text*, ed. Derek Pearsall, York Medieval Texts (London: Edward Arnold, 1978). It is available in facsimile: *Piers Plowman: A Facsimile of Bodleian Library, Oxford, MS Douce 104*, ed. Derek Pearsall and Kathleen Scott (Cam-bridge: Brewer, 1992).

30.   Derek Pearsall, "Manuscript Illustration of Late Middle English Literary Texts, with Special Reference to the Illustration of *Piers Plowman* in Bodleian Library MS Douce 104," in Míceál Vaughan, ed., *Suche Werkis to Werche: Essays on Piers Plowman in Honor of David C. Fowler* (East Lansing: Colleagues Press, 1993), 198. In her catalogue published in *Yearbook of Langland Studies* 4 (1990), 1–86, Kathleen Scott states that the Douce 104 miniature is one of only two pic-tures of Antichrist to survive from fifteenth-century England (p. 71), which, as this chapter shows, is certainly not the case.

31.   Mary Carruthers, *The Book of Memory: A Study of Memory in Medieval Culture* (Cambridge: Cambridge University Press, 1990), 228–29.

32.   Kathryn Kerby-Fulton, *Reformist Apocalypticism and 'Piers Plowman,'* Cambridge Studies in Medieval Literature, vol. 7 (Cambridge: Cambridge Univer-sity Press, 1990).

33.   On this point see Richard K. Emmerson, "'Or Yernen to Rede Redels?' *Piers Plowman* and Prophecy," *Yearbook of Langland Studies* 7 (1993), 27–76.

34. For Hildegard's Antichrist see Bernard McGinn, *Antichrist: Two Thousand Years of the Human Fascination with Evil* (San Francisco: Harper San Francisco, 1994), 128–32; and his chapter in this volume. See also Barbara Newman, *Sister of Wisdom: St. Hildegard's Theology of the Feminine* (Berkeley: University of California Press, 1987), 243–46; Newman's description of "Ecclesia assaulted by the Antichrist" (243) is somewhat misleading, since Hildegard makes it clear that Antichrist arises from within Ecclesia.

35. *Hildegard of Bingen, Scivias,* trans. Mother Columba Hart and Jane Bishop, Classics of Spirituality (New York: Paulist Press, 1990), 493. The standard edition is *Hildegardis Scivias,* ed. Adelgundis Führkötter and Angela Carlevaris, 2 vols., CCCM 43–44 (Turnhout: Brepols, 1978); the color depiction of Antichrist is included in vol. 2. A black-and-white reproduction is published as fig. 13 in Newman, *Sister of Wisdom.*

36. See Lucy Freeman Sandler, "*Omne bonum: Compilatio* and *Ordinatio* in an English Illustrated Encyclopedia of the Fourteenth Century," in Linda L. Brownrigg, ed., *Medieval Book Production: Assessing the Evidence* (Los Altos Hills, Calif.: Anderson-Lovelace, 1990), 183–200.

37. Kathleen Scott, *Later Gothic Manuscripts, 1390–1490,* 2 vols., Survey of Manuscripts Illuminated in the British Isles, vol. 6 (London: Harvey Miller, 1996), 2:193. For the traditional dating and a description of the contents of the manuscript, see *Catalogue of Additions* (London: British Museum, 1907), 324–32; and James Hogg, "Unpublished Texts in the Carthusian Northern Middle English Religious Miscellany British Library MS. ADD. 37049," in James Hogg, ed., *Essays in Honour of Erwin Stürzl on His Sixtieth Birthday,* Salzburger Studien zur Anglistik und Amerikanistik, vol. 10 (Salzburg: Institut für Anglistik und Amerikanistik, 1980), 1:241–84. A partial facsimile is available in James Hogg, *An Illustrated Yorkshire Carthusian Religious Miscellany, British Library London Additional MS. 37049,* Analecta Cartusiana 95 (Salzburg: Institut für Anglistik und Amerikanistik, 1981).

38. For an explication of this visual allegory see Francis Wormald, "Some Popular Miniatures and their Rich Relations," in Francis Wormald: *Collected Writings,* vol. 2: *Studies in English and Continental Art of the Later Middle Ages* (London: Harvey Miller, 1988), 139–46, 171, figs. 125–30.

39. For the four exegetical approaches and their illustration in a fifteenth-century manuscript, see Richard K. Emmerson, "The Apocalypse Cycle in the Bedford Hours," *Traditio* 50 (1995), 173–98.

40. For an edition of Pseudo-Methodius in this manuscript, see "þe Bygynnyng of þe world and þe Ende of worldes," ed. Aaron J. Perry, Early English Text Society, vol. 167 (London: Oxford University Press, 1925).

41. See *Wellcome Apocalypse,* fol. 11, and n. 13 above.

42. For this tradition see Andrew Runni Anderson, *Alexander's Gate, Gog and Magog, and the Inclosed Nations,* Mediaeval Academy Publications, vol. 12 (Cambridge, Mass.: Mediaeval Academy of America, 1932).

43. I am grateful to Michael Twomey, who generously shared with me his research on the English reception of Pseudo-Methodius.

44. See n. 15 above.

45. See Richard K. Emmerson, "'Nowe Ys Common This Daye': Enoch and Elias, Antichrist, and the Structure of the Chester Cycle," in David Bevington, ed., *Homo, Memento Finis: The Iconography of Just Judgment in Medieval Art and Drama*, Early Drama, Art and Music, Monograph Series, vol. 5 (Kalamazoo: Medieval Institute Publications, 1985), 89–120.

46. For the Last World Emperor in Pseudo-Methodius, see G. J. Reinink, "Pseudo-Methodius und die Legende vom römischen Endkaiser," in Verbeke et al., *Use and Abuse of Eschatology*, 83–111. For the legend in general see also Emmerson, *Antichrist in the Middle Ages*, 84–89; McGinn, *Antichrist*, 88–92.

47. On medieval millenarianism see Robert E. Lerner, "The Medieval Return to the Thousand-Year Sabbath," in Emmerson and McGinn, *The Apocalypse in the Middle Ages*, 51–71.

48. The best example of this orthodoxy is Nicholas Love's *Mirror of the Blessed Life of Jesus Christ*, the first work produced in accordance with Archbishop Arundel's Constitutions of 1409. See Nicholas Watson, "Censorship and Cultural Change in Late-Medieval England: Vernacular Theology, the Oxford Translation Debate, and Arundel's Constitutions of 1409," *Speculum* 70 (1995), 852–54.

49. For this manuscript see Otto Pächt and J. J. G. Alexander, *Illuminated Manuscripts in the Bodleian Library, Oxford*, vol. 1 (Oxford: Clarendon, 1966), 55–56, no. 710, pl. 54; Emmerson, *Antichrist in the Middle Ages*, 127, 132, 142, illus. 6; and Wright, *Art and Antichrist*, 170–71, illus. 47, 48.

50. See A. G. Hassall and W. O. Hassall, *Treasures from the Bodleian Library* (New York: Columbia University Press, 1976), 137–39.

51. See Wright, *Art and Antichrist*, illus. 47.

52. Ibid., 170.

53. See Emmerson, *Antichrist in the Middle Ages*, illus. 6.

54. See Wright, *Art and Antichrist*, illus. 48.

55. For this manuscript see M. R. James, *A Descriptive Catalogue of the Manuscripts in the Fitzwilliam Museum* (Cambridge: Cambridge University Press, 1895), 43–51, which dates the manuscript to c. 1480 (p. 43).

56. This French version of the *Legenda Aurea* of Jacobus de Voragine was translated for aristocratic readers in Paris by Jean de Vignay around 1335. See Richard Hamer and Vida Russell, "A Critical Edition of Four Chapters from the *Légende Dorée*," *Mediaeval Studies* 51 (1989), 130–204, which identifies the manuscript as a type C and dates it to c. 1500 (p. 135). No critical edition of the *Légende dorée* is available; for an English translation see *The Golden Legend: Readings on the Saints*, trans. William Granger Ryan, 2 vols. (Princeton: Princeton University Press, 1993). For a study of the *Legenda*, see Sherry L. Reames, *The Legenda aurea: A Reexamination of Its Paradoxical History* (Madison: University of Wisconsin Press, 1985). For discussions of the illustrations in *Légende dorée* manuscripts, see Hilary Maddocks, "Illumination in Jean de Vignay's *Légende Dorée*," in Brenda Dunn-Lardeau, ed., *Legenda Aurea: Sept siècles de diffusion* (Montreal: Éditions Bellarmin, 1986), 155–69; Hilary Maddocks, "Pictures for Aristocrats: The Manu-

scripts of the *Légende Dorée*," in Margaret M. Manion and Bernard J. Muir, eds., *Medieval Texts and Images: Studies of Manuscripts from the Middle Ages* (Chur: Harwood, 1991), 1–23. Unfortunately, neither essay studies the illustrations of Fitzwilliam 22.

57.   On the four methods of gaining power see Emmerson, *Antichrist in the Middle Ages*, 90–95.

58.   Sandler, *Omne Bonum*, 2:24.

6 H. C. Erik Midelfort

Madness and the Millennium at Münster, 1534–1535

ἔλεγον δὲ πολλοὶ ἐξ αὐτῶν, Δαιμόνιον ἔχει καὶ μαίνεται, τί αὐτοῦ ἀκούετε;

Dicebant autem multi ex ipsis: Daemonium habet, et insanit; quid eum auditis?
(Vulgate)

Viel vnter jnen sprachen / Er hat den Teufel / vnd ist vnsinnig / was höret jr jm zu?
(Luther's translation)

And many of them said, He has a demon and is mad; why do you listen to Him?
(King James translation)

John 10:20

An often ignored passage from the gospel of John suggests that at least certain of those who heard Jesus thought him crazy or even demon-possessed.[1] Interestingly, the gospel goes on to refute this charge, not by showing how reasonable or mentally healthy Jesus really was, but by pointing to the wonders he performed. His healing could not, John quotes others as saying, come from a demon. "Can a demon open the eyes of the blind?" (John 10:21, RSV). This is a noteworthy little moment, for it suggests the difficulty we all confront when we deal with strange religious discourse. How easily should one credit the experience of those who travel under the banner of ecstasy, voices, visions, direct revelation, or just personally idiosyncratic interpretations of scripture? Are we all inclined nowadays to think of religious experience and religious language as so irrational, so far removed from empirical science, that anything goes? Does anyone ask, as St. John encourages us to ask, where are the tangible proofs? And do we even agree that a "demon" cannot open the eyes of the blind? How do we know what "demons" can or cannot do? For at least two hundred years, Western Christians have slowly learned not to tie their faith to the supposed proofs of miracles, but that has not impeded the proliferation of wonders: healings, UFOs, freaks of nature figure prominently in our tabloid press, even if we are not sure what they "prove" any more.

115

I am drawn to these vast speculations from my consideration of religious heresy in the age of the Reformation. Now Martin Luther, for his part, was usually careful to steer clear of claims that rested on his own private experience, on his own special insights. He began his Reformation as a doctor of theology, hoping for a public disputation, an open consideration of his ninety-five theses.[2] And within five years of that failed attempt, his German translation of the New Testament was selling briskly. He placed great stock in the tradition of the church, especially of the church Fathers;[3] and when he was consumed by doubts, as he often was, one of the worst doubts was that he might be claiming to be the only one who was right, while all the rest of the church was wrong.[4] So Luther relied on the authority that inhered in his doctorate and in his appointment as a learned professor of biblical theology.

When others took inspiration from Luther but went on to criticize his understanding of baptism, the eucharist, the role of the state, and the social implications of the gospel, Luther was, as we know, eager to argue, perhaps too eager.[5] But he was appalled at the unwillingness of some of his opponents to accept "rational" grounds for discussion—that is, the grounds he had become accustomed to in the university. When Thomas Müntzer cried out against the Wittenberg reformer, blasting Luther for his sellout to secular authority, he based part of his claim on the authority of personal revelations that he, Müntzer, felt came directly from God. Luther remarked that Müntzer seemed to have swallowed the Holy Ghost, feathers and all. But this basic difference deprived the two men of any common grounds for dispute, and soon enough Luther was labeling such people mad, demon-possessed, raging, frantic, hallucinating.[6] He developed a whole vocabulary of folly (*Narrheit*) to describe the blind fools who would not listen to the truth.[7] The mad included, for Luther, the Jews, the pope, the Stoics, atheists and Epicureans, blood-crazed or tyrannical princes, monks who drove themselves insane through lack of food or sleep, and former followers who came to disagree with him over some important issue: the sacramentarians (such as Ulrich Zwingli), the antinomians, the spiritualists, the Anabaptists.[8] They were all mad in their resolute inability (for so it seemed) to listen to reasonable argument.

Of course, in sober moments Luther could also admit that we are all fools, that even the patriarchs had behaved like lunatics at times, that "we" are the children of a church gone mad, and that, in fact, the whole world was insane.[9] Trapped in their worldly and selfish desires, men act as if they were *obsessi* (possessed by the devil), *furiosi* (insane), and *ceci* (blind). When the world spurns deliverance from sin and hell, "Are these not the horrible ragings of darkness?"[10] In this "last age" of the world, men fall into frenzies of lust in ways that men used to avoid in happier days.[11]

We can sense some of the difficulties Luther prepared for himself in the very word he most often used for his spiritualist and Anabaptist opponents: *Schwärmer.* This German word is related to our English *swarm,* and when one *schwärmt,* it was as if bees or bats were swarming in one's head. It could refer to the mental life of one who had fallen off the tracks, or more generally had gone crazy, *verrückt.*[12] We tend to translate the word with "fanatic" these days, but that word, too, has lost much of its original force in English. In its original Latin, and in the English of Shakespeare's and Dr. Johnson's days, the word meant frenzied, mad, possessed by a deity or a demon, a religious maniac.[13] We have trouble with the concept, perhaps, because the word—the origin of our "fan," as in "baseball fan"—has so degenerated; in just the way that "enthusiast" has decayed from its central meaning of divine possession, through a belief in private revelations, to mere heat of imagination, passionate partisanship, vehemence. It is not that we no longer encounter those who claim direct revelations or even spirit possession; instead, it is thought impolite to regard such colleagues and fellow citizens as crazy. As our culture loses its theological moorings, we reach the odd position of being unable to judge the religious views of others, except from one's own often ill-defended religious position or, less often, from a materialist or skeptical position that disregards all religious language. Either way it often just doesn't seem to matter.

But what if some millennium (and not just the turn of a leaf of the calendar) is at hand? What if we are entering a New Age, as the New Agers tell us? What if it is the dawning of the Age of Aquarius, an age of universal brotherhood and enlightenment? Are we then entitled (or required) to behave or think differently? Shall we be transformed by a "higher consciousness" and by widespread appeals to holism? So long as astrology, eschatology, apocalyptic, and even metahistory confine their attentions to telling us where we are in the course of time, our place on the map or the timeline, so to speak, we may not be in a radically different position from those who don't have the advantages of a map. The roads are actually full of cars, and some of the drivers are clearly lost, while others must know their way around. The result is relatively safe for everyone so long as we all follow the same rules of the road. The danger, metaphorically speaking, would seem to come from those whose "maps" tell them that they are now in a new state (perhaps a new state of consciousness) where one may drive at any speed one wishes, or even back up on the freeway. Millennial thought often proposes to tell us what time it is, and how much time is left, but this information does not make much practical difference so long as the old rules of conduct and the old patterns of authority or legitimation still apply.[14]

This digression brings us back to the days of Martin Luther. As his message began to spread, it was hard to tell which of the old rules were still valid. In Strasbourg among the excited heralds of a new age was a married couple, Lienhard and Ursula Jost, evangelical visionaries of such extraordinary strength and confidence that they had a permanent effect upon one of the major figures of the radical Reformation, Melchior Hoffman. Hoffman came to agree with the Josts that after a period of misery true Christians would take control of the whole earth, fanning out from a truly Christian imperial city (Strasbourg, or later Münster) and following the visions of a prophet (Hoffman himself) in the last days.[15] Not everyone agreed with Hoffman in seeing the Josts as apocalyptic oracles, however, and the city of Strasbourg even held Lienhard Jost for several months during 1524 in its *Narrenhaus* or madhouse.[16] For ordinary Christians in ordinary times, ecstasy was hard to distinguish from insanity.

Or take an odd reformer in Schleswig-Holstein, then under the Danish crown. In 1527, while the canons of Schleswig Cathedral were singing their Latin *horae* in the upper choir, down in the lower choir a tumultuous fellow, known to us only as "Mad (*Tolle*) Friedrich," was leading his burgher congregation in singing German hymns, belted out so loudly that the canons lost their place and had to stop. Sermons were now interrupted by hecklers who shouted their objections: "Liar," "Fool." Mad Friedrich's followers urinated in the stoups for holy water, and when they received written reprimands, they used them as toilet paper, "and having dried their arses on it, sealed it and sent it back." Soon Catholic priests and monks were assaulted in the streets, stoned, and accused of being wolves and cannibals, "murderers of souls."[17] But when Mad Friedrich went so far as to criticize Chancellor Wolfgang von Utenhoven for his appropriation of church property, and when he enraged even his evangelical partisans by living simply (and self-righteously) off alms, he was arrested and banished. Was he crazy or only zealous?

Of course, Mad Friedrich was not the only preacher of his day rashly to criticize a ruler or his policy. Luther himself blasted what he called the "insanity of our rulers" for letting the Turks invade parts of Europe. Kings, in his view, all too easily fell into folly or stupidity, or madness.[18] And the folly or madness of kings unfortunately plunged whole peoples into perdition.[19]

In Luther's day the worst example of such insanity was the millennial kingdom established by the Anabaptists at Münster in the German northwest, just forty miles from what is now the Dutch border.[20] This episcopal city was possessed by a Lutheran reformation movement in the years 1532–1533, a movement supported by people from all levels of urban society.[21] But Münster did not follow a familiar course, by which she might have joined the family of ordinary Lutheran or Zwinglian cities. Instead, the town fell captive to a local apocalyptic Anabaptist movement that also enjoyed heavy reinforcements from the ranks of Anabaptist refugees from the Duchy of Jülich-Cleves and from Charles V's Netherlands. Serious research in the last generation has uncovered some of the likely reasons why Münster alone, of all the cities of the empire, found itself unable to resist the slide toward millenarian Anabaptism.[22] At the time it seemed to some like a descent into madness, a judgment shared and repeated by historians down to the present.[23] And so our first assessment of the development of the Anabaptist kingdom of Jerusalem needs to examine a bit more closely how Jan Matthijs and later Jan of Leiden came to control Münster. What was it that made the apocalyptic ideas of Melchior Hoffman so increasingly persuasive?

The first answer is that failing harvests, famine, and the distressed economic conditions brought on by war predisposed the inhabitants of the Netherlands and northwestern Germany in the years after 1527 to think in terms of a currently impending crisis.[24] But it is also true that in Münster radical religious leaders learned to make Münster's medieval civic constitution work for them. In its origins the Anabaptist seizure of power continued to follow a characteristically urban pattern, exploiting the long traditional claims of guildsmen to control their own city. At this stage of their movement, they did not appear crazy or even especially millenarian in their thinking. The most important council in Münster was elected by an electoral college (the *Kurgenossen*) who were in turn annually elected by the *"guden lude,"*—that is, the full citizens divided into six neighborhoods.[25] Just as in most German cities, however, real political power was exercised by a far narrower group of wealthy *Honoratioren*—long-distance merchants and substantial artisans. By the early sixteenth century, it had become customary simply to re-elect the incumbent council. During 1525 a revolt against this system broke out, but despite a strongly anticlerical impulse, this rebellion was not really a movement for Luther's reformation at all. And it achieved none of its purposes, although the council did suffer a loss of prestige and authority in the years that followed.[26] By the early 1530s, as Lutheran ideas were finally spreading in Münster, the council was therefore far less able to control the conjunction of reformation and citizen protest.

In September 1531 the Lutheran missionary Bernhard Rothmann turned to the city authorities in an effort to set up a disputation between a Franciscan, Johann van Deventer, and himself. The idea was to discuss Deventer's doctrine of purgatory publicly and thereby to allow the citizenry of Münster to see just how shaky the doctrine was and to avoid further "harm and corruption of souls."[27] Although the council was firmly

opposed to him, Rothmann continued to press the legal rights of the Münster citizens: his was a position of genuine weight, for it was generally
conceded throughout the empire that citizens had a firm right to obtain
the means of their salvation. This urban right to an exemplary disputation
was exercised repeatedly throughout the early years of the Reformation.[28]

Again and again in 1532 and 1533, Rothmann appealed to the Münster
citizens' pride in self-rule, their rights to participate even in the choice of
clergy and the administration of ecclesiastical institutions. In July of 1532
the united guilds established a Committee of Thirty-Six to control and
check the decisions of the council. Ranke was right when he pointed out
that at this point the city council could hardly suppress its evangelical
competitor, for the old constitution did grant just this sort of popular
influence.[29] On the tenth of August the council approved the appointment
of Lutheran ministers to all of the parish churches in Münster. On February 14, 1533, the bishop of Münster, Franz von Waldeck, acting as the
prince-bishop and lord of the territory, city, and churches of Münster,
accepted this situation; and in March the new council elections brought
in a majority of Lutherans, many of them former members of the Committee of Thirty-Six; but now a new citizen opposition group sprang up in the
place of the old one, and Lutherans in power found themselves opposing a
group led by Bernhard Rothmann, who was on his way to an Anabaptist
religious position.[30] By the spring of 1534, the swelling ranks of Anabaptists had brought their struggle to a successful conclusion, winning the
council election on 23 February.

As Heinz Schilling has argued in a brilliant analysis, the reason Münster
could not halt its slide from Lutheranism to Anabaptism, a slide that all
the other towns of the empire managed to stem, was that the Lutheran
council of 1533 had repudiated precisely the popular urban political
movement that had brought them into power. Influenced as Lutherans
everywhere were by the Peasants' War of 1525 and by the conservative,
authoritarian appeal of the princes, Münster's Lutherans tried to ally
themselves with the Schmalkaldic League and especially with Landgrave
Philipp of Hesse. Therefore, the councillors rejected a proposed church
ordinance in the spring of 1533 because it suggested a Zwinglian doctrine
of the Lord's Supper and a congregational system of running the church,
even though there might have been room here for a balance between council and the congregational forces.[31]

The Lutherans did not strengthen their popular position in the choice
of Dr. Johann von der Wieck as their leader. A learned jurist, sympathetic
to the Roman legal principles of princely government, he seems to have
tried to turn the council into an autocratic organ of almost princely authority, and he complained bitterly when matters discussed in council were

not kept secret from the rest of the townspeople. When Münster held its religious disputation in August of 1533, Rothmann pushed for holding it before a full congregation, but von der Wieck saw to it that only a select group of councillors and guild officials were invited to attend. Although this looked like a Lutheran victory, it further damaged the credibility of the Lutheran urban government from the viewpoint of those eager to defend the autonomy and integrity of the city.

Thus in the course of one year the Lutherans lost control of the communal drive of self-government, coming to look all too much like the recently displaced Catholics. Nor did the Münster Lutherans have a native spokesman of anywhere near the ability of Bernhard Rothmann, and Rothmann for his part was moving (maybe one should say that he felt pushed or pulled) in the direction of an increasingly radical congregationalism. By the fall of 1533 he was denying the council the right to participate in church matters, claiming that they should be left to the "congregatio fidelium" [congregation of the faithful].[32] And it seems plausible that large chunks of Münster's population, regardless of economic or social position, found Rothmann's congregationalism attractive because it coincided perfectly with the constitutional traditions of the town itself, traditions that the Lutherans had apparently abandoned.

The irony is that the Anabaptists used the communal, republican traditions of their city to establish first a prophetic and then a royal regime in 1534 that was anything but republican. When the Melchiorite Anabaptist prophet Jan Matthijs arrived in town, he ordered all godless Lutherans and Catholics to be killed so that "one single body and one single Republic" could be set up to serve the Father peacefully through a new covenant based on new customs and Christian laws.[33] Acceding to milder advice, Matthijs agreed to compromise by merely exiling all who would not accept rebaptism. And so, just four days after the Anabaptists were elected to the council, they ordered the expulsion of all godless men, women, and children, and all remaining persons were rebaptized, a ritual that lasted three days and reconstituted the unity of faith and ritual that the Reformation crisis had unleashed. Following the notion that the separatist congregation had a right to purify itself, these Melchiorite Anabaptists redefined their city as their congregation. The *Gemeinde* (congregation) was once again coterminous with the *Gemeinde* (commune).[34] No one accused them of being mentally unstable or of madly hallucinating up to this point in the history of the Anabaptist takeover of Münster. They were cleverly and effectively using the traditional methods of most successful urban politicians during the late Middle Ages or Reformation.

In the story of the New Jerusalem, we should notice a number of revolutionary shifts in symbol, ritual, and religion that incarnated the new dispensation. Living with a sense that they were ushering in the very last stage of history before the Second Coming of Christ, the Münsterites accepted Jan Matthijs as the Second Enoch and prepared to go forth to assemble the 144,000 rebaptized faithful who would oppose Antichrist (Rev. 7:4, 14:1). The time of suffering and persecution was now at an end. No more Christian blood would be shed, but God would soon destroy every godless tyrant.[35] Following the ideas of Melchior Hoffman, who exerted a remarkable influence even from his prison cell in Strasbourg, the Anabaptists of Münster thought they were participating in the "restitution" of God's law and direct government. In the interpretation of Bernhard Rothmann, Jan Matthijs, and Jan of Leiden, however, they now saw themselves as the active opponents of a "heathen" set of earthly rulers. God's servants must be ready to raise their swords in wreaking vengeance on the godless.[36]

The apocalyptic city went on famously to set up a theocracy. This chapter will not treat the much discussed communism or the polygamy by which the Münsterite leaders used Old Testament and apostolic precedent to cope with unexpected problems of food and shelter for hundreds of newcomers and an extraordinary female surplus (in a town of 11,000, some 7,000 to 8,000 were women, while only 1,500 were able-bodied men).[37] We should look instead at the remarkable new understanding the Münsterites gained of themselves and their mission. In early March after the exodus of the godless, Münster published a general invitation to "All Brothers and Sisters": salvation was at hand in the "new Jerusalem, the City of Saints." God would punish the world, but the truly faithful would be safe in Münster.[38] Jakob Hufschmidt admitted spreading the word that between then and Easter, God would kill off more than nine of every ten persons, but that Münster alone would enjoy peace and security as the city of the Lord, the new Jerusalem.[39] So sure was Matthijs that Christ would return by Easter that he fell into grieving contemplation on the Saturday before Easter, cried out like Christ himself: "Not my will but Thine be done," and, as Easter dawned, rode forth from the city with a few soldiers to do battle with the troops of the bishop, probably expecting a miraculous intervention. Instead, he was hacked into so many pieces that his remains had to be carried back into the city in a basket.[40]

In his place Jan of Leiden arose and established an apocalyptic kingdom that no longer depended on Christ's immediate return for the establishment of the new age. Münster began to enjoy a new millennial dispensation of violently antiurban dimensions. Whereas Matthijs had sponsored a drive to purify Münster by driving out the godless Lutherans and Catholics and inviting in godly Anabaptists from the Netherlands and all around, Jan of Leiden took decisive steps to set up a kingdom and a whole new ritual order. Overturning the old civil constitution with various man-made councils, Jan set up a godly government of the new apostolic age, with "Twelve Elders of the Race of Israel," who had supreme power in all matters secular and ecclesiastical, public and private, distinctions that could no longer be sustained.[41] So thoroughly had Münster renounced its civil rights as an urban community that the bishop could actually claim to be the real defender of the republic, guaranteeing a restoration of "old privileges, liberties and rights held of old" to those who would join him in capturing the city.[42] Under this banner he successfully recruited Protestants to aid him in crushing the self-proclaimed city of God. Religiously the city had cut its ties with the past. All books except the Bible were burned in a huge bonfire. Property was declared common, and people were expected to turn in their foreign coinage. Houses could no longer be locked. The Lord's Supper was celebrated in the streets, before the main gates, using food fit for a peasant wedding: beer, soup, and roast meat.[43] Polygamy was introduced in May of 1534, in an effort to give every single woman (and even girls of barely marriageable age) a patriarchal master. To justify this breach of Christian teachings, the leaders cited the example of the Old Testament patriarchs and the injunction to "be fruitful and multiply" (Gen. 1:28). This often meant that a "main wife" now had to tolerate one or more secondary wives, with Jan of Leiden ultimately taking sixteen wives in all. No other measure in revolutionary Münster provoked so much opposition at the time or so much negative comment since, and it is noteworthy that polygamy was a privilege granted only to men. One woman who took two husbands was executed. A rebellion led by Hinrich Mollenhecke broke out against the Anabaptist leaders, but it was put down with a wave of bloody executions.[44]

At the end of August 1534, following an apparently miraculous victory over the troops of the bishop, Jan of Leiden was declared king of Zion and of the whole world. The constitution changed again as 135 men were named to his royal court.[45] Jan dressed himself in jewels and gold, with robes of purple silk or royal gowns trimmed with fur.[46] He carried a royal scepter and a golden orb bored through with two crossed swords surmounted by a cross to represent his holding both the spiritual and the secular sword of dominion over the world.

Münster witnessed many a strange scene in those days. According to one (admittedly hostile) witness, when the rumor spread that King Jan had received a revelation predicting a miracle on the market square, the people assembled there. In the midst of the ensuing expectancy, Bernd Knipperdolling "jumped up and began to shout and rave" ("tho ropen und tho rasen").[47] He danced strangely before the king, throwing his head back and proclaiming himself the *Geck* (fool, idiot) of the king. "He then

looked at the king as if he were a total fool" ("glich als wie er [Knipperdol-
ling] ein rechte narre were").[48] With a face that went strangely dead, and
with an odd pallor about the eyes, Knipperdolling leaped about "as if
possessed" ("wu dat hei besetten was, als it ouck nicht viel besser was")[49]
and even "rolled about on the ground like a tumbler or a juggler, and behaved just like one who is crazy" ("glich wie ein tummler, ofte ein kocheler,
und heft anders nicht gelevet, ofte bei unsinnigh were").[50] Recovering a
bit of his composure, he went among the populace, blessing some and
threatening others. As our hostile witness put it, "Some people certainly
knew that the devil was in charge of them, but they all had to keep their
silence."[51] For our purposes it does not really matter whether this account
is accurate, for my aim here is to look at the rhetoric within which a movement is described and condemned, and in such cases it goes without saying
that the witnesses will be biased and hostile.

One day in early October, our chronicler tells us, Knipperdolling carried
his ecstatic dancing too far, claiming now that he was the one who should
be king. Jan of Leiden reacted forcefully by declaring that his lieutenant
had gone mad ("want hei en is nicht bei sinne"), but Knipperdolling composed himself enough to apologize for his mad utterance, to ask the king's
forgiveness, and to explain "that he had not known what he did. Thus had
the devil misled him."[52] Jan of Leiden threw his repentant subordinate in
jail for two or three days to punish him for challenging his royal claims.

According to Heinrich Gresbeck, it was not only Knipperdolling who
fell victim to such madness. King Jan, too, gave in to long periods of
speechless possession, acting as if dumb and overcome by "the Anabaptist's spirit" ("des dopers geist"), and when he recovered, he usually
claimed to have had revelations from God. On one such occasion he came
out of his trance and at once ordered the instant execution of one of the
soldiers the city was holding prisoner. Jan of Leiden himself wielded the
sword that cut off the prisoner's head.[53] After Münster was captured, he
admitted that he had personally beheaded "seven or eight" persons.[54]
Gresbeck made it plain enough that in his view the Anabaptist claim to
revelation from God was really a cover for pure demonic possession or
inspiration.[55]

To demonstrate that this really was the messianic kingdom, Jan proceeded to one of the most remarkable exercises in the whole history of
the Münster uprising. On 13 October, after releasing the now repentant
Knipperdolling, Jan of Leiden and his limping prophet, Johann Dusentschur, staged a test of God and his people. Claiming a revelation,
Dusentschur said that (once again) the last days had arrived, that the
Lord's trumpet would sound three times, and that every resident of Münster should abandon the city, so that 2 Esdras 5:4–13 could be fulfilled, a

prophecy that included the detail: "And one shall reign whom those who dwell on earth do not expect"; therefore the city must be deserted that wild beasts might enter in, and the city would become a wilderness. At two-week intervals Dusentschur himself blew the trumpet of the Lord in the streets of Münster, and by mid-October Münster was again ready for the last day.[56] As planned, the whole population gathered at Mount Zion, as the cathedral square was called, ready for the exodus, men in armor, women with baggage and children in tow. In preparation for the apocalyptic breakout, King Jan ordered a set of jousts among the 2,000 men and boys assembled. Repeatedly he was able to turn literal expectation into theater. For after these serious preparations, Jan ordered tables to be set up in the streets and a communion service to be held, a remarkable ritual at which "the King and his first Queen served the bread and wine, pausing to talk with their guests and urging them to be joyful in the Lord."[57] After this communion service, the king gathered all his people together in a crowd and set up a high chair among them from which the preachers took turns explaining the meaning of the Lord's Supper. Finally the king himself ascended the chair and said that God had deprived him of his office, that having provoked God's wrath he was king no more. But then, in an amazing reversal, he proclaimed that the last proclamation requiring everyone to leave the city was not true at all. "It was not God's will but just a test" of their obedience. It seems that King Jan knew well how to spiritualize the expectations of some that the last day was actually, literally, at hand. Catching this note, the limping prophet also ascended the high chair, declaring that it was the preachers who should go forth from the city in all four directions, proclaiming peace to the sinful world. And having nominated twenty-seven preachers for this mission, the prophet reinstated Jan of Leiden as king. It had been a full day for the king of New Jerusalem, a day that symbolized well the new kind of urban visionary religion he had created.

To a certain extent, folly and madness appeared as part of the conscious policy of the Anabaptists in Münster. On one occasion the king and all his queens arrived for a mass meeting in the cathedral, and with them they brought a natural fool named Carl, whom they had dressed in priestly garments and told to conduct Holy Mass. Pretending to be a canon of the cathedral, Carl performed a mock Mass, "and all the people laughed at the fool." Bernhard Rothmann pointed out the moral of this blasphemous spectacle by claiming that all the Holy Masses in the world were in fact no holier than this fool's mass.[58] Robert Scribner has reminded us of many other cases in which a spirit of carnival desacralization helped make the Reformation, but this is the only one I know that literally employed the madness of a fool.[59]

In addition to these examples of madness, ecstasy, and folly, Jan of Leiden and Bernd Knipperdolling also demonstrated a devotion to terror that must have imbued their figures with a frightening awesomeness. Many times Jan himself seems to have enjoyed the pleasure of beheading those who crossed him. Once, he became so enraged at the insubordination of one of his wives that he impulsively beheaded her and then publicly trampled her corpse.[60]

The cruelty and bizarre behavior, the trances and dances, provided critics of Münster with ample evidence that at least the leaders of the city were either insane or demon-possessed, or perhaps both. This is certainly how English readers, such as Robert Burton, thought of the event ninety years later.[61] One of the fullest accounts of the whole episode was Hermann von Kerssenbroch's *Anabaptistici Furoris Monasterium Inclitam Westphaliae Metropolim Evertentis Historica Narratio,*[62] a work that pullulates with the charge that the Anabaptists in general, but their leaders especially, were stark raving mad. They had foamed at the mouth and fallen down in seizures;[63] they had run through the streets possessed by insanity; as the title stated: they were mad. They went unpunished so long "because their insanity had flared ever more hotly," and things had gone "from wickedness to wickedness, from madness to madness."[64]

Interestingly, however, the charge of madness was not the main accusation brought against the Melchiorite Millenarians of Münster. When Bishop Franz von Waldeck enlisted the support of Protestant and Catholic estates throughout the empire, he described the Anabaptist regime and its people as "gruesome, rebellious, faithless, re-baptizing, untrustworthy, covenant-breaking, perjured, godless, disobedient to all orders from the emperor and the empire, and living in violation of the public peace."[65] It is apparent that this legal language was necessary to muster support among estates who might have been much less inclined to throw their weight behind a military siege directed against people described by a Catholic bishop as lunatics or heretics.

And after the city fell, on 25–26 June 1535, not all Lutherans were so stricken with horror at what the Anabaptists had done that they could no longer argue. The best example of this is the extended series of interviews held by Pastors Antonius Corvinus and Johann Kymeus with the captured leaders of Münster, Jan of Leiden, Bernd Knipperdolling, and Heinrich Krechting. These two orthodox Lutheran interrogators were not inclined to view these rebel heretics with charity, and their report begins by blasting Jan of Leiden as a mere "Carnival King," who had "suspended God's Word and placed their [Anabaptists'] own dreams in its place."[66] They were sure that such deep-dyed errors came straight from the devil and accused them of following Bernhard Rothmann's theological teachings in a spirit of "bitterness and insanity."[67] They even suspected that God had given the Anabaptist leaders "a perverted mind because of [their] disgraceful enterprise," and that they unfortunately had "an obstinate head and mind," resistant to God's truth.[68] Nonetheless, they were capable of fairly reasonable discussion. Instead of regarding the fallen rebels as demon-possessed or foaming madmen, Corvinus and Kymeus carried on even-tempered, courteous, even if severely confident investigations of the theological errors into which, especially, Jan of Leiden had fallen. Carefully these Lutheran advisers to Landgrave Philipp of Hesse laid open the false interpretations the Anabaptists had deployed regarding free will, baptism, Christology (their monophysite doctrine of the celestial flesh of Christ), the Lord's Supper, the meaning of the "kingdom of God," and the proper understanding of the Book of Revelation (especially chapters 19 and 20). For over one hundred pages, the account of their interrogation proceeded with a remarkably, even astonishingly, temperate tone, identifying heresy and serious errors in countless areas of Anabaptist thought and practice. According to their account, they even brought Jan of Leiden to the point at which he admitted his errors regarding the kingdom of God and appeared ready to retract his Zwinglian understanding of the eucharist (even though he held firm to his Melchiorite Christology and his opposition to infant baptism).[69] This lengthy "disputation" was evidently regarded as so sound and eloquent that it was even reprinted in the Wittenberg edition of Luther's works, published in twelve volumes (1539–1559),[70] thus achieving a celebrity and distribution it might otherwise have never seen. Apparently the lessons to be drawn from these dangerous heretics could not be properly learned if they were portrayed as simply or totally out of their minds. If we argue with our opponents, it seems that we have to assume a basic rationality at some level.

We find something like this in Martin Luther's reactions to Münster, too. In his little work defending the right of civil magistrates to punish the Anabaptists (published in 1536), Luther accused the rebels of falling into the errors of the ancient Manicheans and Donatists. Nowhere did he call them mad or possessed by the devil. Instead they were "stubborn" heretics, who had been "deluded by the devil."[71] Their errors needed sharp correction. In his 1535 introduction to Urbanus Rhegius's attack on the Münsterite theology, Luther likewise accused the Anabaptist "mutineers" of being "hardened" (*verstockt*), as Pharaoh had been hardened in his heart, but they were not crazy. They were wrong.[72] Dealing with the basic problem of argument, Luther remarked in frustration: "What more should one or could one say or do if, with great energy, fidelity, and seriousness, we bring such deep, certain, and public truths and scriptures clearly and powerfully into the light against such a gross and foolish (even if wrathful and wicked) spirit?"[73]

In another little preface, also from 1535, Luther reacted to the latest news of Jan of Leiden's regime by exclaiming that it was perfectly obvious that the devil had set up a household in Münster, or rather that the demons were "piled up thick as toads" there.[74] It was just lucky, in Luther's view, that the devil in Münster was playing such coarse and obvious tricks. Even so, one had cause to worry. "If God is angry and allows the devil to blow on a spark, even a tiny spark can become a blaze that can consume the world."[75] The only reliable weapon against such seductions, therefore, was the "sword of the spirit, God's Word." And so Luther undertook, even in just a page or two, to refute the Melchiorite notion that Christ had not taken on flesh from his mother, but was formed instead from celestial flesh; he also attacked Münsterite errors with respect to baptism, community of goods, and marriage.[76] Crucially, despite his revulsion, he did not label the people or leaders of Münster insane. They were proud, stubborn, demon-led, and mistaken.[77]

One can even detect this attitude of respect in the earliest portraits of the Münster Anabaptist leaders by Heinrich Aldegrever of Soest. His copperplate engravings of Jan of Leiden and of Bernd Knipperdolling, completed in 1536, breathe an air of quiet dignity, of firmness or perhaps even indifference to what the viewer or others think of them.[78] Art historians have found the grandeur of these two portraits similar to the grandeur of many contemporary portraits of princes. Aldegrever clearly found his subjects interesting, even moving. Except for their chains, swords, and scepters, there is no graphic hint of their worldly pretensions, and no mark or gesture signaling any presumed mental defect or obsession. Sharply contrasting with these serene and dignified portraits is a later depiction of Jan of Leiden sitting among naked men, probably in order to associate him with fleshly lusts and Anabaptist indecency, or a mid-sixteenth-century bathhouse scene by Virgil Solis depicting the amorous indecencies of the Anapabtists.[79] In these pictures we are invited to condemn the immoral excesses of religious enthusiasm. It seems almost as if distance made it easier to ridicule the Anabaptists and to depict them as libertine immoralists. Perhaps it is easier to think another mentally ill or essentially wicked if we do not know him or her very well.

Luther and his followers all shared the intense mood of eschatological expectation so common among the Anabaptists at Münster.[80] Such millenarian beliefs, however, did not necessarily produce rebellion or revolution, as some have thought.[81] But the heady sense that a new age was dawning, together with a sense that the old rules and patterns were no longer valid, released the fantasies of some visionaries and prophets, while prompting others to believe that arguably manic utterances were the latest dispensations from on high. In the estimation of Catholic and Lutheran opponents, the millenarian Anabaptists at Münster went well beyond holy scripture and fell into frantic and desperate madness. My point, however, is not the simple and reassuring one that traditionalists and conservatives have regularly drawn from such episodes.[82] Instead, if religious experience and prophecy are so precariously close to madness, we will have to take seriously the warning of the apostle John: "Do not believe every spirit, but test the spirits to see if they are from God, because many false prophets have gone out into the world" (1 John 4:1). Robert Burton knew this lesson well,[83] and we may be well advised to learn it again, not because frightful error is in fact so close to mental disorder, but because the very founders of our Western tradition, whether Socrates or Jesus, sank their roots into layers where we cannot so easily say that they were not beside themselves or mad. But as Martin Luther, Antonius Corvinus, and Martin Bucer learned, one cannot so easily dismiss fantastic ideas or visions of the millennium as merely deluded and mad. Or rather, we *can* perhaps be dismissive and contemptuous, but there is a cost to pay for our presumed superiority. When a group finds that others consider their views lunatic or crazy, those labeled crazy may then give up all attempts to explain themselves. And in this process of mutual alienation, opposing ideas can become (and often do become) even more angry and alienated, madder and more autistic, sealed off from any requirement that they explain themselves and hold themselves (and us) to a standard of mutual intelligibility. When Corvinus and Bucer and Luther undertook discussions and arguments with the visionaries in their midst, they did not find themselves unable to test their spirits, but they did find that the "fanatics" who had terrified them at a distance were much more ordinary when interrogated closely. Scholars, perhaps especially, need to recover what Luther and his companions so clearly had: the learned ability to argue with those who claim special or personal access to a wisdom that passeth human understanding.

Notes

1. In Mark 3:21 Jesus' kinsmen act to take charge of Jesus because people were saying he was out of his mind. See Michael Screech, "The 'Mad' Christ of Erasmus and the Legal Duties of His Brethren," in Norris J. Lacy and Jerry C. Nash, eds., *Essays in Early French Literature Presented to Barbara M. Craig* (York, S.C.: French Literature Publications, 1982), 119–27, and more generally idem, *Ecstasy and the Praise of Folly* (London: Duckworth, 1980), chap. 4, section 3: "The Madness of Christ."

2. Jaroslav Jan Pelikan, *Obedient Rebels: Catholic Substance and Protestant Principle in Luther's Reformation* (New York: Harper and Row, 1964); idem, *Luther the Expositor: Introduction to the Reformer's Exegetical Writings* (St. Louis: Concordia, 1959), 46–47.

3. Alister E. McGrath, *The Intellectual Origins of the European Reformation* (Oxford: Blackwell, 1987).

4. Karl Holl, "Martin Luther on Luther," trans. H. C. Erik Midelfort, in Jaroslav Pelikan, ed., *Interpreters of Luther: Essays in Honor of Wilhelm Pauck* (Philadelphia: Fortress Press, 1968), 9–34.

5. Mark U. Edwards, *Luther and the False Brethren* (Stanford: Stanford University Press, 1975); idem, *Luther's Last Battles: A Study of the Polemics of the Older Luther, 1531–46* (Ithaca: Cornell University Press, 1983).

6. I often cite both the critical edition, *D. Martin Luthers Werke. Kritische Gesamtausgabe* (Weimar: H. Bohlau, 1883–) [hereafter *WA*], and the English translation, when available, ed. Helmut T. Lehmann and Jaroslav J. Pelikan, *Martin Luther, Works* (St. Louis: Concordia, 1955–1986) [hereafter *LW*]. For the point just mentioned see *WA* 10.1.1 (Kirchenpostillen): 132, 205, 218, 234, 387.

7. For examples, *WA* 43 (Lectures on Genesis): 186, 276, 363.

8. *WA* 43:417, 276; cf. *LW* 3:269; 4: 71, 125, 195, 346, 407. See Dale Jonathan Grieser, *Seducers of the Simple Folk: The Polemical War against Anabaptism (1524–1540)* (Th.D. diss., Harvard University, 1993).

9. "Narren sind wyr": *WA* 10.1.1: 698; *LW* 1:222; *LW* 2:235.

10. *WA* 43:423; *LW* 4:400.

11. *LW* 4:378.

12. The Grimms' *Deutsches Wörterbuch* cites the following early modern usages *s.v.:* "Mein herr thut grausam schwermen und fluchen ich soll sein tochter wider suchen" (J. Ayrer); "habe ich der tollen und immerschwermenden welt die eitelkeit unsers zeitlichen lebens in einem offentlichen spiell wollen fürbilden" (Hollonius); "in dem höheren grade dieser störung schwarmen durch das verbrannte gehirn allerlei angemaszte überfeine einsichten" (Immanuel Kant); "das talent . . . regellos verfahren und schwärmen zu lassen, würde vielleicht originale tollheit abgeben" (Kant); "der fanatiker (visionär, schwärmer). . . , ist eigentlich ein verrückter von einer vermeinten unmittelbaren eingebung und einer großen vertraulichkeit mit den machten des himmels" (Schuppius); "der schwärmer ist einem phrenetisch-rasenden gleich, der sich in wütenden konvulsionen wirft" (Bürger).

13. See *Oxford English Dictionary,* second ed., 5: 712–13. The Latin *fanum* means "temple," and so a *fanaticus* was a person "inspired by orgiastic rites, enthusiastic, fanatic, frantic." Livy (38.13.12): "cum iactatione fanatica corporis vaticinari." L. Annius Florus, *Epitome Bellorum Omnium Annorum,* DCC, 2.7 (3.19.4): "fanatico furore similato." Samuel Johnson thus defined "fanaticism" as "enthusiasm" or religious frenzy, and the "fanatick" as "a man mad with wild notions of religion." *Johnson's Dictionary of the English Language,* 9th ed. (London, 1805), vol. 2, *s.v.*

14. James M. Stayer, *Anabaptists and the Sword* (Lawrence, Kan.: Coronado Press, 1972), 239–51.

15. Klaus Deppermann, *Melchior Hoffman. Social Unrest and Apocalyptic Vi-*

sions in the Age of Reformation, trans. Malcolm Wren, ed. Benjamin Drewery (Edinburgh: T & T Clark, 1987), 204–13.

16. By 1538 Hoffman's disciples were also ready to reject Lienhard Jost as a *Narr* (ibid., 204–5, 364). Cf. Klaus Deppermann, *Melchior Hoffman: Soziale Unruhen und apokalyptische Visionen im Zeitalter der Reformation* (Göttingen: Vandenhoeck und Ruprecht, 1979), 179, 318.

17. Ibid. (English ed.), 99–100; (German ed. 87).

18. *WA* 44:153–54; *LW* 6:206–07.

19. *WA* 44:154–55; *LW* 6:207–11.

20. For decades the best-known account of Münster in English was the concluding section of Norman Cohn, *The Pursuit of the Millennium: Revolutionary Millenarians and Mystical Anarchists of the Middle Ages* (1957), rev. ed. (Oxford: Oxford University Press, 1970), 252–80. More discriminating general accounts include Stayer, *Anabaptists and the Sword,* 211–80; George H. Williams, *The Radical Reformation,* 3d ed. (Kirksville, Mo.: Sixteenth Century Journal Publishers, 1992), 553–88.

21. Karl-Heinz Kirchhoff, *Die Täufer in Münster 1534/35: Untersuchungen zum Umfang und zur Sozialstruktur der Bewegung* (Münster: Aschendorff, 1973), 42.

22. Karl-Heinz Kirchhoff, *Die Täufer in Münster 1534/35;* Heinz Schilling, "Aufstandsbewegungen in der stadtbürgerlichen Gesellschaft des Alten Reiches. Die Vorgeschichte des Münsteraner Täuferreichs, 1525–1534," in Hans-Ulrich Wehler, ed., *Der deutsche Bauernkrieg, 1524–1526* (Göttingen: Vandenhoeck und Ruprecht, 1975), 193–238; Ronnie Po-chia Hsia, "Münster and the Anabaptists," in Ronnie Po-chia Hsia, ed., *The German People and the Reformation* (Ithaca: Cornell University Press, 1988), 51–70, D. Jonathan Grieser, "A Tale of Two Convents: Nuns and Anabaptists in Münster, 1533–1535," *Sixteenth Century Journal* 26 (1993), 31–47, takes issue with Schilling's now nearly orthodox view. Along these lines see also Taira Kuratsuka, "Gesamtgilde und Täufer: Der Radikalisierungsprozess in der Reformation Münsters: Von der reformatorischen Bewegung zum Täuferreich 1534/35," *Archiv für Reformationsgeschichte* 76 (1985), 231–70. The most copious review of the literature is found in Karl-Heinz Kirchhoff, "Das Phänomen des Täuferreiches zu Münster 1524/35," *Der Raum Westfalen* 6, part 1: *Fortschritte der Forschung und Schlußbilanz* (989), 277–422.

23. To take a casual and therefore revealing example: Heinrich Bornkamm, *Luther's World of Thought,* trans. Martin H. Bertram (St. Louis: Concordia, 1958), 23: Writing of Luther from 1535 on, Bornkamm remarks in passing, "Even the Anabaptists occupied him but little. . . . the mad spectre of Münster merely confirmed Luther's belief that the devil was playing a role there." See also the excerpts printed in Richard van Dülmen, *Das Täuferreich zu Münster 1534–1535* (Munich: Deutscher Taschenbuch-Verlag, 1974), 286–94.

24. Deppermann, *Melchior Hoffman* (English trans.) 162–67, 268–73, 325–28.

25. Schilling, "Aufstandsbewegungen," 197.

26. Ibid., 199–207; Otthein Rammstedt, "Stadtunruhen 1525," in Wehler, *Der deutsche Bauernkrieg,* 234–76.

27. Schilling, "Aufstandsbewegungen," 210.

28. Bernd Moeller, "Zwinglis Disputationen: Studien zu den Anfängen der

Kirchenbildung und des Syndalwesens im Protestantismus," *Zeitschrift der Savigny Stiftung für Rechtsgeschichte, Kanonistische Abteilung* 56 (1970), 275–325, and 60 (1974), 213–365.

29.   Leopold von Ranke, *Deutsche Geschichte im Zeitalter der Reformation,* ed. Paul Joachimsen (Meersburg: F. W. Hendel, 1933), 3: 307.

30.   Schilling, "Aufstandsbewegungen," 219–20.

31.   Ibid., 221. Schilling recapitulates and extends this argument in two major chapters of his *Religion, Political Culture, and the Emergence of Early Modern Society: Essays in German and Dutch History* (Leiden: Brill, 1992), 61–134, 135–87, esp. 103–16 and 140–52.

32.   Ibid., 224.

33.   Van Dülmen, *Das Täuferreich zu Münster,* 71.

34.   See H. C. Erik Midelfort, "Social History and Biblical Exegesis: Community, Family and Witchcraft in 16th-Century Germany," in David C. Steinmetz, ed., *The Bible in the Sixteenth Century* (Durham, N.C.: Duke University Press, 1990), 7–20.

35.   Deppermann, *Melchior Hoffman* (English trans.), 333–39.

36.   Ibid., 342–48.

37.   Van Dülmen, *Das Täuferreich zu Münster,* 18–19.

38.   Ibid., 78, 80.

39.   Ibid., 82.

40.   Ibid., 105, 108–9.

41.   Ibid., 112–14.

42.   Announcement of 17 March 1534: ibid., 101.

43.   Ibid., 120.

44.   Hermann Homann, *Drei Käfige am Turm: Aufstieg und Fall des Wiedertäuferreiches in Münster 1534/35* (Münster: Coppenrath, 1977), 128–36.

45.   Van Dülmen, *Das Täuferreich zu Münster,* 154–57.

46.   Ibid., 158–59.

47.   Carl Adolf Cornelius, ed., *Berichte der Augenzeugen über das münsterische Wiedertäuferreich* (Münster: Aschendorff, 1983), 142–43.

48.   Ibid., 143.

49.   Ibid., 144.

50.   Ibid.

51.   "Ein deil luede merckeden wol, dat der duvel so mit innen regierde. Ein ieder moiste stil schweigen." Ibid., 145.

52.   "So hat sich Knipperdollinck der furiger rede beclagt und heft den koningk umb gnade gebedden, er en wuste nicht, wat er gedain hedde; so hat oem der duvel verliet." Ibid., 150.

53.   Ibid., 113–14. For a different account of what was perhaps the same episode, see Williams, *Radical Reformation,* 573–74.

54.   Cornelius, *Berichte,* 344.

55.   Ibid., 101–3, 113; "dat die wiederdoper einen eigen geist hedden, der sie plach tho plagen. So khan ein ider wol gedenckhen, dat et moist gein guit geist sein gewest. Got behoede uns alle fur solchem geist." Ibid., 102.

56. Günther List, *Chiliastische Utopie und radikale Reformation* (Munich: Fink, 1973), 218.

57. Horst Karasek, *Die Kommune der Wiedertäufer: Bericht aus der befreiten und belagerten Stadt Münster 1534* (Berlin: Wagenbach, 1977), 118.

58. Cornelius, *Berichte*, 151.

59. Robert W. Scribner, "Reformation, Carnival, and the World Turned Upside Down," *Social History* 3 (1978), 303–30, reprinted in his *Popular Culture and Popular Movements in Reformation Germany* (London: Ronceverte, 1988).

60. Elisabeth Wantscherers had criticized Jan's royal style of high living at a time of hardship for most residents of Münster. Van Dülmen, *Das Täuferreich zu Münster,* 256–57.

61. Robert Burton, *The Anatomy of Melancholy,* ed. Holbrook Jackson (New York: Dutton, 1977), 3:371: "It is a wonder to reveal what passages Sleidan relates in his Commentaries, of Cretink, Knipperdolling, and their associates, those madmen of Munster in Germany; what strange enthusiasms, sottish revelations they had, how absurdly they carried themselves, deluded others; . . . we may say of these peculiar sects, their religion takes away not spirits only, but wit and judgment, and deprives them of their understanding; for some of them are so far gone with their private enthusiasms and revelations, that they are quite mad, out of their wits."

62. The only reliable edition is by Heinrich Detmer in 2 vols. (Münster: Theissing, 1899–1900).

63. Van Dülmen, *Das Täuferreich zu Münster,* 164–65.

64. "Impunitos, dum eorum insania ardentius flagraret"; "a scelere in scelus, a furore in furorem." Detmer, *Anabaptistici Furoris,* 191.

65. "Diese grausamen, aufrührerischen, abtrünnigen, wiedertäuferischen, treulosen, bundbrüchigen, meineidigen, gottesvergessenen, des Reiches und allen kaiserlichen Befehlen ungehorsamen und dem öffentlichen Frieden zuwiderlebenden Einwohnern der Stadt Münster." Van Dülmen, *Das Täuferreich zu Münster,* 230.

66. Acta: Handlungen: Legation und schriffte: so durch den durchleuchtigen hochgeboren Fürsten und Herrn Philipsen, Landgraven zu Hessen ect [sic] Inn der Münsterischen sache geschehen, zusamen gepracht. . . . Item. Gespreche und disputation Antonii Corvini und Joannis Kymei, mit dem Munsterischen König, mit Knipperdolling und Krechting, ehe denn sie gerechtfertigt worden sein, gehalten in Jenner Anno MDXXXVI (Wittenberg, 1536), fols. A2, A3.

67. Ibid., fol. B4v: "sind sie gar erbittert und unsinnig worden."

68. Ibid., fol. F4.

69. Ibid., fols. f3–h3v.

70. See WA 60:464–95, esp. 471, 479. And see Martin Luther, *Werke,* vol. 2 (Wittenberg: Hans Lufft, 1557), fols. 363v–399v.

71. *Das weltliche Oberkeit den Wiederteuffern mit leiblicher straffen zu wehren schuldig sey* (Wittenberg, 1536): *WA* 50: 6–15.

72. *WA* 38: 338–40.

73. Ibid., 339.

74. *WA* 38: 341–50, at 347.

75. Ibid., 348.

76. Ibid., 348–49.

77. In Strasbourg in 1533 during the crisis over spiritualism and Anabaptism there, Martin Bucer, too, had disputed carefully and at length with the visionaries. Deppermann, *Melchior Hoffman* (English trans.), 295.

78. Jochen Luckhardt and Angelika Lorenz, eds., *Heinrich Aldegrever und die Bildnisse der Wiedertäufer* (Münster: Westfälisches Landesmuseum für Kunst und Kulturgeschichte, 1985), 19–20, 42–45.

79. Ibid., 140–43.

80. Robin Barnes, *Prophecy and Gnosis: Apocalypticism in the Wake of the Lutheran Reformation* (Stanford: Stanford University Press, 1988).

81. This is part of Norman Cohn's thesis (*Pursuit of the Millennium*), to which Robert E. Lerner, *The Powers of Prophecy. The Cedar of Lebanon Vision from the Mongol Onslaught to the Dawn of the Enlightenment* (Berkeley: University of California Press, 1983), and William Lamont, *Godly Rule. Politics and Religion 1603–1660* (London: Macmillan, 1969), provide effective counterarguments.

82. For this tradition see Michael Heyd, "The Reaction to Enthusiasm in the Seventeenth Century: Towards an Integrative Approach," *Journal of Modern History* 53 (1981), 258–80; Richard Golden, "Religious Extremism in the Mid-Century: The Parisian Illuminées," *European Studies Review* 9 (1979), 195–210. I also thank Sara T. Nalle for showing me her unpublished essay, "Between Hope and the Devil: The Treatment of False Messiahs in the Iberian World," September 1997.

83. See n. 61 above.

7 *David M. Bethea*

Apocalypticism in Russian Literature
A Brief Portrait

In recent times culture has been compared to a kind of "supraconscious-ness" hovering over the physical globe in a circumambient cloud.[1] It ma-nipulates on a massive scale the same communicative codes that every human being operates in his or her individual world. Building on discover-ies in cell biology, organic chemistry, and brain science, the Russian theo-rist and literary scholar Yury Lotman devised the term "semiosphere" to capture this notion of human communication writ large as cultural eco-system: the place where intracranial brain function (i.e., the relationship between right and left hemispheres), meaning production, and the shapes and symbols we project onto (or extract from) the external world coalesce into our collective organism's psychic drive for growth and discovery.[2] That this site is a *metaphor,* a product of language and therefore invisible like the atmosphere over the earth, does not make it any less "real" to those constructing meaning out of their interactions with others. In this regard, literature has traditionally been seen as a rich source of communi-cation (i.e., new information) because, potentially, many different codes and "languages" (in the sense of stylistic registers, dialects, idiosyncratic speech patterns, etc.) can coexist and be artfully juxtaposed within its boundaries.

Russian literature of the modern period (roughly from 1800 to the pres-ent) has played a dynamic, even crucial, role in the larger "ecosystem" of

Russian culture. To appreciate this role, let us propose another meta-phor—an interior photograph, an MRI, of the Russian literary "brain." This figure of speech, of course, registers likeness more than difference (as all metaphors do), and it cannot do justice to subtle changes over time or to the historical specificity of certain phenomena. Still, as a means of isolating global psychic tendencies that become, as it were, imprinted on the larger social organism's memory, it is not without heuristic value. Exceptions to these tendencies exist, but the fact that these exceptions *take the tendencies into account*—they thwart them or undermine them, but they do not *ignore* them—means that this "psychic mapping" is not invisible. Why these tendencies and not others have become salient in the Russian context is buried deep in the past, and is as much a question of cultural mythology, including Russians' sacred legends about themselves and their destiny as a people, as of history per se. The list could, of course, be expanded, but in order to provide a general picture of the apocalyptic character of Russian literature, I focus on the following traits: religious sensibility, maximalism, the writer as secular saint, literature as social conscience, the problem of personality, space–time oppositions (East versus West, old versus new), and the combination of eros and national myth.

Religious Sensibility

Perhaps the first and arguably the most important formative influence to come to mind is Russian culture's pervasive spirituality (*dukhovnost'*) and, correlatively, the written word's traditionally sacred status. Apocalypticism, if it has any meaning at all, insists on the existence of a genuine alterity (or otherness) and on the understanding that words are not uttered self-reflexively but are the occasion for disclosing (the Greek *apoka-luptō*, uncover, reveal) an ultimate reality beyond them. Russia (Kievan Rus') was Christianized under Prince Vladimir in the year 988, and from roughly that point until well into the seventeenth and eighteenth centuries, the entire notion of literature for secular pleasure or edification was largely moot. There were saints' lives (*vitae*), sermons, chronicles, and even epics (e.g., *The Igor Tale*), but the category of fiction (i.e., a self-contained world wholly created through words that is understood by its reader to be artificial, hence "untrue") came late to Russian literature. Indeed, it can be argued that much of the attraction of the great works of Russian literature is due to this tendency of reader reception/perception: Russian "fictions" about the world are more "real" than the real-life context into which they are read and absorbed. Russian writers have long operated under the conviction that they are writing, not one more book, but versions, each in its way sacred, of the Book (the Bible). Thus, when some modern Russian writers have taken a militantly materialist, antispiritualist approach to reality, the fervidness and single-mindedness of their commitment to new belief systems often suggest a replay of various medieval models of behavior, replete with the latter's thematics of conversion. This is not the absence of theology, but rather its negative ("apophatic") assertion.[3] Likewise, Lev Tolstoy presents his anticlericalism and his sharp criticism of Orthodox dogma and ritual not in the name of Voltairean enlightenment and urbane secularism, but in that of a *new* religion, which came to be known as "Tolstoyanism."

This religious sensibility continues in the shadow life of some of the most influential Russian poems, novels, and dramas through the transposing of medieval forms of sacred writing (especially hagiography) to later secular works. Examples include Ivan Turgenev's "Living Relics," Nikolai Chernyshevsky's *What Is to Be Done?*, Fyodor Dostoevsky's *The Idiot* and *The Brothers Karamazov*, Sergei Stepnyak-Kravchinsky's *Andrei Kozhukhov*, and Maxim Gorky's *Mother*. What the *vita* requires is that the personal become sanctified, monumentalized, subsumed within the impersonality of holiness. If one considers how much the modern novel in the European and Anglo-American bourgeois traditions depends on individual, concrete examples of an open, *developing* biography and history (e.g., the *Bildungsroman*), this means that the Russian novel will often be acting against prevailing trends in Western practice. Saintly behavior can be actively submissive (the "meek" model of the martyred brothers Boris and Gleb) or defiantly subversive (the "holy warrior" model of Alexander Nevsky), but what it cannot be is consciously concerned with its own needs as a separate ego with a merely personal mission.

Another important attribute of the literary expression of Russian spirituality is the emphasis on what might be termed, after the pioneering work of the mathematician-priest Pavel Florensky, liminality or "iconic space."[4] The icon, with its physical materials (painting on wood), its otherworldly, two-dimensional figures, and its notion of divine authorship (the icon painter is merely the instrument of the higher power), is not perceived by the viewer as a representation of holiness, but *as holiness itself*: when the penitent individual kisses the icon, he or she steps, as it were, *through* its frame from the realm of the profane to the realm of the holy. There is no middle ground or expandable space en route to this miraculous transformation, just as the icon itself cannot be understood in Western terms of mediation (i.e., the three-dimensional figures that increasingly, as a result of the Renaissance, *stood in for* humanity in representational paintings). One could argue that when a writer like Dostoevsky describes heroes and situations that are constructed around the psychological dynamics of liminality—Myshkin before the portrait of Nastasya Filippovna and the

Holbein painting of Christ (*The Idiot*); Alyosha Karamazov recalling his half-crazed mother in the context of an icon of the Virgin (*The Brothers Karamazov*)—we are in the presence of this same iconic space: the space of religious conversion (or, in its demonic opposite, the space wherein all faith is lost).

The *iurodivyi* (holy fool, fool-in-Christ) is a potent figure in Russian literature, from Alexander Pushkin's character who says to the tsar what no one else dares (*Boris Godunov*) to Yury Olesha's Ivan Babichev, who tells campy versions of gospel parables to the drunks and outcasts of Soviet society (*Envy*). The reason is that he captures in one person, with great economy and expressive force, this principle of iconic liminality. He voluntarily humiliates himself, thus retraversing Christ's path, in order to, as it were, rub society's nose in its own pride and exclusionary logic (ostracizing the "pure" from the "impure"). By plunging into the midst of "polite society" naked or with the carcass of a dog strapped to his waist, the *iurodivyi* forces the issue of his own degradation and marginalization.[5] And the reader must make a choice: is this simply a fool or a fool whose antics reveal the workings of divine wisdom? Do I judge and join the ranks of the modern Pharisees, or do I imitate Christ and celebrate the Bakhtinian carnival logic of role-reversal, laughter, and folly?

Maximalism

Russian spirituality has a powerful maximalist streak—hardly surprising in light of the tragic character of Russian history. "There are," as the philosopher Nikolai Berdyaev once wrote in *The Russian Idea*, "two dominant myths which can become dynamic in the life of a people—the myth about origins and the myth about the end. For Russians it has been the second myth, the eschatological one, that has dominated."[6] Likewise, some of the best-known works in modern Russian literature (Pushkin's *Bronze Horseman*, Nikolai Gogol's *Dead Souls*, Dostoevsky's *The Devils*, Gorky's *Mother*, Andrei Bely's *Petersburg*, Alexander Blok's *The Twelve*, Evgeny Zamyatin's *We*, Andrei Platonov's *Chevengur*, Mikhail Bulgakov's *The Master and Margarita*, Boris Pasternak's *Doctor Zhivago*) have possessed a "deep structure" of biblical/apocalyptic or utopian myth. Meaning is sought in a dramatic, usually violent, "right-angled" resolution: either God the Author, standing outside/beyond, decides to put a flaming end (*ekpyrosis*) to his story (human history), or else mankind, realizing that it is the sole author (God is dead) and that perfectability on earth is possible, devises its own ideal *polis* (a secular City of God) as a conclusion to history's plot.[7] In either case, whether meaning comes from without or from within, an equals sign is placed between "revelation" (the final truth) and "revolution" (violent social/political upheaval). Charismatic popular leaders (Stenka Razin, Emelyan Pugachov) and their rebellions were inevitably portrayed as apocalyptic scourges striking at the godless state with its "new" religion; Peter the Great, perhaps the most famous of all tsars, was viewed among some segments of the populace (e.g., the Old Believers) as the Antichrist and among others (e.g., Pushkin) as an archrevolutionary.

But it is not only historical conditions that have forced on Russians this maximalist mentality. One can argue that the very structure of their religious imagination has in a way guaranteed certain outcomes. For example, Russian holy men and religious thinkers have traditionally shown great impatience with any axiologically neutral or "middle ground"—from the Purgatory of the Catholic church, where one can *gradually* (cf. the notion of "progress") atone for one's sins en route to Paradise, to the notion of "middle-class values," where one can see to one's individual well-being even as those less fortunate are excluded or allowed to become invisible. Likewise, it has been traditional for Russians to evince a profound skepticism about the rhythms of everyday life (*byt*): it seems this quotidian space-time can only, with great difficulty, "mean." Furthermore, as Lotman and others have shown, Russians, and perhaps Slavs in general,[8] have felt that such compromising notions as "negotiation" and "agreement" (*dogovor*) are the province of the devil, whereas in the Western tradition of Roman law and the Catholic church such concepts were more or less unmarked: one could "arrange" one's position (or one's loved one's) in the other world by doing good deeds, making donations, or offering prayers in this one.[9] But as in Florensky's iconic space, where any believer can instantaneously step through the frame from the profane to the holy, this concept of agreement, or "giving with strings attached," has often proved anathema to the "all or nothing" Russian religious mind. It is by no means strange in this context, therefore, that Russian culture has produced a number of modern thinkers, most notably Vladimir Solovyov and Nikolai Fyodorov, whose ambitious visions for the realized transfiguration of humanity are virtually unimaginable in the West. Solovyov, for instance, made the case for a theocratic marriage of Western and Eastern Christian churches, while Fyodorov assayed nothing less than the actual biological (molecule by molecule!) resurrection of our ancestors. Moreover, these and other philosophers (including the already mentioned Florensky) exerted considerable influence on modern writers: their ideas surface in modified form in the works of Gorky, Fyodor Sologub, Blok, Bely, Vladimir Mayakovsky, Bulgakov, Platonov, Nikolai Ognyov, Nikolai Zabolotsky, Pasternak, and others.[10]

The Writer as Secular Saint

Because Russian society was slow to adopt the worldly ways of the West and because the written word was carefully scrutinized and censored by church and state (its "sacred" status thereby implicitly recognized and controlled), the writer, and the poet in particular, became a secular saint and, very often, a martyr (or suffering "holy fool"). The Ur-text in this regard was Pushkin's 1826 poem "The Prophet" (*Prorok*), whose speaker has his formerly sinful tongue ripped out by a six-winged Seraph (the source is Isaiah) and whose words are henceforth meant to "burn the hearts of people" with their message.

The list of "martyred" writers is very long, and the role of "suffering for the faith" must be acknowledged as one of the truly defining traits of the Russian literary imagination: Vasily Trediakovsky, Alexander Radishchev, Pushkin, Mikhail Lermontov, Gogol, Chernyshevsky, Dostoevsky, Blok, Velimir Khlebnikov, Nikolai Klyuev, Zamyatin, Isaak Babel, Osip Mandelstam, Anna Akhmatova, Marina Tsvetaeva, Bulgakov, Pasternak, Alexander Solzhenitsyn, Varlam Shalamov, Andrei Sinyavsky, Joseph Brodsky. Even famous suicides—Radishchev, Sergei Esenin, Mayakovsky, Tsvetaeva—did not "simply" kill themselves but were written into this larger martyrology (i.e., they were "killed" by society/the state). The Russian writer became a lightning rod (or scourge) in a society that was anything but "civil" and in a faceless, sprawling bureaucratic state (tsarist, then Soviet) that had little respect for individual rights and the rule of law.

How did this martyrology work? What were its psychic mechanisms? In the poet Vladislav Khodasevich's phrase (borrowed again from Pushkin), Russian society and its writers entered into a kind of fatal contract, or "bloody repast" (*krovavaia pishcha*). It was a contract with little of the spirit of compromise about it. The poet-martyr was persecuted and eventually killed (like Christ) because of his service to a higher ideal (Russian culture, the Russian poetic word), while society played the role of Pontius Pilate or the Roman soldiers at the foot of the cross. The persecutors could not, according to this logic, act otherwise. By bringing the sainted figure to his death, they were fulfilling a larger dispensation: giving the Christ-figure the chance *to redeem them* through his sacrifice. Even those who survived persecution (Akhmatova, Pasternak) or those who emerged alive from the hell of the camps (Solzhenitsyn, Shalamov) did so with the martyr's aureole intact and the myth of their semireligious witness confirmed. Hence one of the more fascinating questions of Russian literary studies is how poets have seemed to fashion their own "fated" ends (Pushkin's is again the archetypal example) out of this "contract" with their wayward, needful flock. Rather than meekly accepting God's will, as in the famous *vita* of the murdered brothers (and first "passion sufferers") Boris and Gleb, the Russian poet has tended to model his life on that of the indomitable and "plain-speaking" Archpriest Avvakum, who was burned alive with his sectarian followers in 1682 for not accepting the official faith of the church and state.

Literature as Social Conscience

"People can be killed for poetry here—a sign of unparalleled respect—because they are still capable of living by it," Nadezhda Mandelstam wrote.[11] She was, of course, speaking not only about poetry (and literature) in general, but also about the work of her husband, Osip Mandelstam, one of the great poets of the twentieth century, who died in a Stalinist labor camp because his writing was judged to be a crime against the state (and, more crucially, an affront to its leader). The point is that, ironically, the state has until very recently shown "unparalleled respect" through its relentless persecutions of its writers because its attempts to silence them have only further emphasized the roar of independent protest in their written words. And because the state has not only failed to protect the individual, but has actually made a mockery of any notion of basic human rights, it has traditionally been literature's job to serve as social conscience: advocate for the downtrodden (peasant, "little man" *chinovnik*/bureaucrat, factory worker, women and children) and critic of the despotic tsarist regime, with its instruments of power (censorship, secret police, court system, labor camps). This tendency to give voice to concerns that are incapable of being uttered through other social institutions—even if that voice is muffled by censorship and "Aesopian" encodings and circumlocutions—has given Russian literature its strong didacticism and sense of moral rectitude. It is arguable that this same urge to use "literature" (broadly defined) in the service of social change has always been present in Russian culture, but its rise in modern times is usually associated with the name of the great *raznochinets* critic Vissarion Belinsky and his literary journalism of the 1830s and 1840s. The questioning titles of works by leading practitioners of the "Belinskian line" speak forcefully of this notion of literature as conscientious opposition to the status quo: Alexander Herzen's novel *Who Is to Blame?* (1847), Nikolai Dobrolyubov's essays "What Is Oblomovism?" (1859) and "When Will the Real Day Come?" (1860), Chernyshevsky's novel *What Is to Be Done?* (1863).

The Problem of Personality

Closely related to Russian literature's function as social conscience is the problem of *lichnost'* (personality, personhood). Whereas the tradition of Belinsky and the civic critics relentlessly exposed the negative sides of Russian existence (what the state had denied its citizens in terms of basic dignity and self-respect), other writers sought a *positive content*—expressed in the search for a "positive hero" (*polozhitel'nyi geroi*)—for *lichnost'*.[12] Russian literature of the nineteenth and twentieth centuries is heavily populated by personality "types": the "superfluous man" (*lishnii chelovek*), who is gifted and often "noble" (in both senses) but has no historically viable arena for action and thus repeatedly suffers a loss of will (Alexander Griboedov's Chatsky, Turgenev's Rudin, Ivan Goncharov's Oblomov); the "new man" of the 1860s (and then of the Soviet period), who is precise, unsentimental, scientific, materialist, but who inevitably must wait for society to "catch up" to him (Turgenev's Bazarov, Chernyshevsky's Rakhmetov, Gorky's Pavel Vlasov); and the "strong woman," who is often made to represent Russia's hidden potential and who possesses the courage and resolute idealism that the weaker male characters lack (Pushkin's Tatiana Larina, Goncharov's Olga Ilyinskaya, Fyodor Gladkov's Dasha Chumalova, Bulgakov's Margarita). Again, in a way that suggests a religious/"maximalist" as opposed to secular/"skeptical" approach to the written word, the Russian reading public has often made a *direct, prescriptive link* between the portrayal of charismatic activity in fiction and the rules for behavior in phenomenal reality outside the text. As is the case with Florensky's iconic space, the word does not stand in, metaphorically, for the person, but *is* the person, his most real, sacred trace.

Space–Time Oppositions: East/West, Old/New

From the time of its earliest formation, Russia has faced the problem of how to view itself in the "history of nations": which version of Christianity, Eastern or Western, should it choose? Many of the turning points in its history, and many (if not most) of its cultural monuments, have centered on the issue of whether this increasingly vast and diverse country and its people(s) are "Western," "Eastern," or some significant, new combination of the two. Ignored until recently is how the temporal opposition between old and new is simultaneously embedded in the spatial opposition between East and West. In other words, these oppositions, which are necessary for constructing meaning, can in certain highly charged situations be viewed *as extensions of each other.* Their respective values (plus/minus, good/bad, we/they) can change depending on the circumstances, but that they are implicated in each other in the Russian historical imagination seems by now beyond doubt.

Thus Hilarion, in his early "Sermon on Law and Grace" (c. 1037–1050), likens the "new" faith of the Russians to the enfranchised bride Sarah (hence to *New* Testament grace) but the "old" faith of Byzantium to the handmaiden Hagar (hence to *Old* Testament law). Several centuries later, the Archpriest Avvakum will reverse these values during the Great Schism (*raskol*) of the 1660s, so that the "new" Nikonian reforms imposed by the church/state are now perceived as the province of the Antichrist and a betrayal of the Old Belief. Likewise, Moscow's role as Third (and last) Rome, with its tsar as *basileus* (the emperor who is simultaneously spiritual and secular leader of the Christian realm), becomes clear when Constantinople (the "Second Rome") falls to the Ottoman Turks in 1453. And Peter the Great's reforms, including his spelling with a foreign alphabet, his passion for Western architecture, and his new calendar, galvanized the Old Believer sectarians precisely because these innovations conflated and made interchangeable the unholy categories of new and Western: they demonstrated that this tsar could not be the true *basileus* and so had to be an impostor—which is to say, the Antichrist. In recent centuries these binaries have become especially marked in Russia's myth-saturated geography: the "old," more native city of Moscow versus the "new," more Western city of St. Petersburg. Generally speaking, Russian cultural and political figures, and writers *a fortiori,* tended to face the problematic present by either looking to a positive future ideal (a modern urban or technological utopia emerging out of new/Western ideas) or to a positive past ideal (an archaic village utopia—the peasant *mir/obshchina*—emerging out of old/native ideas).

Eros and the National Myth

The pagan roots of Russian/Slavic culture were not forgotten with the coming of Christianity. Indeed, as the scholar Boris Uspensky has indicated, those roots were often "remembered" *through inversion* in the forms of the adopting mythology: the pre-Christian gods became the devils of the Russian Christian world (from Volos/Veles to *volosatik,* wood goblin).[13] In this respect, one of the inevitable developments in the mythologization of Russian time and space by its writers and thinkers is that the pagan concept of "Mother Earth" (*mat' syra zemlia*) and the Christian concept of "Holy Russia" (*Sviataia Rus',* a term first used in the sixteenth century by Prince Andrei Kurbsky in his correspondence with Ivan IV) were telescoped—again, *made extensions of each other.* As a result, perhaps the greatest of all modern Russian literary plots, expressed in a stunning variety of works over the past two centuries, involves the rescuing/ redeeming of a heroine, who represents the country's vast potential, by a Christ-like paladin. The logic of the fairy tale and the logic of the Christian hierogamy (the marriage of the Lamb and the Bride in Revelation) join hands.

This means that the national Russian myth has, at its core, become profoundly eroticized and at the same time strangely sublimated/abstracted: personal love cannot "mean" outside this higher calling. Pushkin's Tatiana, Dostoevsky's Nastasya Filippovna, Tolstoy's Anna Karenina, Solovyov's Sophia, Blok's Beautiful Lady/Stranger, Bulgakov's Margarita, Pasternak's Lara—all these heroines, and more, have their fates linked with Russian history (broadly speaking), primarily in its tragic incarnation. Many of them die for their love. In a sense their lives and loves cannot have a "happy ending" until the right "Prince Charming" appears in a historical context *that is ready for him*—and this, given the belatedness of Russian culture, is almost never. Even the great women poets, Tsvetaeva and Akhmatova, participate as suffering wives, mothers, and lovers in the tragedy that is Russian historical time: Tsvetaeva's roles as Amazonian freedom fighter (it is *she* who must rescue the swain) and as archetypal heroine trapped in male role-playing (Ophelia, Gertrude, Phaedra); Akhmatova's realized metaphor of Suffering Mother in the cycle *Requiem* (her first husband, the poet Nikolai Gumilev, was executed by firing squad, her close friend Mandelstam died in a Stalinist camp, her son Lev also served time in prison). In sum, the erotic theme in Russian literature has traditionally been played for infinitely higher stakes than bourgeois love and family happiness. If the heroine is portrayed as some combination of heavenly mother and earth-bound demiurge—the Stranger is both streetwalker and otherworldly enchantress, Margarita is both the spirit of hope/ forgiveness and a witch who flies naked, Lara is both a Mary Magdalene figure and an image of Russia waiting to be reborn—then the hero is likely to appear as Christ-like paradox: the leader of marauding Red Guard disciples as androgynous apparition (*The Twelve*), the poet-doctor Zhivago as weak-willed Red Cross Knight, the Master as a great artist who is also hopelessly paranoid and on the verge of insanity.

With some notable exceptions (e.g., Pushkin), therefore, Russian literature of the modern period is plagued with its own special brand of cultivated repression or Victorianism. Sex for its own sake, as a source of bodily pleasure, or sex merely for the sake of procreation, to produce children, can be equally insulting to the quixotic Russian truth-seeker. A striking number of influential writers and thinkers (Solovyov, Fyodorov, Blok, Bely, Mayakovsky, and more) felt the act of copulation to be essentially humiliating, the prospect of biological children frightening, or both. The philosopher Vasily Rozanov championed sex and family life in their everyday, nonhieratic guises, but this rare exception was scandalous for its time and only proves the general rule. The fear was not so much sin, as in the Catholic and Protestant West, but cosmic indifference, meaninglessness. Perhaps the strongest condemnation of the "demonic" source of erotic pleasure in all Russian literature belongs to Tolstoy's novella "Kreutzer Sonata"; Tolstoy, in typical maximalist fashion, would prefer celibacy, and hence the end of the human race itself, to "sex without meaning."

Russian literature and culture are suffused with an apocalyptic mentality that continually sees the present as end-determined. As I have pointed out elsewhere, Russian novelists and poets have often deployed the image of the horse and rider (or its modern mechanical counterpart, the train) to telescope in one semantic field the notions of divine judgment (the principal source here, of course, being Rev. 6:1–8), historical crisis, and secular "progress" run amok.[14] An all-powerful tsar's equestrian statue comes back to punishing life in Pushkin's famous narrative poem; a breakneck troika ride is placed strategically at the end of the first part of Gogol's *Dead Souls;* an autobiographical hero takes a deadly train trip in Venedikt Erofeev's *From Moscow to the End of the Line.* In each case the question of who is behind the often tragic forward thrust of history is never far from the surface of the modern Russian literary consciousness. Even the challenging (not to say gleeful profanation) of the high moral calling and the sacred myths of Russian literature undertaken by writers and thinkers in the post-*glasnost* era, including Viktor Erofeev, Vladimir Sorokin, Dmitry Prigov, and Lev Rubinstein, has nothing gradualist about it, but is itself "apocalyptic" or, to reinvoke Epstein, "apophatic,"[15] in the totality of its negation.[16] Only with the coming of the new millennium will we see if this thousand-year history of imagining *Endzeit* will begin to take the shape of something else.

Notes

1. This chapter has been updated and adapted from my longer article "Russian Literature," in Nicholas Rzhevsky, ed., *Cambridge Introduction to Russian Culture* (Cambridge: Cambridge University Press, 1999), 161–204.

2. See discussion in Iu. M. Lotman, "O semiosfere," in *Izbrannye stat'i,* 3 vols. (Tallinn: Aleksandra, 1992–1993), 1:11–24.

3. On the "apophatic" in Russian culture and its version of the collective unconscious, see Mikhail Epshtein (Epstein), *Vera i obraz* (Tenafly: Hermitage, 1994), 5–28.

4. See Steven Cassedy, "P. A. Florensky and the Celebration of Matter," in

Judith Deutsch Kornblatt and Richard F. Gustafson, ed., *Russian Religious Thought* (Madison: University of Wisconsin Press, 1996), 95–111.

5. See A. M. Panchenko, "Smekh kak zrelishche," in D. S. Likhachev and A. M. Panchenko, eds., *"Smekhovoi mir" drevnei Rusi* (Leningrad: Nauka, 1976), 91–183; Harriet Murav, *Holy Foolishness: Dostoevsky's Novels and the Poetics of Cultural Critique* (Stanford: Stanford University Press, 1992), 1–31.

6. Nikolai Berdiaev, *Russkaia ideia* (Paris: YMCA, 1946), 35.

7. See David M. Bethea, *The Shape of Apocalypse in Modern Russian Fiction* (Princeton: Princeton University Press, 1989), 3–61.

8. One assumes here that Lotman has in mind primarily the *Eastern* Slavs.

9. Iu. M. Lotman, "'Dogovor' i 'vruchenie sebia' kak arkhetipicheskie modeli kul'tury," in *Izbrannye stat'i,* 3 vols. (Tallinn: Aleksandra, 1992–1993), 3:345–55.

10. See Irene Masing-Delic, *Abolishing Death: A Salvation Myth of Russian Twentieth-Century Literature* (Stanford: Stanford University Press, 1992), 1–122.

11. Nadezhda Mandelstam, *Hope Abandoned,* trans. Max Hayward (New York: Atheneum, 1974), 11.

12. See Rufus W. Mathewson, Jr., *The Positive Hero in Russian Literature,* 2d ed. (Stanford: Stanford University Press, 1975).

13. B. A. Uspenskii, "Kul't Nikoly na Rusi v istoriko-kul'turnom osvesh-chenii," *Trudy po znakovym sistemam [Uchenye zapiski Tartuskogo Gos. Univ.]* 463 (1978):86–140.

14. Bethea, *Shape of Apocalypse,* 44–61.

15. Epstein, *Vera i obraz,* 5–28.

16. See, e.g., Viktor Erofeev, comp., *Russkie tsvety zla (rodnaia proza kontsa XX veka)* (Moscow: Podkova, 1997).

PART 3

APOCALYPTICISM IN
TWENTIETH-CENTURY THOUGHT

8 *Paul Boyer*

The Apocalyptic in the Twentieth Century

For understandable reasons, media coverage of the apocalyptic strain in contemporary America has typically linked it to fringe groups and all too often to violence: sometimes self-destructive, suicidal violence; sometimes violence perpetrated by society against the group; sometimes murderous violence directed outward toward society as a whole. The litany has become only too familiar: Jim Jones and the People's Temple, David Koresh and the Branch Davidians, Aum Shinriko, the Order of the Solar Temple, Heaven's Gate, the Aryan Nation, Christian Identity—all those cults and fringe groups among us whose world view includes a strong millennialist or apocalyptic strain.[1] As we learned after the Heaven's Gate mass suicides, Marshall Applewhite and his companion Bonnie Lu Nettles were avid students of Bible prophecy who became convinced that they were the Two Witnesses mentioned in the Book of Revelation.

But such groups are only the outer fringe of a vast company of Americans who ground their world view in a particular reading of Bible prophecy. Literalistic prophecy belief is easy to ridicule, difficult to take seriously. It is associated with sleazy television evangelists, zany theories about the number 666, lurid tabloid headlines, and nervous jokes about vaguely understood apocalyptic terms:

"Knock, knock."
"Who's there?"

149

"Armageddon."

"Armageddon who?"

"Armageddon outta here!"

And now, of course, the approach of the year 2000 has brought its own wave of pop-culture exploitation. Just as hundreds of companies cashed in on the word "atomic" after 1945, we now have Millennium vacuum cleaners, Millennium slot machines, Millennium undergarments from Maidenform, and dozens of other products incorporating the potent word. The Miller Brewing Company has named itself Official Sponsor of the Millennium.[2]

Perhaps it's time to move beyond the kitsch and the jokes to confront the seriousness with which millions of Americans read the biblical apocalypses—not as allegory, not as spiritual consolation, not as a source of images that have inspired great art, but as prewritten history, a precise if symbolically expressed guide to events soon to unfold before our very eyes.

I was forcibly reminded of this fact in January 1988 as I sat in a lounge at Los Angeles International Airport, waiting for an incoming passenger. I was then researching the book that became *When Time Shall Be No More,* so I had brought along a paperback entitled *How to Recognize the Antichrist.* At the bar, an African American couple laughed and talked, seemingly oblivious of my presence. But as they left, the man stopped at my table and somberly asked: "Well, do you think you'll recognize him?" Caught off guard, I mumbled a noncommittal answer. "I think he exists now," the man said earnestly. "Actually, I'm kind of pleased, because the sooner the better." And with that he disappeared into the busy airport throng.

The belief that the Bible reveals a series of end-time events that will culminate in a reign of peace and justice is, in fact, extremely ancient, having arisen in the apocalyptic genre that pervaded Jewish and early Christian writings from around 200 B.C.E. to 100 C.E.[3]

Let us fast forward to twentieth-century America and to the most popular contemporary system of interpreting the apocalyptic scriptures: premillennial dispensationalism. This system was formulated by the nineteenth-century British dissenter and transatlantic revivalist John Darby, a founder of the Plymouth Brethren. It was popularized in America by many prominent late nineteenth- and early twentieth-century churchmen, most notably Cyrus Scofield, whose 1909 Reference Bible has sold as many as twelve million copies.[4]

Premillennial, of course, means that Christ will return before the millennium. *Dispensational* means that God has dealt with mankind in a series of distinct epochs, or dispensations. Popularizers buttress this belief system with proof texts from Daniel, Ezekiel, Matthew, Mark, 1 Thessalonians, 2 Peter, and Revelation—texts written over hundreds of years, but assumed by dispensationalists to unveil a coherent sequence of end-time events, like a jigsaw puzzle correctly assembled. To cite all these proof texts and to explain the meaning dispensationalists place upon them would be a book-length undertaking, but suffice it to say that they were woven together with great ingenuity by Darby and others, and the scenario they created has become an article of faith for millions.

According to this scheme, as history nears its climax, probably very soon, a series of "signs" will alert the faithful that the end is near. Wickedness and natural disasters will increase. The founding of the state of Israel in 1948 and Israel's recapture of the Old City of Jerusalem in 1967 are considered prophetic signs of the first importance.

These signs will culminate in the Rapture, a doctrine drawn from 1 Thessalonians 4:16. In this event of cosmic import, set to occur at some unknown future time—perhaps today—all true believers will join Christ in the air. The Rapture will spread terror among those left behind, especially airline passengers flying with a raptured pilot. After the Rapture comes the seven-year Great Tribulation, prophesied by Christ in Matthew 24, a nightmarish interval during which Antichrist, also referred to in Revelation as the Beast, will arise and rule the world.

As the seven years end, Antichrist's forces will gather at Megiddo, an ancient battle site in Israel, to fight a vast army from the East—hence the Battle of Armageddon (literally, the hill of Megiddo), mentioned in Revelation 16. As the armies assemble, however, Revelation foretells that Jesus Christ will return with his raptured saints to destroy his foes and launch a thousand-year reign—the Millennium. After a solemn Last Judgment, human history ends. A New Heaven and a New Earth arise, with Christ reigning forever.[5]

This belief system remains very strong in contemporary America. Forty percent of Americans regard the Bible—including the apocalyptic texts—as "the actual Word of God, to be taken literally, word for word." A 1983 Gallup Poll found that 62 percent of us have "no doubt" that Jesus will return to earth again. In a major 1996 study of U.S. and Canadian religious attitudes conducted by the Angus Reid Group, 42 percent of the U.S. respondents agreed with the statement: "The world will end in a battle in Armageddon between Jesus and the Antichrist." In other words, perhaps 100 million Americans embrace a central tenet of premillennial dispensationalism.[6]

Several large denominations espouse this doctrine, including fast-growing pentecostal or charismatic groups such as the 2.2-million-member Assemblies of God Church. Prophecy belief pervades the independent Bible churches and Bible fellowships proliferating across the land. Sixty-three percent of Southern Baptist ministers are premillennial, and perhaps an even larger proportion of the fifteen million Southern Baptist laity—the largest Protestant denomination—hold these beliefs. The Mormons, Jehovah's Witnesses, and Seventh-day Adventists, with their millions of members, espouse particular versions of end-time belief.[7]

The prophetic word is spread by paperback books that sell hundreds of thousands of copies, including Hal Lindsey's *The Late Great Planet Earth,* which was *the* nonfiction bestseller of the 1970s and is still in print.[8] Religious broadcasters, including such luminaries as Oral Roberts, Jerry Falwell, Jack Van Impe, and Pat Robertson, promulgate premillennialism worldwide.

Prophecy belief is disseminated by touring evangelists; by America's 6,000 Christian bookstores (a $3 billion-a-year business); by fundamentalist seminaries and Bible schools, most notably Dallas Theological Seminary; by tape, film, videocassettes, and Internet discussion groups; by tracts, Christian comic books, Rapture wristwatches that proclaim, "One Hour Nearer the Lord's Return," and bumper stickers that warn: "Caution: If the Rapture Occurs, This Car Will Be Driverless."[9]

Prophecy belief has seeped into mass culture through such movies as *The Omen* of 1976 and *The Rapture* of 1991 and rock songs such as Barry McGuire's "Eve of Destruction" and David Bowie's "[We've Got] Five More Years." Bob Dylan, during his born-again phase in the late seventies and early eighties, released many songs with apocalyptic lyrics such as "When He Returns" of 1979.[10]

Nor is end-time prophecy belief confined to a mythic southern "Bible Belt." The 1996 study finds dispensational belief in all regions. The highest level, predictably, is in the South; but even in the area where it is lowest, New England, more than a quarter of the respondents answered yes to the questions about "Armageddon." Madison, Wisconsin, a university town and state capital, with a generally affluent and well-educated population, boasts over fifty churches where prophecy is regularly expounded and seven Christian bookstores offering the latest prophecy paperbacks. While end-time belief is strongest among poorer, less well educated Americans, it is found at all educational and income levels.[11]

How do we account for the remarkable tenacity of these beliefs? From one perspective, this phenomenon is simply a by-product of America's pervasive piety and wide-open religious marketplace. A 1995 study of comparative religious attitudes reported in the *International Social Science Journal* included a survey that asked: "Is God very important in your life?" In France, 13 percent said yes; in Great Britain, 19 percent; in the United States, 58 percent![12]

Lacking an established church, America's *laissez-faire* religious culture has always nurtured innovators, from Anne Hutchinson and Roger Williams to Joseph Smith, Mary Baker Eddy, Charles Taze Russell of the Jehovah's Witnesses, Ellen White of the Seventh-day Adventists, and Herbert W. Armstrong of the Worldwide Church of God. From this perspective, Hal Lindsey and other prophecy popularizers are simply present-day exemplars of this historical pattern.

Prophecy interpretation is the quintessential populist theology: anyone can play. Cyrus Scofield had little formal education and no theological training. Indeed, the lack of theological credentials is an asset, guaranteeing that one has not been tainted by the skepticism of elite universities or liberal seminaries.[13]

And dispensationalism happily coexists with our modern scientific and technological order. The popularizers incorporate allusions to modern technology in their end-time scenarios, as evidence that Antichrist's rule is near, while simultaneously using these same new technologies, from communications satellites to the Internet, to spread their message.

Bible-based apocalypticism also gains strength from a body of secular social thought rooted in an apocalyptic mind set. In the 1970s and 1980s, such books as *Future Shock, The Population Bomb, The Fate of the Earth, The Closing Circle, Megatrends,* and *The End of Nature* echoed the dispensationalist popularizers in warning of cataclysm ahead.[14]

A current example of the secular apocalyptic genre is the bestseller *The Fourth Turning* by William Strauss and Neil Howe. Though an ostensibly "secular" work, *The Fourth Turning,* with its revealing subtitle "An American Prophecy," has all the earmarks of a dispensationalist tract: it views history as predetermined; it sees American history unfolding in four long cycles that approximate the human life span. Each of these cycles, in turn, includes four stages, the final two of which, called "Unravelings" and "Turnings," sound remarkably like the Great Tribulation and Armageddon. And, indeed, the next "Turning" is imminent: Strauss and Howe place it between 2005 and 2025—and thus assure their book a long run. Such works of "secular apocalyptic" both draw upon the popular belief in Bible prophecy and help sustain the market for the real thing.[15]

The enduring power of premillennial dispensationalism is also rooted in its flexibility—a flexibility enhanced by the symbolic language of the apocalyptic texts. While Darby's core system remains intact, new events are constantly incorporated, while events or individuals that fail to fulfill their expected prophetic roles quietly vanish. From the 1920s through 1945, for example, many prophecy writers built a persuasive case for Mussolini as Antichrist. With Il Duce's death, this theme simply dropped away. In the 1930s, Social Security numbers and the NRA's Blue Eagle were trumpeted as forerunners of Antichrist's rule. With the end of the New Deal, popularizers downplayed these themes and found new evidence in the daily headlines.[16]

The historian, reading hundreds of prophecy books published over a span of several centuries, can clearly see this technique of inserting current events into an archaic belief system. The ordinary believer, encountering the genre for the first time, is stunned by its uncanny timeliness.

The remarkable "prophetic fulfillments" trumpeted by the popularizers as they match the prophecies with current events help buttress evangelical faith. With the post-Darwinian erosion of natural theology, which found proof of God's existence in the harmony and symmetry of nature, prophecy belief finds evidence for the divine in the harmony and symmetry of history.

Prophecy belief also finesses the ancient dilemma of free will versus determinism by embracing both positions. For prophecy believers, history's overall course is determined. But within this predestined order lies a crucial realm of freedom: by accepting Christ, individuals can control their own eternal destiny and escape the horrors ahead by way of the Rapture.

Above all, prophecy belief gives meaning and drama to history, and to one's individual life. In contrast to the textbook version of history, the prophecy writers' version is ordered, purposeful, and teleological: it is moving toward an ultimate fulfillment. As John F. Walvoord of Dallas Theological Seminary put it in 1971: "The twentieth century is a stream moving exactly in the pattern of the prophetic word."[17] In the nineteenth century, allegedly secular historians like George Bancroft often invoked divine providence.[18] But with the history profession's banishment of God as a direct causal force, the prophecy interpreters stepped in to fill the popular longing for transcendent meaning in history.

Above all, dispensationalism is at heart a utopian system. Beyond the terror and bloodshed ahead lies a golden age. The Tribulation and Armageddon are but way stations to the millennium: a new age of peace, harmony, and justice—the antithesis of the present tragically flawed social order.[19]

Can we wonder that so many millions of Americans have embraced dispensationalism with such tenacity and enthusiasm?

Even if we acknowledge the pervasiveness and appeal of dispensationalism, does it really merit our close attention? I believe it does, not only because any belief system embraced by millions demands notice, but also because a great many Americans view global events, domestic politics, and contemporary social issues through the prism of end-time Bible prophecy belief.

Of course, prophecy is not the only factor shaping the world view of believers. World views have complex sources and are rarely wholly consistent. For example, despite Ronald Reagan's well-documented belief that Russia's destruction is foretold in Ezekiel, he ended his presidency by strolling in Red Square with Mikhail Gorbachev.[20] While Bible prophecy is not the only guide by which believers interpret current events, it represents one very important source. A glance at how dispensationalist popularizers in the Cold War era viewed the nuclear threat, the Soviet Union, Israel and the Jews, the emerging global economic order, and the fate of America illustrates that this belief system does have important "real world" ramifications.

The advent of the atomic bomb in 1945 stimulated intense interest in prophecies of the earth's final destruction. As 2 Peter 3:10 memorably puts it: "The heavens shall pass away with a great noise, and the elements shall melt with fervent heat, the earth also and the works that are therein shall be burned up" (King James trans.). Zechariah 14:12 offers an even more chilling vision: "[The people's] flesh shall consume away while they stand upon their feet, and their eyes shall consume away in their holes, and their tongue shall consume away in their mouth."

Scores of post-1945 popularizers of dispensationalism found atomic war foretold in such texts. Despite their claims to biblical literalism, these writers and evangelists freely transformed the bows and arrows and spears of the apocalyptic scriptures into missiles, missile launchers, and ICBMs.

The popularizers insisted that they were not advocating nuclear war. They were simply viewing current events in the light of prophecy. But in finding atomic war foretold in the Bible, they encouraged passivity toward the threat. Why resist the inevitable, especially when it will probably come after the Rapture? Disarmament talks were a cruel deception, they argued, offering a mirage of peace when the prophecies said otherwise. Only Christ's return would end the nuclear threat.

The more scrupulous writers noted that Armageddon is not a human war, but a divine intervention. But nuclear war and Armageddon easily melded in the popular mind. A 1984 survey found that 39 percent of Americans believed that the Bible's end-time prophecies did, indeed, refer to thermonuclear war.[21]

Russia, too, loomed large for Cold War prophecy popularizers. This was not a new theme. When Napoleon and Alexander I of Russia carved up Prussia in 1807, Prussian Bible scholars such as Wilhelm Gesenius soon identified Russia as "Gog," the northern kingdom whose destruction is foretold in Ezekiel 38. Some argued that the Hebrew phrase translated as "chief prince" in the King James version of Ezekiel 38 actually means "Prince of Rosh"—another arrow pointing to Russia. John Darby found Russia's destruction foretold in Ezekiel, as did Cyrus Scofield's 1909 Reference Bible. The 1917 Bolshevik Revolution added further weight to this interpretation.[22]

This strand of the dispensationalist scenario reached hysterical proportions during the Cold War, as paperback popularizers, television preachers, and touring expositors endlessly proclaimed the coming destruction of Russia.[23] Once again, most denied any intention of fomenting war with the Soviets. Russia's end would be by divine intervention, not human means, they insisted. But their endless preaching of Russia's approaching doom added eschatological fuel to Cold War paranoia and passivity. If Russia's destruction was foreordained, why resist the inevitable?

A third point of intersection between prophecy belief and current events relates to the Jews.[24] In Genesis 15, God promises Abraham all the land from the Euphrates to the "river of Egypt," often identified as the Nile. In this text, dispensationalists find a foretelling not only of Israel's rebirth as a nation but also of a vast expansion of its boundaries to include all or parts of Lebanon, Syria, Iraq, Jordan, Saudi Arabia, and Egypt. The more scrupulous interpreters place this expansion in the millennium, not in the present dispensation, but the popularizers typically blur this distinction.

They also cite texts that they believe foretell the rebuilding of the Jerusalem Temple, destroyed by the Romans in 70 C.E.—a site now occupied by two sacred Islamic shrines, the Dome of the Rock and Al Aqkba Mosque. Wrote prophecy interpreter Ray C. Stedman in *What's This World Coming To?* (1970): "[How the Jews will] surmount the problem of rebuilding a temple on the place now occupied by an Arab holy place is anyone's guess. But rebuild it they shall, for as Jesus said . . . , 'The scriptures cannot be broken.'"[25]

Again, these writers insist that they are simply interpreting prophecy, not making political judgments. Yet the anti-Muslim implication is clear. As Arthur Bloomfield put it in 1971: "When all the Jews return . . . , God says He will lay the land of the Arabs waste and it will be desolate. . . . This may seem like a severe punishment; but the provocation is going to be very great. The terms of covenant must be carried out to the letter."[26]

However, the same writers who glory in Israel's thrilling prophetic destiny also portray the long cycles of anti-Semitic persecution as God's "chastisement" of his wayward people. In 1991, when I visited the Yad Vashem Holocaust memorial in Jerusalem, with its harrowing scenes of the Nazi horrors, a fundamentalist prophecy believer murmured to me:

"Surely when Jews see this, they must realize what a mistake they made in rejecting Christ."

And the Jews' plight will worsen as the end draws near. Citing a passage from Zechariah, many dispensationalist popularizers teach that during the Tribulation, two-thirds of all Jews will be slaughtered by Antichrist's armies.[27] This, too, of course, is part of God's plan, beyond human power to avert. As Arthur Bloomfield put it in *How to Recognize the Antichrist* (1975):

Antichrist's persecution will be much more terrible than Hitler's. Hitler used gas chambers; he got rid of six million Jews, but Antichrist's purpose will be to do away with all Jews of all nations. That many Jews cannot be driven into gas chambers, but they could be driven into Egypt. Egypt has great deserts where Jews could be sent to die and their bones would not clutter up good ground.[28]

When I asked the dispensationalist expositor J. Dwight Pentecost of Dallas Theological Seminary in 1989 if the approaching Jewish holocaust could be avoided, his response was consistent with this belief system: "Prophetically, the only thing that could prevent it is Israel's repentance."[29] In short, Jewish holocausts past and future are part of God's plan—tragic and lamentable, but inexorably inscribed in the prophecies.

Apart from some fringe groups, the prophecy popularizers who predict a new holocaust are not overtly anti-Semitic. They deplore what lies in store for Jews. They write feelingly of Jewish sufferings under Hitler and other persecutors. Nevertheless, their interpretation of the prophecies leads them to view these events as foreordained and beyond human control.

The popularizers also foresee a standardized, regimented world order where all individuality will be stamped out. The emerging global economy, they believe—with its computers, laser scanners, and credit cards—is preparing the way for Antichrist's rule and the dread "Mark of the Beast" foretold in Revelation 13:

And [the Beast] causeth all . . . to receive a mark in their right hand, or in their foreheads. And . . . no man might buy or sell, save he that had the mark, or the name of the beast, or the number of his name. . . . Let him that hath understanding count the number of the beast; for . . . his number is Six Hundred three score and six.[30]

The mysterious number 666 exerts a special fascination. The ancients often gave numerical values to letters, and most Bible scholars view "666" as an allusion to the Emperor Nero, whose resurrection and renewed persecution of Christians was widely feared in Asia Minor in the late first century.

Over the centuries, however, the fateful number was applied to the pope, Saladin, Napoleon, Hitler, Mussolini, Anwar Sadat, Henry Kissinger, and many others. At the grassroots level, the fascination continues. In the 1980s, some interpreters noted that each of Ronald Wilson Reagan's three names has six letters! The Internet is full of systems by which the name of Bill Gates, the head of Microsoft, can be made to total 666.[31]

Recent prophecy popularizers are less interested in pinpointing an individual than in exposing the global economic system that Antichrist will exploit. Some point out that if you assign the letter A the value 6, B the value 12, C 18, and so on through the alphabet, adding six each time, then the letters "C-O-M-P-U-T-E-R" total 666! (So does "New York City," by the way.)[32] Along with computers, credit cards, multinational corporations and international banks, they also cite global television, hysterical rock concerts, and manipulative political campaigns as precursors of Antichrist. He will not initially seem monstrous, they suggest, but charismatic—brilliantly using the electronic media to further his evil purposes.

This theme clearly taps into the anonymity and alienation many feel in an age of mass culture, global corporations, and media-driven politics. Indeed, the dispensationalists' conspiratorial view of a tightly controlled world system uncannily resembles the New Left rhetoric of the 1960s, which also saw capitalism as an omnipotent global system controlling government and the mass media. The politics differs; the apocalyptic sensibility is similar.

And what of the United States in prophecy? The popularizers cite an array of evidence—from secularism and materialism to AIDS, pornography, radical feminism, and the New Age movement—to prove that America has become wicked and apostate as the end nears. Indeed, these popularizers display a kind of perverse patriotism in placing America in the forefront of the plunge into wickedness that will end with Antichrist.[33]

This bleak view of America's prophetic destiny represents a radical interpretive shift. The New England Puritans, Jonathan Edwards in the eighteenth century, and many nineteenth-century churchmen saw America as divinely favored, perhaps even the site of the millennial kingdom. As the Puritan leader Edward Johnson assured the people of New England in 1653: "For your full assurance, know this is the place where the Lord will create a new Heaven and a new earth . . . , new Churches and a new Commonwealth together."[34]

Except for the Mormons and a few other groups who still view America as the New Zion, such a blend of patriotism and eschatology is rare today. In writing of the United States, the popularizers see not divine favor but growing Satanic influence. The federal government, once viewed as an instrument of God's purposes, has become a force for evil, oppressing the righteous, legalizing abortion, banning school prayer, promoting homo-sexuality, thrusting its tentacles into every facet of life. As God's timetable unfolds, they insist, Washington, D.C., will be unmasked as a linchpin of Antichrist's global system.

The prophecy writers' dark view of current social trends emerges starkly in their accounts of the Tribulation. *The Beast,* a 1985 prophecy novel, describes one woman's horror as she drives through New York City after the Rapture:

> She could see cars overturned and on fire. Trash littered the streets. Shop windows had been smashed and the merchandise inside stolen. It was like a scene from hell, she thought to herself. There didn't seem to be any restraint left anywhere. . . . Some great restraining hand had been lifted from the earth. The delicate veneer that kept mankind from the laws of the jungle had been jostled by an accident of cosmic proportions and the ooze of primitive man was escaping.[35]

These two motifs, social chaos and social regimentation, while super-ficially contradictory, in fact tap into two prime sources of uneasiness in contemporary America: fears of underclass turmoil and violence, and fears of an emerging economic and technocratic order that will destroy individual freedom. The two converge in descriptions of the Great Tribula-tion as a time of initial social disintegration and then of absolute regimen-tation under Antichrist's brutal dictatorship.

As we near the end of the 1990s, is not this interpretive scheme somewhat dated? The Cold War is over, Russia is enfeebled, the nuclear threat has faded, Israel and the Palestinians, prodded by Washington, at least pay lip service to a peace process. What will happen to the dispensationalist scenario now? In fact, this infinitely adaptable genre has always accom-modated itself to altered global realities. As the portentous year 2000 ap-proaches, the outpouring of works linking current events to Bible proph-ecy actually seems to be on the rise. Pat Robertson's prophecy novel *The End of the Age* briefly topped the bestseller lists in 1995. A projected twelve-volume series of premillenialist novels by Tim LaHaye and Jerry Jenkins recounting the events of the last days from the Rapture through the Battle of Armageddon, published by Tyndale House of Wheaton, Illi-nois, is selling at a phenomenal pace. As of the end of 1998, the first four volumes—*Left Behind, Tribulation Force, Nicolae,* and *Soul Harvest*—had sold more than 3 million copies. Tyndale House's home page on the Worldwide Web (*leftbehind.com*) provides full information. A junior edition is summed up by the publisher as "Four Kids Face Earth's Last Days Together." A "Left Behind" radio serial and a movie version are in preparation.[36]

Other prophecy popularizations that did very well in the post–Cold War years include John Hagee's *Beginning of the End;* Ed Dobson's *The End;* Hal Lindsey's latest entries, *Planet Earth—2000 A.D.* and the prophecy novel *Blood Moon;* and a Jack Van Impe paperback and videotape, *2001: Countdown to Eternity.*[37]

Many of these books are marketed not only in Christian bookstores but also in mass outlets like Wal-Mart, Borders, and Barnes & Noble—illustrating the genre's spillover into the so-called secular culture. Bible prophecy can mean big profits in the current climate, and publishers are cashing in. As a spokesperson for Zondervan, a major prophecy house, told *Publisher's Weekly:* "Any savvy publisher will recognize that when you go from one millennium to the next, you have a great deal of interest in eschatology. . . . The turn of the millennium provides a context for renewed interest in the future."[38]

These post–Cold War dispensationalist popularizers are shaping a new prophetic paradigm, similar to the one I have sketched, but with different emphases, different biblical passages highlighted, some themes muted and old themes revived, to reflect contemporary realities and fears.

As they have for centuries, the prophecy writers insist that at this precise moment all the pieces of the jigsaw puzzle are at last falling into place. As Lindsey asserts in *Planet Earth—2000 A.D.*: "Never before in the history of the planet have events and conditions so coincided as to set the stage for [the Rapture]."[39] Of course, that's what he said in *The Late Great Planet Earth* a quarter of a century ago—but never mind.

Initially some popularizers of the nineties, seeking to salvage the familiar script, warned that the apparent Soviet collapse was just a trick. After all, do not the scriptures warn: "When they shall say peace and safety, then sudden destruction cometh upon them."[40]

But the Islamic Menace soon emerged as a new controlling motif. During the Persian Gulf War, some writers fingered Saddam Hussein as Antichrist, and this theme has gained popularity since. Joseph Chambers' 1997 paperback *A Palace for the Antichrist* describes Saddam's rebuilding of Babylon, the wicked city whose end-time destruction is foretold in Revelation 18. Since Babylon obviously cannot be destroyed until it is rebuilt, Saddam's reconstruction project is being invested with profound eschatological significance.[41]

The Islamic menace is actually an ancient theme in popular Christian eschatology. For centuries, prophecy interpreters routinely identified Islam and the Ottoman empire, sometimes along with Russia, as the demonic end-time power foretold in scripture. When the Ottoman empire collapsed and the Soviet Union emerged after 1917, the popularizers simply downgraded Islam and moved Russia to center stage.[42]

With the Cold War over and Islamic fundamentalism much in the news, this ancient theme was revived. Lindsey's *Planet Earth—2000 A.D.* identifies the Muslim world with Ishmael, Abraham's illegitimate son by Sarah's handmaiden Hagar, who is cursed by Jehovah in Genesis 16: "He shall be a wild man, his hand against every man, and every man's hand against him."[43]

As the dispensationalist scenario is updated, environmental themes loom larger as well. As the popularizers tirelessly point out, the Book of Revelation describes the ultimate ecological disaster: the sun and moon darken; the seas become "as the blood of a dead man"; earthquakes, searing heat, monstrous insects, and hideous sores make life a torment.

Current fears about global warming, radioactive waste, toxic pollution, and ozone depletion can easily be made to fit John's apocalyptic vision. In Robertson's apocalyptic novel *The End of the Age,* a massive meteor strikes in the Pacific Ocean, setting off tidal waves and volcanoes that destroy Los Angeles and much of the West Coast. Lindsey in *Planet Earth—2000 A.D.* offers a litany of alarming environmental developments, from earthquakes and volcanoes (which he claims are increasing in frequency decade by decade) to ozone-layer depletion, deforestation, global warming, and the freakish meteorological effects of El Niño and concludes: "The physical tribulations of the Earth and its environment has been one of the most significant developments—prophetically speaking— since I authored *The Late Great Planet Earth* 25 years ago."[44]

As in the past, books in the "secular apocalyptic" vein echo the prophecy writers' end-time scenario. The title of Rodney Barker's 1997 book *And the Waters Turned to Blood,* about deadly micro-organisms in the nation's waterways, deliberately plays upon apocalyptic fears.[45]

But above all, the emerging global system of international banks, multinational corporations, and satellite communications dominated post–Cold War prophecy popularizations. Such books as *The Coming Cashless Society* and *Final Warning: Economic Collapse and the Coming World Government* combined current economic fears with premillennial dispensationalist doctrine.[46]

Pat Robertson—founder of the Christian Broadcasting Network and the Christian Coalition—offered a truly paranoid account of this global system in his 1991 book *The New World Order.* For Robertson, history is absolutely determined. "A giant plan is unfolding," he writes. "Everything perfectly on cue."[47] The Bavarian Illuminati, the Masonic Order, Baron Rothschild, Colonel House, Woodrow Wilson, the United Nations, the Trilateral Commission, the Council on Foreign Relations, the Beatles, Hollywood, the multinational corporations, George Bush, Visa and Mastercard—all are part of a giant conspiracy pointing to one outcome: the rise of Antichrist. Robertson even suggests that international bankers (implicitly identified with the Jews) arranged the Cold War as a hoax to tighten their global financial grip and thus prepare the way for the Evil One.

And at the center of the conspiratorial web is the federal government. During the Cold War, the sharp apocalyptic division of all reality between good and evil was projected onto a global stage, with Moscow the focus of evil. Today's prophecy popularizers apply this Manichean formula to the domestic realm, with Washington, D.C., replacing Moscow. Indeed, Robertson translates the phrase "Novus Ordo Seclorum" on the Great Seal of the United States (which appears on every dollar bill) as "New World Order." For all its past greatness, Chambers sadly concludes in his *A Palace for the Antichrist,* America "will continue to disintegrate as we approach the end."[48] The fact that the United States has played such a leading role in the development of television, computers, credit cards, space satellites, and other technologies that Antichrist will employ reinforces the conspiratorial view.

Dispensationalism thus feeds antigovernment hostility in 1990s America, just as it earlier fueled anti-Soviet hatred. This strand of the popularizers' scenario deepens believers' view of Washington as not merely inefficient, wasteful, and meddlesome, but, quite literally, demonic.

Once again, the secular media supply fodder for the dispensationalists' nightmare of Antichrist's total control. A 1996 article in the *New York Times Magazine,* "The True Terror Is in the Card," offered a grim vision of government control of individuals through a national ID card. Powerful forces, the author warned, are promoting "an identity card with a fingerprint, digitized photo, eye retina scan or some other biometric identity device." The article was illustrated with a photograph of a man with shaved head and a bar code tattooed across the back of his neck.[49] Such material quickly makes its way into prophecy paperbacks foretelling the rise of Antichrist. Suspicion of "the New World Order" is not limited to cranks, cults, and survivalist groups in Montana and Idaho. It is endemic in a society where millions of citizens remain convinced, on the basis of their reading of Bible prophecy, that national and world trends are rushing toward their final crisis.

Nothing better illustrated dispensationalism's successful transit to the post–Cold War era, and its brilliant repackaging for the 1990s, than Tim LaHaye's and Jerry Jenkins' "Left Behind" series. Though these bestsellers surely made the authors rich, one ought not dismiss them as merely opportunistic. LaHaye, founder in 1983 of the American Coalition for Traditional Values, based in Washington, D.C., and his wife, Beverly, head of

Concerned Women for America, are prominent on the religious right, and these novels clearly promote their larger conservative agenda.[50]

Left Behind tells of the Rapture from the perspective of Rayford Steele, a pilot on a transatlantic flight, who, while not raptured himself, suddenly confronts the disappearance of 100 passengers. In the sequel, *Tribulation Force,* Steele joins a small group of "Tribulation Saints" who realize their error, accept Christ, and join the New Life Community Church to learn what lies ahead. *Tribulation Force* offers the classic dispensationalist scenario in modern dress: the head of the United Nations, a charismatic Roumanian named Nicolae Carpathia, is really Antichrist. After the Rapture, Carpathia presents a bold plan for global disarmament that wins universal praise. As he proclaims: "My motives are pure, my goals are peaceful, and my audience is global."[51]

Most of the world's leaders, including liberal Protestant churchmen—who, of course, haven't been raptured—endorse Carpathia and announce plans for a new world religion. The international bankers introduce a single global currency. A craven and naive U.S. president, completely deceived by Carpathia, surrenders America to the New World Order. Carpathia moves the UN to a rebuilt Babylon and signs a treaty with the leaders of Israel, who hail him as the messiah. The little band of Tribulation Saints, aware of what is happening, prepare for the persecution ahead by building underground bunkers. In short, LaHaye's apocalyptic fiction reiterates his right-wing political message: international organizations are suspect, politicians are naive at best and traitorous at worse, true Christians and patriots must prepare for the worst.

Tribulation Force is also a novel of the nineties. The Tribulation Saints follow events on CNN, communicate by e-mail, and pursue their prophetic studies via the Internet. LaHaye and Jenkins weave in the pop psychology that pervades today's evangelical scene. As the Tribulation unfolds, Rayford Steele's daughter Chloe, a beautiful and independent young college student, ponders whether she can find happiness with Cameron Williams, a middle-aged journalist transformed by the trauma of the Rapture from a tough careerist into a sensitive New Age guy who is in touch with his feelings and cries easily. In short, John Darby joins with Oprah Winfrey and Dr. Joyce Brothers.

And the alluring utopian glow persists. For all the terrors they foretell, the prophecy books of the 1990s, like their predecessors, end with the promise of final triumph. In the last milliseconds of human history, says Pat Robertson in *The New World Order,* just as Satan's victory seems inevitable, Christ will return and establish his kingdom. "*God's* new world order," Robertson concludes triumphantly, echoing a centuries-old theme, "is coming much nearer than we believe. . . . [Its] triumph . . . is certain."[53]

Let me conclude with a modest prophecy of my own. So long as premillennial dispensationalism continues to meet the emotional and psychological needs of a great many Americans and so long as the popularizers of Bible prophecy continue to weave our deepest collective anxieties into their end-time scenarios, this ancient belief system, with its infinite adaptability and its imaginative, drama-filled vision of history, will remain a significant shaping force in our politics and culture. To fail to understand the enduring power of these ancient apocalyptic texts is to fail to understand contemporary America.

Notes

1. David Chidester, *Salvation and Suicide: An Interpretation of Jim Jones, the People's Temple, and Jonestown* (Bloomington: Indiana University Press, 1988); Paul Boyer, "Apocalypse in Waco: David Koresh and the Branch Davidians," in William Graebner, ed., *True Stories from the American Past* (New York: McGraw-Hill, 1996), 151–271; "With World Still Intact, Sect Draws More Critics," *New York Times* (2 March 1997), 26 [on Elizabeth Clare Prophet]; David E. Kaplan and Andrew Marshall, *The Cult at the End of the World* [Aum Shinriko] (New York: Crown, 1996); Michael Barkun, *Religion and the Racist Right: The Origins of the Christian Identity Movement* (Chapel Hill: University of North Carolina Press, 1994); Southern Poverty Law Center, "Sovereign Nation, Under God," *Klanwatch: Intelligence Report* (Spring 1997), 10–12.

2. "The Pending Millennium," *Harper's* (August 1997), 29. See also "Gearing Up for Millennial Fervor," *Publisher's Weekly* (13 January 1997), 38–40.

3. John J. Collins, *The Apocalyptic Imagination: An Introduction to the Jewish Matrix of Christianity* (New York: Crossroads, 1984); Paul D. Hanson, *The Dawn of Apocalyptic* (Philadelphia: Fortress Press, 1975). In *Cosmos, Chaos, and the World to Come: The Ancient Roots of Apocalyptic Faith* (New Haven: Yale University Press, 1993), Norman Cohn traces the Zoroastrian roots of the apocalyptic genre. For a brief overview of the early history of the genre, see Paul Boyer, *When Time Shall Be No More: Prophecy Belief in Modern American Culture* (Cambridge: Harvard University Press, 1992), 21–24.

4. Donald Kraus (Senior Editor, Bibles, Oxford University Press) to author, 14 June 1990 [on Scofield Bible sales]; Clarence B. Bass, *Background to Dispensationalism: Its Historical Genesis and Ecclesiastical Implications* (Grand Rapids: Baker, 1977); Ernest R. Sandeen, *The Roots of Fundamentalism: British and American Millenarianism, 1800–1930* (Chicago: University of Chicago Press, 1970); Timothy P. Weber, *Living in the Shadow of the Second Coming: American Premillennialism, 1875–1925* (New York: Oxford University Press, 1979); Boyer, *When Time Shall Be No More,* 86–100.

5. With countless variations and embellishments, this scheme may be found in literally hundreds of popularizations of Darby's system. See, for example, Frederick A. Tatford, *God's Program of the Ages* (Grand Rapids: Kregel, 1967). For

summaries by historians, see Weber, *Living in the Shadow of the Second Coming,* 18–23; Boyer, *When Time Shall Be No More,* 87–88.

6. Angus Reid Group Cross-Border Survey, "Canada/U.S. Religion and Politics," 80. Printout of results, dated 11 October 1996, supplied to author by Professor Mark Noll, Department of History, Wheaton College, Wheaton, Illinois. The pollsters interviewed a scientifically selected sample of 3,000 Americans and 3,000 Canadians. Among the U.S. respondents characterizing themselves as "conservative Protestants," 69 percent professed belief in a future Battle of Armageddon between Jesus Christ and Antichrist.

7. Boyer, *When Time Shall Be No More,* 4.

8. Hal Lindsey with C. C. Carlson, *The Late Great Planet Earth* (Grand Rapids: Zondervan, 1970; reissued by Bantam Books, 1973); Ray Walters, "Paperback Talk: Apocalypse," *New York Times Book Review* (12 March 1978), 45; Weber, *Living in the Shadow of the Second Coming,* 4; Boyer, *When Time Shall Be No More,* 5–6.

9. "Christian Bookstores Take a Worldly Lesson," *New York Times* (25 July 1996); "Stirring the Waters of Reflection: How the Anguish of the 1960s Transformed the Role of Religion [*sic*] Publishing," *Publishers Weekly* (125th anniversary special issue, July 1997), 73–74; "All in the Family—CBA Style," *ibid.,* 76–78, 80 [on the Christian Booksellers' Association]; "Christian Radio Stations, Riding a Wave of Change, Keep Their Popularity," *New York Times* (10 January 1994); Boyer, *When Time Shall Be No More,* 5–7.

10. Boyer, *When Time Shall Be No More,* 8–9; Jonathan D. Lauer, "'Pray That I Don't Die of Thirst, Baby, Two Feet from the Well': Last Songs on Bob Dylan's Studio Albums, 1974–1993," *On the Tracks,* 5 (15 June 1997), 14–23.

11. Boyer, *When Time Shall Be No More,* 13–15. The Angus Reid Survey (n. 6 above) contains data broken down by region that confirm the generalization that prophecy belief, and dispensational premillennialism specifically, knows no regional boundaries. Two germane sociological studies are James Davison Hunter, *American Evangelicalism: Conservative Religion and the Quandary of Modernity* (New Brunswick: Rutgers University Press, 1983); idem, *Evangelicalism: The Coming Generation* (Chicago: University of Chicago Press, 1987).

12. Mattei Gogan, "The Decline of Religious Beliefs in Western Europe," *International Social Science Journal* (September 1995), 405–18.

13. Boyer, *When Time Shall Be No More,* 304–11.

14. Alvin Toffler, *Future Shock* (New York: Random House, 1970); idem, *The Eco-Spasm Report* (New York: Bantam Books, 1975); Paul R. Erlich, *The Population Bomb* (New York: Ballantine Books, 1968); Jonathan Schell, *The Fate of the Earth* (New York: Knopf, 1982); Barry Commoner, *The Closing Circle: Nature, Man, and Technology* (New York: Knopf, 1971); Bill McKibben, *The End of Nature* (New York: Anchor Books, 1990). For a discussion of the links between biblical apocalyptic and this "secular apocalyptic" genre, see Michael Barkun, "Divided Apocalypse: Thinking about the End in Contemporary America," *Soundings* 66 (1983), 257–80.

15. William Strauss and Neil Howe, *The Fourth Turning: An American Prophecy* (New York: Broadway Books, 1997).

16. Boyer, *When Time Shall Be No More,* 107–8.

17. John F. Walvoord, "Where Is the Modern Church Going?" in Charles Lee Feinberg, ed., *Prophecy and the Seventies* (Chicago: Moody Press, 1971), 121.

18. Dorothy Ross, "Historical Consciousness in Nineteenth-Century America," *American Historical Review* 89 (1984), 909–28; Boyer, *When Time Shall Be No More,* 312–13.

19. For one example among many of prophecy writers' portrayal of the millennium as earth's "golden age," see Kenneth S. Wuest, *Prophetic Light in the Present Darkness* (Grand Rapids: Eerdman's, 1955), 117–18. Boyer, *When Time Shall Be No More,* 318–24, contains further citations. For a general historical treatment, see Lorraine Boettner, *The Millennium* (Philadelphia: Presbyterian and Reformed Publishing Co., 1957).

20. James Mills, "The Serious Implications of a 1971 Conversation with Ronald Reagan: A Footnote to Current History," *San Diego Magazine* (August 1985), 141, offers first-hand evidence of Reagan's deep and longstanding belief in Bible prophecy. See also Boyer, *When Time Shall Be No More,* 142–46, and chap. 4, nn. 79–83 (pp. 378–79).

21. For an influential early assertion that atomic war is foreshadowed in the Bible, see Wilbur M. Smith, *This Atomic Age and the Word of God* (Boston: W. A. Wilde, 1948), an expansion of Smith's 1945 booklet of the same title that was condensed in the January 1946 *Reader's Digest.* For a fascinating mid-1980s study documenting how prophetic belief underlay fatalistic views of nuclear war in Amarillo, Texas, home of the Pantex Corporation, a hydrogen-bomb assembly facility, see A. G. Mojtabai, *Blessed Assurance: At Home with the Bomb in Amarillo* (Boston: Houghton Mifflin, 1986). For my own fuller treatment of this topic see *When Time Shall Be No More,* chap. 4, "The Atomic Bomb and Nuclear War," 115–51 (the 1984 survey is reported on p. 144).

22. Dwight Wilson, *Armageddon Now! The Premillenarian Response to Russia and Israel since 1917* (Grand Rapids: Baker, 1977); Boyer, *When Time Shall Be No More,* 152–57.

23. Lindsey, *The Late Great Planet Earth* (Bantam ed.), 48–60; Thomas S. McCall and Zola Levitt, *The Coming Russian Invasion of Israel* (Chicago: Moody Press, 1974). For an extended discussion of this theme, with many more examples, see Boyer, *When Time Shall Be No More,* chap. 5, "Ezekiel as the First Cold Warrior," 152–80.

24. Wilson, *Armageddon Now!;* Grace Halsell, *Prophecy and Politics: Militant Evangelists on the Road to Nuclear War* (Westport, Conn.: Lawrence Hill, 1986); Hertzel Fishman, *American Protestants and a Jewish State* (Detroit: Wayne State University Press, 1973); James L. Guth, Cleveland R. Fraser, John C. Green, Lyman A. Kellstedt, and Corwin E. Smith, "Religion and Foreign Policy Attitudes: The Case of Christian Zionism," paper presented at the annual meeting of the American Political Science Association, Washington, D.C., 2–5 September 1993. The authors write in their abstract: "We find that religious tradition and doctrinal dispensationalism are powerful predictors of support for Israel among religious and political elites, as well as in the mass public." See also Boyer, *When Time Shall Be No More,* chap. 6, "The Final Chastisement of the Chosen," 181–224.

25. Ray C. Stedman, *What's This World Coming To?* (Ventura, Calif.: Regal Books, 1970; 2d ed., 1986), 39.

26. Arthur Bloomfield, *Before the Last Battle: Armageddon* (Minneapolis: Bethany House, 1971), 65.

27. Zech. 13:8: "And it shall come to pass, that in all the land, saith the Lord, two parts therein shall be cut off and die; but the third shall be left therein." For Hal Lindsey's interpretation of the long history of persecution and slaughter of the Jews, and their impending fate, as expressions of God's "disciplinary action" against a disobedient people, see *The Late Great Planet Earth,* chap. 4, "Israel, O Israel," 32–47 (Bantam ed.). One section of this chapter is wittily entitled "God's Woodshed" (p. 35). Writes Lindsey: "Israel's history of misery which has exactly fulfilled prophetic warnings should be a sign to the whole world—a sign . . . that God means what He says, and says what He means" (p. 37). For a more extended discussion, see Boyer, *When Time Shall Be No More,* 208–24.

28. Arthur E. Bloomfield, *How to Recognize the Antichrist* (Minneapolis: Bethany Fellowship, 1975), 139–40.

29. Author's telephone interview with J. Dwight Pentecost, 13 July 1989.

30. Rev. 13:16–18; Boyer, *When Time Shall Be No More,* chap. 8, "Antichrist, 666, and the Mark of the Beast," 254–90.

31. Robert Fuller, *Naming the Antichrist: The History of an American Obsession* (New York: Oxford University Press, 1995); Bernard McGinn, *Antichrist: Two Thousand Years of the Human Fascination with Evil* (San Francisco: Harper San Francisco, 1994); "Filling in the Potholes in the 'Road Ahead,'" *New York Times* (28 November 1996) [article on Bill Gates, including mention of the Gates-as-Antichrist theories on the Internet].

32. Jack Van Impe, *11:59 and Counting* (Royal Oak: Jack Van Impe Ministries, 1983), 115.

33. For typical recitals of contemporary America's manifold sinfulness by an influential prophecy popularizer see David Wilkerson, *The Vision* (New York: Pyramid Books, 1974), 43, 44, 50, 97, and idem, *Set the Trumpet to Thy Mouth* (Lindale, Texas: World Challenge, 1985), 1–2, 20–21. For other examples, see Boyer, *When Time Shall Be No More,* 230–41.

34. Edward Johnson, *Wonder-Working Providence* (1653), quoted in M. H. Abrams, "Apocalypse: Theme and Variations," in C. A. Patrides and Joseph Wittreich, eds., *The Apocalypse in English Renaissance Thought and Literature* (Manchester: Manchester University Press, 1984), 357. See also Ernest Tuveson, *Redeemer Nation: The Idea of America's Millennial Role* (Chicago: University of Chicago Press, 1968); Nathan O. Hatch, *The Sacred Cause of Liberty: Republican Thought and the Millennium in Revolutionary New England* (New Haven: Yale University Press, 1977); James H. Moorhead, "Between Progress and Apocalypse: A Reassessment of Millennialism in American Religious Thought, 1800–1880," *Journal of American History* 71 (1984), 524–42, esp. 531–33.

35. Dan Betzer, *The Beast: A Novel of the Future World Dictator* (Lafayette, La.: Prescott Press, 1985), 109, 151, 155–56, 162.

36. Pat Robertson, *The End of the Age: A Novel* (Dallas: Word, 1995); information about the LaHaye and Jenkins series from Tyndale House marketing staff, 19

September 1997 and 5 January 1999, and statement by Jerry B. Jenkins on *amazon.com* website, 31 December 1998. The last of the planned twelve novels, tentatively scheduled for 2002, will complete the saga with Christ's Second Coming.

37.   John Hagee, *Beginning of the End: The Assassination of Yitzhak Rabin and the Coming Antichrist* (Nashville: Thomas Nelson, 1996); Ed Dobson, *The End* (Grand Rapids: Zondervan, 1997); Hal Lindsey, *Planet Earth—2000 A.D.* (Palos Verdes, Calif.: Western Front, 1994); idem, *Blood Moon* (Palos Verdes, Calif.: Western Front, 1996).

38.   Lyn Cryderman, an executive at Zondervan Publishing Co., quoted in "Gearing Up for the Millennium," *Publishers Weekly* (13 January 1997), 38.

39.   Lindsey, *Planet Earth—2000 A.D.*, 306.

40.   1 Thess. 5:3. See, for example, "Beware of the Soviets," *Bible Prophecy News* (January–March 1991), 6.

41.   Joseph Chambers, *A Palace for the Antichrist: Saddam Hussein's Drive to Rebuild Babylon and Its Place in Bible Prophecy* (Green Forest, Ark.: New Leaf Press, 1996). See also Charles H. Dyer with Angela Elwell Hunt, *The Rise of Babylon: Sign of the End Times* (Wheaton, Ill.: Tyndale House, 1991). At the time his book was published, Dyer was associate professor of Bible exposition at Dallas Theological Seminary.

42.   Boyer, *When Time Shall Be No More,* 326–31.

43.   Lindsey, *Planet Earth—2000 A.D.*, chap. 10, "The New Islamic Threat," 169–84.

44.   Robertson, *The End of the Age,* 96; Lindsey, *Planet Earth—2000 A.D.*, 81–100, quoted passage on p. 90. See also James L. Guth, John C. Green, Lyman A. Kellstedt, and Corwin E. Smidt, "Faith and the Environment: Religious Beliefs and Attitudes on Environmental Policy," paper delivered at the annual meeting of the Southern Political Science Association, Savannah, Ga., 4–6 November 1993.

45.   Rodney Barker, *And the Waters Turned to Blood: The Ultimate Biological Threat* (New York: Simon & Schuster, 1997). Not only the title, but also the publisher's ads for this book, with blood-red background and references to "a terrifying new plague" and fishermen "plagued by lesions that would not heal," underscored the implicit link to biblical apocalyptic imagery. See, for example, the advertisement in the *New York Times Book Review* (6 April 1997), 19.

46.   Thomas Ice and Timothy J. Demy, *The Coming Cashless Society* (Eugene: Harvest House, 1996); Grant Jeffery, *Final Warning: Economic Collapse and the Coming World Government* (Eugene: Harvest House, 1996).

47.   Pat Robertson, *The New World Order* (Dallas: Word, 1991), 176.

48.   Chambers, *A Palace for the Antichrist,* 101.

49.   Robert Ellis Smith, "The True Terror Is in the Card," *New York Times Magazine* (8 September 1996), 58–59, quoted passage, 59.

50.   On the LaHayes' activism on behalf of conservative causes, including opposition to abortion, the United Nations, gay rights, and many other issues, and their view of the U.S. government as irretrievably evil, debased, and antireligious, see *The Religious Right: The Assault on Tolerance and Pluralism in America* (New York: Anti-Defamation League, 1994), passim. LaHaye has written: "America is a nation based on biblical principles. Christian values should dominate our gov-

ernment. The test of those values is the Bible. Politicians who do not use the Bible to guide their public and private lives do not belong in office." Ibid., 107. LaHaye's emergence as a popular novelist in the 1990s quite clearly represented a pursuit of his long-time conservative agenda by other means.

51. Tim LaHaye and Jerry B. Jenkins, *Tribulation Force* (Wheaton, Ill.: Tyndale House, 1996), 149.

52. Robertson, *The New World Order,* 247, 268.

9 *Michael Barkun*

End-Time Paranoia
Conspiracy Thinking at the Millennium's Close

It is a truism that we live in a culture that seems obsessed with conspiracies, where a major motion picture bears the title *Conspiracy Theory,* announced by an advertisement that says, "The Paranoia Begins August 18."[1] Every unexplained event seems to call forth ever more baroque plots, whether the crash of TWA Flight 800 or the spread of AIDS. *The X-Files* becomes a cult television hit by suggesting conspiracies so powerful that even the FBI cannot expose them. Increasing numbers of Americans find the most compelling explanations of events to be those dominated by deceptions, coverups, and intrigue.

An obvious question posed by these luxuriant conspiratorial growths is, Why now? Conspiracy theories abound in part because they are great simplifiers at a time when reality seems inordinately complex. At the same time, they reinforce apocalyptic concerns, the extravagant fears and expectations generated by the approach of a new millennium. As we shall see, these two forces—the drive to simplify reality and the expectations created by a new millennium—feed upon each other.

The need to simplify the world is a product of the dramatic international political transformations that began in the late 1980s. While the end of the Cold War has been cause for general rejoicing, it has not come without costs. The nature of those costs was suggested some seventy years ago by the writer André Maurois in a charming story he called "The War Against the Moon,"[2] an episode he placed in the then-future world of 1963.

In Maurois's imagined future, humanity had just survived a calamitous world war, followed by a time of extraordinary peace, consolidated by the efforts of a global circle of media tycoons. The danger that this new world faced was not the danger of violence but the danger of boredom, peace having produced an ennui so suffocating that it threatened to convert minor quarrels into major conflicts as a way of lifting the oppressive stability. Reflecting upon this strange and unexpected danger, one of Maurois's media giants remarked of the world's people, "They are getting bored with the era of understanding and international reasonableness that we have set up." To which one of his colleagues responded that the answer was to find an enemy, because, he said, "It doesn't in the least matter against whom we unite," as long as the enemy seems sufficiently mysterious and threatening.[3]

We do not, of course, face so complete and boring a peace as Maurois described in 1927. But the end of the Cold War, the dissolution of the Soviet Union, and the effective removal of the threat of superpower nuclear war have at one stroke not only deprived us of an enemy but dissolved a simple picture of the world—a dualistic vision of good against evil, of the "Free World" against the "Evil Empire." Whatever anxieties this vision produced were counterbalanced by its comforting simplicity and completeness. Virtually every quarrel or conflict could be incorporated within it. Instead, we now face a world which, while it may be objectively less threatening, has been filled with complicated and ambiguous conflicts, whether in Bosnia, Zaire, Afghanistan, Cambodia, or Haiti. Thoughts of conspiracy take us back to the comforting simplicity of an earlier time, producing the appearance of order not by identifying a concrete military and political adversary, but by conjuring up powerful, hidden cabals that seem all the more frightening for their very invisibility.

If the end of the Cold War provides one explanation for the rise of conspiratorialism, the other is surely the approach of a new millennium. For millenarianism has always encouraged dualistic world views, with sharply defined spheres of good and evil. To be sure, this dualism has sometimes been muted, as it was among American millenarian revivalists in the 1830s.[4] But the millennialism that fastens on the year 2000 seizes upon that date in part because it is seen as a boundary between perfect and imperfect time. And those who believe perfect time will arrive suddenly, in an instant, often join that to a belief in a coming final battle between the forces of light and the forces of darkness. These opponents are destined to meet in a last struggle, a literal or metaphorical Battle of Armageddon.

These "catastrophist millenarians" (in Catherine Wessinger's evocative phrase)[5] consequently tie a millenarian future to a climactic disaster. The closer we come to the year 2000, the more vivid the sense of an imminent clash. This occurs in part because the time remaining keeps contracting, imparting ever-greater apprehension and urgency. But it is also because millenarians have always found it easier to describe the evil they detest than the perfection they desire. Perhaps because we live in an imperfect world, we find perfection difficult to describe other than by saying what it is not: it is not the world we know. Far easier, therefore, to describe the enemy, the malign forces preventing the consummation of history. They are allegedly even now marshaling for a last titanic effort at obstruction.

The human imagination, so impoverished in conceiving what the millennium itself will be like, turns out to be endlessly resourceful in picturing the forces of evil. And so millenarians require conspiracies in order to play out their scenarios of the last battle, to which they bring a clarity and detail missing from their fuzzy portraits of the millennium itself. The stronger the millenarian impulse, the more complex, vivid, and ominous the conspiratorial forces appear.

The conspiracy theories that incorporate these representations of evil fall into two categories. One consists of what might be called episodic or segmented conspiracies, plots believed responsible for some single, limited phenomenon or event, whether the Kennedy assassination, UFOs, or crack in the inner city. The sheer proliferation of such theories is itself indicative of a deep unease, but significant though they are, they throw less light on the contemporary apocalyptic mood than the other category of conspiracy theories: what I here call the systematic theories. Systematic conspiratorialism speaks in terms not of limited plots but of vast, convoluted intrigues, malevolent combinations so sweeping that they purportedly explain all of the world's evil. This evil can then be traced back through circuitous paths to a single, unimaginably powerful and corrupt source. There have been many such systematic conspiracy theories in the past. Some have identified the plotters with Jews, some with Freemasons, some with the Catholic church, yet others with global capitalists.

Our own time has the dubious distinction not only of generating such ideas in unprecedented numbers, but of producing a convergence among them. Whether they originate in fundamentalist religion, extremist politics, or the speculations of the New Age, the systematic conspiracy theories of our own time increasingly speak a common language. Different in details, the enemy is always the same: it is always something called the "New World Order." To religious fundamentalists like Pat Robertson, the New World Order represents the forces of Antichrist as they make a last attempt to wrest the world from the godly.[6] To militia groups, the New World Order is a world government about to be imposed upon the United States by the United Nations.[7] To white- or Aryan-supremacist groups like the Christian Identity movement—the dominant religious position on the radical right—the New World Order is the latest manifestation of a Jewish conspiracy to control the world.[8] To some believers in UFOs, the New World Order is a cabal of the wealthy and powerful intent on preventing the world from learning the truth about the extraterrestrials who allegedly have made contact with us.[9] And to some antiabortion groups, the New World Order is the constellation of political forces that have established a right to abortion. When in June 1997 the FBI released letters written by the presumed bombers of an Atlanta abortion clinic, a group that called itself the "Army of God," the letters' author chose to end the communications with "Death to the New World Order."

These disparate visions of coming evil predate George Bush's popularization of "New World Order" in the early 1990s in connection with the Gulf War. Bush, seeking a phrase that would communicate a commitment to new forms of collective security, unknowingly stepped into a religious and political minefield. For by that time both right-wing conspiratorialists and many fundamentalists were already employing the phrase to denote the rising power of evil in the world. Although there is as yet no complete history of the term, "New World Order" was in relatively widespread use by the 1970s, two decades before it entered common political usage. It is not yet clear whether it gained separate, simultaneous acceptance in both religious and political circles, or whether it began in one and was appropriated by the other. However, it seems likely that it initially was employed by religious millenarians to denote the time of persecution associated with the end-time reign of Antichrist. It appears to have migrated from there into the somewhat more secular milieu of the extreme right, where it came to stand for a world dictatorship presided over by such organizations as the UN, the Trilateral Commission, and a world Jewish conspiracy. Its continuing diffusion into such areas as UFO literature suggests its remarkable adaptability.

In a few years' time, these very different subcultures have adopted the New World Order vocabulary as a common conspiratorial language. They all envision a single conspiracy of immense cunning and power that seeks to establish a global dictatorship. The ends to which the conspiracy's power is put vary, from suppressing information about extraterrestrials, to advancing the cause of Satan, or placing America under UN control. The ends are different, but they are all a product of what has functioned since the early 1990s as a "generic" or "ecumenical" conspiracy theory whose shared characteristics make it equally attractive to a wide range of outsider groups. George Bush's unwitting adoption of a term that apocalypticists had for at least the preceding decade or two used to denote absolute evil[10] seemed to conspiratorialists not a coincidence, but rather public confirmation of the plotters' brazenness and power. The spread of both religious and secular New World Order visions has changed America's apocalyptic landscape. The result is a new phenomenon, a single apocalyptic vision, not based exclusively in scripture but manifested in an array of religious, political, and New Age variations.

This theory, broadly stated, argues that much of the world's political and economic life is controlled by a secret set of interlocking decision-makers. What they do not already control, they are prepared to seize quickly. These conspiratorial forces allegedly constitute the world's real government, pulling the strings that determine what publicly visible governments do, while most of the world's people either remain ignorant or have allowed themselves to become the conspiracy's tools.

New World Order theory comes in weak and strong versions. The weak version—what might be called "New World Order Lite"—is epitomized by the writings of Pat Robertson. Like others in the genre, his book *The New World Order* emphasizes a coming UN dictatorship brought about by the machinations of a secret society of Illuminati,[11] but provides little in the way of additional detail.

The "strong" version, less widely known to the general public but increasingly widely disseminated, adds such embellishments as concentration camps to incarcerate "patriots" run by FEMA, the Federal Emergency Management Agency; and microchips implanted under the skin to monitor individuals' movements, at the same time fulfilling the Book of Revelation's "Mark of the Beast" prophecy (an idea, by the way, with which Timothy McVeigh appears to have been familiar).[12] For those who accept either version, such a world view has two advantages. First, it contains room for virtually all of the enemies that figured in the plots of earlier eras: there is room for the Rothschilds and the Rockefellers, the Jews, the Masons and the Vatican, the Council on Foreign Relations and the Trilateral Commission. The New World Order conspiracy is a grand superconspiracy in which all lesser plots can be conveniently nested. In the second place, New World Order theory, like all systematic conspiracy theories, cannot be falsified. While it purports to provide an empirically verifiable picture of the world, in fact there is no information skeptics could produce that would induce believers to have serious doubts. The response of believers is always the same: any contrary evidence, they say, has been concocted or planted by the conspiracy itself to mislead and deceive, demonstrating just how clever the conspirators are. New World Order theory also unites religionists and secularists. Whether one thinks the conspirators are minions of Antichrist or merely greedy plutocrats, the basic outlines of the theory remain intact. Its vocabulary of secret societies and invisible governments serves as a lingua franca uniting believers and nonbelievers.

I am well aware that these are ideas that are difficult to take seriously. In part they are easy to dismiss because to most of us their contents are, to put it kindly, bizarre—for example, their obsession with the symbolism of the Great Seal of the United States, found on the back of the one-dollar bill, and widely believed in conspiratorial circles to encode secrets of the New World Order. Thus, they translate "Novus Ordo Seclorum" as "New World Order" and identify the eye atop the pyramid with the "all-seeing eye of Lucifer," allegedly part of the Illuminati's insignia.[13] If such notions invite ridicule, other New World Order speculations induce revulsion. This is a rhetoric saturated with hatred of the federal government, deemed to be a puppet of the evil forces bent on destroying the Constitution itself. It is also a body of ideas particularly congenial to anti-Semitism; consider the specter of international Jewish bankers found in Pat Robertson's *The New World Order*, the use of *The Protocols of the Elders of Zion* by such UFO writers as William Cooper, or the strident anti-Semitism and racism of Christian Identity, which sees "Aryans" as the descendants of the tribes of Israel and Jews as the offspring of Satan.

In any case, quite apart from the ideas themselves, it is difficult to take seriously the ideological products of socially marginal subcultures. Surely this motley array of antigovernment militants, religious fundamentalists, and dabblers in the occult and crank "science" have little claim on our time or attention. But to conclude that their pariah status makes them insignificant is, in my judgment, to fall into a common but dangerous fallacy—namely, that only the ideas found in respectable academic discourse are worthy of serious consideration. Unfortunately, ideas not blessed by the academy have had a way of securing significant followings, and I would suggest that New World Order theories fall into precisely this category. They are important not because they are true (indeed, I think they are false), but because so many people *believe* them to be true.

Increasingly, as we approach the year 2000, New World Order conspiracy theories furnish a common structure for millenarian speculation. They provide the raw material for that dualism so vital to millenarians. They identify the enemy and endow it with sufficient power to fulfill its necessary role in a coming cosmic struggle for supremacy. At the same time that New World Order ideas make Armageddon possible by conjuring up a suitably demonic adversary, they also provide an escape hatch for frustrated millenarian expectations. For if the millennium does not arrive, there is now a ready answer: the enemy is too powerful; the forces of evil have succeeded in delaying the consummation of history, so that the saved and enlightened must redouble their efforts. If the putative enemy is strong enough, millenarians need not fear the embarrassment of failed prophecies. Unlike the Millerites in the 1840s, who set millennial dates only to find that they came and went without the Second Coming they had predicted,[14] New World Order millenarians have constructed a nearly foolproof explanation for frustrated eschatological hopes.

Millenarians of every stripe claim to possess special knowledge. Only they know what controls the dynamics of history, whether by an esoteric reading of scripture or a theory of class struggle. In similar fashion, the New World Order purports to endow its believers with special knowledge. They are the chosen, not only because they see themselves as salvationist instruments, but because they claim to have seen through the curtain that obscures the vision of the rest of us.

Theirs is a world view in which there is room for neither coincidence nor chance. It is a vision that rests on three beliefs: that nothing happens by accident, that everything is interconnected, and that nothing is as it seems. While at one level this is a vision based on dissimulation and intrigue, on another level it is oddly reassuring, for it tells believers that the world is governed by purpose and design, even if the purposes advanced are sometimes those of Lucifer and his surrogates. The saved and chosen see themselves as fighting not in a meaningless universe but on an ordered cosmic battlefield in which every interaction counts for one side or the other.

The emphasis upon intentionality, interconnection, and deception produces in New World Order literature a bizarre kind of pseudo-scholarship. Millenarians who have adopted New World Order ideas regard history not as a story to be told but as a puzzle to be solved. Since there are deemed to be no random events, every occurrence, no matter how seemingly inconsequential, must be plumbed for its true meaning. Since all events and institutions are linked, students of the New World Order engage in an endless search for points of contact between apparently dissimilar and unconnected organizations, in an attempt to unmask the invisible interlocking directorate that allegedly rules the world. And, since nothing is as it seems, those who appear powerful may actually be impotent puppets, while the truly powerful lie concealed and must be exposed. The result is revisionist history on a grand scale.

As New World Order ideas spread, their implications have changed. The most important change has been the "mainstreaming" of the New World Order. Ideas once found only in the obscure writings of marginal sectarians have begun to seep into the mainstream of American culture. They could be found in Pat Buchanan's 1996 campaign speeches and in the films and television programs that now retail conspiratorialism to mass audiences. These are no longer notions for which one has to search exclusively in ideological undergrounds. They have surfaced, and as they have done so, they have set in motion new consequences. On the one hand, the more widely and frequently such ideas appear, the more respectable they seem. They gradually lose the stigma associated with the pariah groups that developed them. They become part of public debate, openly acknowledged even by those who oppose them. On the other hand, their growing acceptability may, paradoxically, also reduce their attractiveness to some millenarians. The more widely accepted a set of ideas is, the less easy it is to characterize it as special knowledge, and the less privileged are those who believe it. Part of the attraction of New World Order theory is that much of it is made up of what I have called "stigmatized knowledge,"[15] factual claims rejected by such knowledge-validating institutions as universities. To believers, the fact that such institutions reject some factual claims is taken as evidence that those claims are really true. Since prestigious institutions are believed to be part of the conspiracy, anything they accept is *ipso facto* false, while whatever they reject must necessarily be true. Why else would they reject it, if not because it threatens the work of the conspiracy? Therefore, as the New World Order concept spreads, it is difficult to know whether its influence will rise as a function of newfound popularity or fall as those who once gave it credence draw away.

The rising popularity of the New World Order theory not only partially destigmatizes it; it also makes it appear more plausible. If so many people, representing so many constituencies, believe it to be true, does that not make it true? To be sure, such a conclusion is spurious, for repetition provides only the appearance of confirmation, not the substance. But as with popular opinion generally, the more a message is repeated, the more credible it appears.

The reduction of stigma and increasing levels of perceived credibility would count for little were it not for the fact that belief in a New World Order conspiracy has behavioral as well as ideological consequences. It can affect what people do as well as what they believe. It effectively lifts from the shoulders of believers any sense of responsibility for the world's problems. Those are seen as the result not of identifiable human actions, but of unseen forces. If there are evils in the world, then the plotters and their lackeys are at fault. The only obligation incumbent upon New World Order devotees is to expose and defeat the conspiracy. Unfortunately, quite apart from the fact that that involves dueling with a chimera, the results are apt to be socially destructive and quite possibly violent.

In the first place, the very secrecy in which the conspiracy is said to shroud itself engenders an urge to expose it. In the eyes of conspiratorialists, the invisible plotters taunt them with appearances that seem to announce the conspiracy's presence while at the same time maintaining a frustrating barrier. A number of the most extensive conspiracy theories feature faceless symbols of evil—the black helicopters, for example, whose sightings are an obsessive concern for militia members, who believe they are the conspiracy's favored vehicles for transportation and surveillance;[16] or the mysterious "men in black" who make their appearance in UFO theories as well as in *The X-Files* as a sinister force intimidating those who know too much.[17] (By the way, the "men in black" of UFO folklore have nothing in common with the movie buffoons of the same name.)

This desire to expose leads to a search for scapegoats: clearly identifiable individuals and groups on whom responsibility for the New World Order can be placed. To a striking degree, those who are singled out are often the same groups scapegoated in earlier periods: Jews, Freemasons, and Catholics. Indeed, as I comb through recent conspiratorial literature, I am struck by the increasing emphasis on such ideas as a "Jesuit-Masonic conspiracy," ideas with deep roots in nineteenth-century American nativism.[18] Those who traffic in such charges piously declare their freedom from bias and are careful to say that most Jews, Masons, and Catholics are innocent of sinister intentions. It is only "bad" Jews, Masons, and Catholics who allegedly need to be brought to justice. Such disclaimers, however, seem disingenuous attempts to deflect criticism by conspiratorialists who do not trouble to indicate how "good" and "bad" group members can be distinguished.

It is, of course, possible that some who follow this route are in fact unaware of the dangers of the ideas with which they are dealing. Pat Robertson appeared genuinely shocked when articles in the *New York Review of Books* demonstrated that *The New World Order* was shot through with anti-Semitic references.[19] Similarly, militia organizations make much of their openness to members of every race and religion. Perhaps they are as open as they claim. But the logic of New World Order ideas suggests that regardless of their claims of openness, an inexorable logic pushes believers to identify in increasingly specific terms the groups they consider demonic.

This logic has already begun to play itself out in the interactions between New World Order apocalypticists and the federal government. They see in the federal government the conspiracy's public face. From their point of view, federal employees are the conspiracy's agents, and federal laws and regulations are tools to entrap "patriots." In their view, the federal government has either totally lost its legitimacy or is well on the way to doing so. The more seriously such ideas are taken, the greater the likelihood that the most mundane demands for legal compliance will be defied, that governmental personnel may be attacked, and that conspiratorialists will stand in armed confrontation with law enforcement agencies, willing Armageddon into existence. We have already seen this dynamic in action in Garfield County, Montana, during the spring of 1996, when the Freemen retreated into an armed enclave in a standoff with the FBI. The Freemen's chief of security, Rodney Skurdal, had earlier written that no genuine Christian or patriot could apply for a Social Security card, a building permit, or a driver's license without committing an unspeakably idolatrous act of submission to Baal.[20] The Freemen standoff fortunately ended without violence. But events might have taken a different course, and there is little reason to regard the 1996 standoff as an isolated event.

An increasing number of Americans believe that the millennium is at hand, its attainment blocked only by the conspiratorial forces that allegedly represent and advance the New World Order. Most have limited their expression to the written and spoken word. Others, however, have armed themselves in the conviction that a battle of titanic scope lies just ahead. They do not agree on a precise date. For some, it is the late 1990s; for others, the year 2000; for still others, the years immediately thereafter. What seems certain, however, is that regardless of disagreements about the specifics of the apocalyptic scenarios, the century and millennium will close with episodes of real or potential violence.

The danger of systematic conspiracy theories lies therefore in their capacity to generate self-fulfilling prophecies. Those who see conspirators everywhere more readily adopt the lifestyles of the besieged. They may retreat into survivalist enclaves, organize paramilitary forces, or experience an alienation so profound that they doubt the legitimacy of all social institutions. In so doing, they create the very dualism that they predict, as they construct a world of opposed forces. It is a world we have already glimpsed outside Waco,[21] on the Montana prairie, and in the militia groups that dot rural America. The forces that drive such groups are unlikely to ebb in the next few years. Indeed, if anything, they seem likely to grow stronger. To keep their violent propensities in check will require a complex and sophisticated balancing of liberty concerns with order concerns, a balancing that was egregiously absent at Waco but that the resolution of the Freemen episode suggests may yet be possible. Let us hope it is, for if it is not, the passage into the next millennium will indeed be tumultuous.

Notes

1. Advertisement, *New York Times* (3 August 1997).
2. André Maurois, *The Next Chapter: The War against the Moon* (New York: E. P. Dutton, 1927).

3. Ibid., 32.

4. Michael Barkun, *Crucible of the Millennium: The Burned-over District of New York in the 1840s* (Syracuse: Syracuse University Press, 1986), 24–29.

5. Catherine Wessinger, "Millennialism with and without the Mayhem," in Thomas Robbins and Susan J. Palmer, eds., *Millennium, Messiahs, and Mayhem: Contemporary Apocalyptic Movements* (New York: Routledge, 1997), 47–60.

6. Pat Robertson, *The New World Order* (Dallas: Word, 1991).

7. This literature is vast, but see, for example, the following: Jack McLamb, *Operation Vampire Killer 2000: American Police Action Plan for Stopping the Program for World Government Rule* (Phoenix: American Citizens & Lawmen Assoc., 1992); Mark Koernke, *America in Peril,* videotape.

8. Michael Barkun, *Religion and the Racist Right: The Origins of the Christian Identity Movement,* rev. ed. (Chapel Hill: University of North Carolina Press, 1997).

9. See, for example, Milton William Cooper, *Behold a Pale Horse* (Sedona, Ariz.: Light Technology, 1991), which is read widely in both UFO and militia circles.

10. The earliest appearance of the phrase "New World Order" has yet to be established, but one relatively early example is *Witchcraft and the Illuminati* (Pontiac, Mo.: Covenant, Sword and Arm of the Lord, 1981), published by a now-defunct Christian Identity commune. I discuss New World Order conspiracy theory in greater detail in "Religion, Militias and Oklahoma City: The Mind of Conspiratorialists," *Terrorism and Political Violence* 8 (1996), 50–64.

11. Conspiracy literature on the Bavarian Illuminati extends back to the late 1700s. David H. Bennett, *The Party of Fear: The American Far Right from Nativism to the Militia Movement,* rev. ed. (New York: Vintage, 1995), 23–26. The actual Bavarian "Order of Illuminists" lasted little more than a decade, from 1776 to about 1787. However, since the late 1700s, conspiracy theorists have insisted that its dissolution was merely a ploy that allowed it to go underground in order to wreak greater political and economic havoc.

12. Barkun, *Religion and the Racist Right,* 259.

13. E.g., *Witchcraft and the Illuminati,* 40.

14. Barkun, *Crucible of the Millennium,* 39–41.

15. Michael Barkun, "Conspiracy Theories as Stigmatized Knowledge: The Basis for a New Age Racism?" in Jeffrey Kaplan and Tore Bjorgo, eds., *Nation and Race: The Developing Euro-American Racist Subculture* (Boston: Northeastern University Press, 1998), 58–72.

16. For a presentation sympathetic to militia views, see Jim Keith, *Black Helicopters over America: Strikeforce for the New World Order* (Lilburn, Ga.: IllumiNet Press, 1994).

17. Peter J. Rojcewicz, "The 'Men in Black' Experience and Tradition: Analogues with the Traditional Devil Hypothesis," *Journal of American Folklore* 100 (1987), 148–60.

18. Bennett, *The Party of Fear,* 49.

19. Michael Lind, "Rev. Robertson's Brand of International Conspiracy The-

ory," *New York Review of Books* 42 (2 February 1995), 21–25; Michael Lind and Jacob Heilbrunn, "On Pat Robertson," ibid. (20 April 1995), 65–71.

20. "Common Law Memorandum, Rodney O. Skurdal vs. de facto corporation state of Montana, Roundup, Montana, October 28, 1994." I discuss the document further in *Religion and the Racist Right,* 286–87.

21. James D. Tabor and Eugene V. Gallagher, *Why Waco? Cults and the Battle for Religious Freedom in America* (Berkeley: University of California Press, 1995).

PART 4

HOPE AND FAITH AT THE END OF THE MILLENNIUM

TWO HOMILIES

10 *Archbishop Rembert G. Weakland, O.S.B.*

Hope in the Face of Crisis

I therefore, the prisoner in the Lord, beg you to lead a life worthy of the calling to which you have been called, with all humility and gentleness, with patience, bearing with one another in love, making every effort to maintain the unity of the Spirit in the bond of peace. There is one body and one Spirit, just as you were called to the one hope your calling, one Lord, one faith, one baptism, one God and Father of all, who is above all and through all and in all. But each of us was given grace according to the measure of Christ's gift. . . . The gifts he gave were that some would be apostles, some prophets, some evangelists, some pastors and teachers, to equip the saints for the work of ministry, for building up the body of Christ, until all of us come to the unity of the faith and of the knowledge of the Son of God, to maturity, to the measure of the full stature of Christ.

Ephesians 4: 1–7, 11–13

To experience the crossing over from one millennium to another is a special gift of God to our generation. It is important that we Christians use this gift in a positive and constructive way. Already we find some among us who want to convince us that the end is at hand, that Christ is coming in all His glory. We hear also that this coming will be preceded by a cataclysm—the signs of which are all around us. As Christ tells us in the Gospels, we do not know the time or the hour. These prophets may be right, not because it is the millennium but because we do not know the day or the hour. We live waiting, but prepared. The end-times began with the birth of Christ, God-among-us. They began with His preaching that the Kingdom of Heaven was at hand. But He also warned us that we do not know the day or the hour: such knowledge is reserved to God alone. It is our imagination that has decided that the day or the hour is somehow to be connected with the turning of a millennium. We should be leery of trusting our own fascination that thrusts us into playing the role of God.

But the transition from one millennium to another can be of great importance to us Christians. What should the millennium celebration do for and to us? How would God want us to use this gift? What will be special to our generation as disciples of Christ living through this moment that other generations did not have? What is this *kairos* (a special time set by God, as opposed to *kronos* or linear time) to mean in our lives? These are

185

the questions we must ask ourselves, whether the world ends tomorrow or in the year 2000 or 2001 or 2999 or whenever.

Ultimately the answer should be a sharper realization that God in His love is truly and forcefully in command, that God in His love has a plan for us and for this earth as a part of the fulfillment of His Kingdom, that all our hope must be placed in that same loving and saving God. The millennium should help us reflect on the larger picture, the vast plan God has for the universe and for all of us who are a part of that Kingdom. In the midst of all of our daily problems and sufferings, our cares and concerns, our anguishes and griefs, joys and trials, we can say, "God is in command, and God loves us, never abandons us, and has a greater destiny for us and this world in the fulfillment of His Kingdom than we can ever be able to imagine." Our trust in God is the basis of our hope. The millennium forces us to look beyond our daily drudgeries to see that larger picture.

During this time we will naturally be hearing more and more from the apocalyptic literature of the New and Old Testaments. We will have the chance of hearing the apocalyptic passages in a fresh way, with fresh ears, with fresh insights, with fresh understanding. That is the gift God gives to us of this generation that will experience the millennium. I would like to mention five special aspects of our Faith that the millennium should reinforce, all of them being a part of our hope and trust as we face the future, all of them found in that apocalyptic literature, all of them in one way or another being but different strains of the same theme.

First, the millennium and our apocalyptic literature will seek to strengthen our larger vision of who Jesus Christ is. The vision of Christ for the millennium takes the Jesus of the Gospels (who, in all His humanity, we confess to making at times into a cozy and sentimental companion) and portrays Him as the Christ who is Lord of history, majestic in His divinity, and more than a human brother to us all. Ephesians used the term "Son of Man," so dear to the Book of Daniel, to describe that apocalyptic vision of Christ. We are reminded that we are growing into the fullness of Christ, reaching our full stature as persons loved by God. Or should I say that Christ is reaching His full stature and assimilating us to Him, to His Body? This image of Christ is one of completion, of fullness. It is one that is not abstract, not out there somewhere; its fulfillment takes place here in our midst. We are growing into the fullness of Christ's Body. Christ and His Body, the baptized, are now one. That is why we can say one Spirit, one baptism, one Lord of us all.

John the Seer's vision of Christ in the Book of Revelation is the same: Christ is Lord of all, Lord of history, Lord of the Church. In His awesomeness He stands before the throne of the Almighty. The apocalyptic literature makes us stretch our vision of Jesus to embrace that "high" Christology that we may have been avoiding of late. The Christ of the end-times stands before us in majesty but does not hesitate to take us up into that same fullness of life that is His. We may prefer to meditate on the human Jesus of Nazareth; but when we are faced with larger issues, such as the ultimate destiny for ourselves and for this earth, we find consolation in knowing that the same Jesus Christ who taught in the synagogues, who cured the sick, who talked about God's love for the poor, who forgave sinners, stands before the throne of the Almighty as our Lord, the Lord of all. The message we must understand is this: with Christ as the Lord of our history, why should we fear?

Second, the apocalyptic literature has an immediacy about it that has been lost through the centuries. We have relegated the coming of Christ to some time out there, so far away that we do not see it as relevant. These times force us to ask why we have lost a sense of urgency that was characteristic of the New Testament literature. That same presence of the risen Lord that is to come must stand in our midst now. In the Book of Revelation Christ stands in the middle of His Church. Each Easter we say that He is risen, He is here. Then we go our ways and forget Him. The excitement of the Easter narratives of discovery, whether they be about Mary at the tomb, or John and Peter, or the disciples on the way to Emmaus, must be ours. How their hearts were on fire when He was in their midst! Do we continue to seek Him in His Word and in the breaking of the bread? What has happened to our excitement? We may laugh when we read a bumper sticker that says "If the rapture comes this car will be empty," but it may well be the occasion for us to examine ourselves and ask why we do not have that same enthusiasm for Christ's presence among us now.

The urgency and excitement of the apocalyptic literature will be for us these days a constant examination of conscience. Do not try to escape it. Try, instead, to enkindle in your own hearts that same desire for the full presence of Christ in our midst that was so clear in the early Church. It should also mean that we eagerly seek every sign of the presence of Christ in Church and world today. Let the immediacy of the coming of Christ as described in the apocalyptic literature become a reminder of the immediacy of Christ's presence in the here and now. The two are intimately linked together. The degree of expectation of one equals the degree of expectation of the other. It is the same Christ we are constantly seeking.

Third, there is something very special about this millennium for our culture. We moved from an Enlightenment concept of the human person and human society—one of gradual perfection and fulfillment through reason—to disillusionment. We humans, in our pride, thought we could bring ourselves to perfection. Perfectibility was within our grasp, we thought. Some even believed they could structure rational plans for a perfect society, if reason would only be followed. Secretly, we all hoped that these theories could be right, even if we saw as well the proclivities toward sin and evil in our midst. This Enlightenment vision fell apart with the recent wars and with our own inabilities to face up to the injustices in the world. Our idealism was in for a shock. In this postmodern period, there can so easily follow a tendency to cynicism, to skepticism, to selfishness.

The millennium and the literature that we will hear will give us reason to say that total fulfillment is not of our making. We know that only Christ can bring such fulfillment and such perfection, both to us as individuals and to societies. We yearn for it, but we are now too smart to believe that we will of ourselves create it. Perhaps it was necessary for us to go through such a purging of our naive idealism based on human means alone before we could come to rely totally on Christ and see that our perfection will come about only insofar as we are lifted up by him. A false humanism is replaced with a real one, a Christocentric one. A false perfection is replaced by a genuine one, a Spirit-animated one. We are not left hopeless, but have a new and more solid hope in Christ. The letter to the Ephesians makes this hope real. As members of Christ's Body, we can be lifted up and made whole in him. As St. Augustine said so long ago, our hearts are restless till they rest in Christ. Only there is true peace and assurance. It is amusing how often in history we humans have to be brought down to our size again. We are always building our towers of Babel. The apocalyptic literature will again remind us that market economy, democratic processes, and all the lip service we give to seeking solutions to racism, violence, exploitation of others, and what have you will not work until we are remade into Christ's image and likeness, till we take our discipleship seriously and let Christ remake us. Through the celebration of this millennium we may then come to a new realism that lets Christ be Christ— namely, the savior in our midst.

In fourth place, the apocalyptic literature will also help us form ourselves into a people, a Church, a People of God. One thing is sure: in that literature no one stands alone. Christ is present to one and to all. The role of the Church becomes clear. It is a gathering of all the elect. We are present, like the lamp-stands in the Book of Revelation, with Christ before the throne of the Father. The passage from Ephesians makes it clear that we do not wait for the coming of Christ alone; we wait as a people. That sentiment is also much needed in our day. We form community as we wait because it is a shared waiting, not a lonely, isolated vigil. As we wait we are being formed into the living Body of Jesus Christ. The spirituality of our day is very self-centered. It often corresponds to and reinforces the worst part of our egotistical culture. Instead of challenging the "me-ism" of our culture, it encourages it. The apocalyptic literature will be the best antidote to such isolationism that we could find. It sees all God's people together. We are tied in, one to another, in our destiny before Christ. There is one Church, one baptism, one Lord, one Spirit. Oneness dominates in this literature. Christ unites: He does not divide. As the Ephesians had to be taught that truth, so do we.

I would hope that the celebration of the millennium could be used to strengthen the bonds that unite us all as the one people of God, as the one Church, the *una sancta*. The sociologists tell us that the younger generation is indeed very spiritual, prays much, and has an instinct for the holy. We are also told that they have an aversion to the institutional Church. We must ask why and in the light of the apocalyptic literature seek an answer. Why is it not in the Church that the presence of Christ becomes real to that generation? Why do they fear the Church or disregard it? Perhaps, as they hear the apocalyptic passages read in the assembly, they will see that one of the important aspects of our belief in Jesus Christ and in the Church that He founded is that it must contain that Spirit of unity and oneness and be a catalyst for bringing people together, not dividing them. Am I too naive in hoping that the millennium could be used for a new vision of the Church as well, first for its importance in the whole plan of God, and second for its nature as a visible place for the presence of the Risen Christ to shine forth?

Last, the apocalyptic literature tells us much about how we should live in the end-times as we wait. Sometimes it strikes us as too negative, and we claim that it would not pass the examination of modern psychologists. The term so often used is "patient endurance." So much of this literature was written in a time of persecution. That virtue was most important so that there would be no backsliding, no reverting to the pagan ways that looked so much easier and less full of suffering. "Patient endurance" became a way of saying that one believed in God's presence among us, that all was in God's hands, that there was never reason for despair or for depression. Patient endurance is a sign of hope in God.

The aim of such endurance is not just stoicism; rather, it leads to new life. Because it is waiting with Christ, it cannot be in vain. This vision also sees the Church as in the midst of a kind of battle. Some of us do not like this military image, but the apocalyptic literature will remind us that there is evil in the world, that all is not of itself right, that we must fight against forces that are not on the side of Christ. I do not believe that the sides in this battle can so easily be determined by us humans. Evil or good is not the total possession of one or the other person or institution. Good and evil create a ragged line down through all people and all human constructs.

Evil must be fought against, within ourselves, in our Churches, in our society, in the world. The apocalyptic literature will not let us be naive about evil. We are not to be tossed about like children, but to be mature and face that evil without fear, with the weapons that Christ Himself gave us.

There will be tendencies in our day to form a perfect society among ourselves, the elect, to the exclusion of the others. There will be a tendency to see ourselves as the saved and the others as the condemned, as the evil ones. The literature we will hear could easily lead to such an atmosphere. But we must resist that temptation. The letter to the Ephesians would not have been written to them if all the evil people had been excluded, if everyone who did not agree had been excommunicated. Now is not the time to turn ourselves into the final judge—we leave that to Christ—but, rather, to seek to take from our own hearts and minds all that keeps us from being aware of Christ's presence in others, in the Church, in society, in the world. It would not be a bad gift to us this millennium if we had a heightened sense then of evil and sin and sought to name the causes of violence and division among us. The Ephesians were simply told that they must now act as a new people, a Christ-like people. That in itself is the lesson we must hear.

As the millennium approaches, we can thus see it as a moment of special grace for all of us. I hope we will not seek to close ourselves off from others as if that was the only way to ensure that we will be among the saved. I hope we recapture the urgency of the Gospel without falling into a false interpretation of the signs of the times—a knowledge reserved to God alone.

But more than anything else I hope the apocalyptic literature we will hear proclaimed in the assembly will be a grace to us as we meditate on it in these special times. May it heighten and deepen our Faith and our trust in God and in the power of His Spirit in the Church. May we rest in the peace of knowing that God's Kingdom is being brought to fulfillment by Jesus Christ and that we are privileged to be part of His Body.

This will be a time of grace if our waiting for Christ becomes a search for His Presence in our midst in the here and now. If that happens, the millennium will have been truly God's gift to our generation, and we will be waiting, as we should, in renewed hope, not only in the year 2000, but for all the future time God gives us and this universe.

Christian Faith and Witness amidst Political Oppression
A Glance Back to Church Life in East Germany, 1970–1990

The theme "Waiting in Fearful Hope: Approaching the New Millennium" evoked spontaneous endorsement in some of my German friends and in myself. Although at times we feared that the Communist rulers might draw people away from the Christian belief and, slowly but surely, cause the Church to die, we also had hope in our hearts that the Lord would lead us to a new and deeper perception of His revelation. We read in the Book of Revelation, chapter 13, the story about the beast and the dragon and their dangerous power. But we also listened to chapter 15 and therefore to the song of the Lamb, holy and victorious and king of all nations:

> Great and wonderful are thy deeds,
> O Lord God the Almighty!
> Just and true are thy ways. . . .
> All nations shall come and worship thee. (15: 3–4, RSV)

So this theme, fearful hope, recalls the pattern of the East German pilgrimage and underlines our experience of the power of God's coming Kingdom. Despite the very different political systems in West and East Germany, and in particular the cultural and historical distinctions between the United States of America and Germany, we perceive in the theme of the conference that we are all together, looking forward to the new millennium, feeling fear and needing hope, and we are asking God for renewal of our belief in His prophetic revelation.

I would like to present a meditative report about the faith and witness of Christian parishes during the final decades of Communist rule in East Germany. East Germany is a very small part even of Europe, and its fate is not a very special one among the suffering people on earth! Yet our Christian pilgrimage in isolated East Germany illustrates in part what it means, in practical terms, to believe in God's coming Kingdom. I will attempt a brief sketch of this bird in flight.

Political Events

The Communist rulers' policy toward the Church did not remain the same over the years but showed a certain development. The Communists slowly changed their behavior from violent actions after 1945 against the so-called enemies of socialist progress to a program of rationally calculated administrative measures. These developments in the state's policy for church affairs were normally linked directly or indirectly to important political events.

The first important event was the death of Stalin in March 1953. He was rightly seen as the definitive representative of brutality in the Soviet Union before, during, and after the Second World War. His death led—slowly but surely—to internal conflicts in the Soviet Union itself. As a first consequence, the Soviet government issued, as we know now, in June 1953 a secret command to the East German rulers to end the persecution of Christian congregations and to follow a course of "normalizing" relations with the churches.

The second important political event was in 1968, the development known as the "Prague Spring." The Czech Socialist party decided to develop a socialist system "with a human face" and thus established—indirectly but concretely—a certain political independence from the Soviet Union. First of all, they wanted democratic reforms. This was "too much." You doubtless remember the suppression of this hopeful movement by military force, and Leonid Brezhnev's declaration of the "limited independence of the socialist countries."

On May 3, 1971, Walter Ulbricht, a notorious hard-liner, was replaced by Erich Honecker, who was not much better than Ulbricht, but smarter and predisposed to think before acting. He longed for political recognition of the GDR, the German Democratic Republic, within the world community, and thus he was interested in good international relations. Willy Brandt, the West German chancellor at that time, did his best to lessen the contrast between East and West Germany. In 1979 the so-called Basis

Pact between East and West Germany was developed and finally signed by both sides through Brandt's initiative. This made way for the first officially sanctioned contacts between people in the East and the West—by telephone, for example; sometimes, for "humanitarian" reasons, even permission to travel was granted.

It was in 1973—which was also an important year for the East German people—that the Helsinki Conference on Security and Cooperation in Europe started its work, inviting and, finally, including representatives from both parts of Germany. In 1975, documents containing statements on human rights were signed by all participants, including those from the East German government. On November 10, 1980, the Polish *Solidarnosc* movement led by Lech Walesa was approved by the Polish government. This development alarmed the East German government.

Finally, in March 1985, Michail Gorbachev was elected general secretary of the Soviet Party. He coined the two terms *perestroika* and *glasnost. Perestroika* meant reforms, and *glasnost* meant the openness of Soviet society to alternative political patterns. These became terms of hope for many East German people. Gorbachev's slogan was repeated from mouth to mouth: "Who comes late (with reforms) will be punished by life itself." Recalling the progress made through these political events of the last twenty years, I remember the old Christian saying: "The Church of Christ lives *in* the world, but does *not* live *by* the world."

Marks of Spiritual Development

The main effect of political oppression on people whose religious and moral convictions differed from the official state ideology was that Christian people found themselves compelled honestly to test the reliability of their Christian belief and the truth of the biblical message. More than that: oppressed Christians had to learn to find understandable words to express their belief and bear witness to the mighty atheists, because they, as Christians, were questioned and sometimes mocked and suspected. The East German Christians lived through all the decades in the Communist system in a more or less cooling head-wind. In general it was easier to say, "I am an atheist," than it was to confess, "I am a Christian." Officially, Christians were judged to be either fools or political enemies. Through the years, although the climate was not comfortable for practicing Christians, it ultimately strengthened and clarified their spiritual identity.

Three main fields of conflict between Marxist ideology and Christian belief were education, careers, and military service. First, as we read in Revelation, 19, "Praise our God, all you his servants, . . . for the Lord our God the Almighty reigns. Let us rejoice and exult and give him the glory"

(5–7). "God is." "God reigns." This is and was our confession. "No!" runs the Marxist antithesis, taught and printed again and again. "There are only human beings in the world, living in either reactionary or progressive social structures, men and women with their physical and moral possibilities." After the successful launch of the first Sputnik with Yuri Gagarin aboard, we were told that the pilot had not met any God in the sky. Marxists asserted that only modern natural sciences and their methods could state and express reality and truth.

Second, as Christians we said, "Only God, only the Lord Jesus Christ, is able to develop and to complete full humanity in us human beings." Our Christian belief says: we are created in God's image; but we have perverted that image and we are encircled by our selfish egos.

For its followers Marxism represented something like a secular eschatology; they could be seen as secular zealots. It was their conviction that all the people of the working class, holding and using all the political power, will bring society close to social perfection. Man is good, they said; men and women are fundamentally good, unless they are exploited by the mighty and the rich. There was a substantial difference between Marxist and Christian anthropology. It was this anthropological misconception in Marxist ideology which, over the years, led to economic disaster. It is not true that people who have a good job, an adequate salary, and a strong socialist education will do their best to work for the benefit of the general public. It is more realistic to admit that people with a good job and an adequate salary will do their best to find a better job for themselves with a higher salary, and so on.

Third, as Christians, we said: "God alone is merciful. God's mercy is the main inalienable premise for a healthy society." We were and are convinced: God's mercy authorizes us to work toward understanding and reconciliation among people in our own country and around the globe. And God's mercy forbids us to support hate and revenge.

This may look like an academic and theoretical antithesis. But it was this conflict which finally motivated Christian work for peace, alternative military service, and conscientious objectors. It gave us the inner power to reject hatred toward the people in West Germany. Yet such ongoing discussions about these Christian convictions on different levels sapped energy from many parish members, especially the young ones, who were being constantly criticized and examined at school.

The shape of our East German spirituality developed gradually through the years. At first, the old question of the meaning of human suffering was raised among us. Why was it just us in the East? I remember many studies based on biblical passages like 2 Corinthians 4:17–18: "For this slight momentary affliction is preparing for us an eternal weight of glory beyond all comparison, because we look not to the things that are seen, but to the things that are unseen." Or Acts 14:22, where they strengthened "the souls of the disciples, exhorting them to continue in the faith, and saying that through many tribulations we must enter the kingdom of God.'" In both passages the coming Kingdom of God, the eschatological perspective of His ruling the world, is expressed as a strong encouragement for Christians living between fear and hope. I clearly remember that there was no theoretical discussion among us about the possibility or impossibility of God's coming Kingdom. We also discovered this eschatological discussion in the Gospel of St. Matthew (24–25) and even in some parts of the Old Testament prophets. Challenged by our exhausting situation, the biblical message of God's coming Kingdom carried its own conviction and shone in our hearts.

The atheistic propaganda—in schools and universities, in theaters and films, by literature, by the mass media—combined with "some" political pressure on professional careers and in other areas influenced many people to leave the Church. Through the years it was a shock to learn that even a moderate head-wind is enough to drive many traditional Christians away from the Church. Many left. It is probably well known that in East Germany not more than 20 percent of the total population belong to *any* of the Christian churches. And among the secularized 80 percent, even the knowledge of the Christian roots of our culture has enormously diminished. I must clearly say that the dwindling membership of East German people in any of the churches and the extremely slight knowledge of our Christian background and of Christian values was and is the most harmful result of the Communist education system after forty-five years.

Faced with this development, we did not choose resignation but reacted creatively. By God's grace many small Christian groups—normally with ten to twenty members—came into being amidst local parishes. I would like to call them "charismatic groups." Christian men and women wanted to bring their individual natural and spiritual gifts together, to strengthen one another for their daily lives in socialist society, to improve their understanding of the Bible, and to train their endurance when faced with critical challenges. They often identified themselves spiritually with Apostolic passages like 1 Corinthians 12 and Ephesians 4, witnessing the one divine spirit and a variety of gifts, as one spiritual body with many members. They had a strong commitment to build up and renew Christian congregations by the message of the coming Kingdom of God in which joy, justice, and peace would be all-embracing. The eternal Lord is here! The inner basis in such groups was mutual trust between the members—a precious precondition in our land. The invisible, living, and coming Lord was their focal point, experienced and witnessed as a strong help in their present life; as we read in Hebrews 11:1, "Now faith is the substance of things hoped for, the evidence of things not seen." In the late 1980s, even the East German civil rights and human rights groups (having more or less Christian roots) lived on in this special tradition of charismatic groups.

Another example: we worked hard to develop the Christian education of baptized and also nonbaptized children in the parishes. The all-powerful secular school had thrown pastors and catechists out of the classrooms. It was a fight between David and Goliath. We could not overcome the extensive socialist education system, but we did our best to teach the full Gospel and to live with the children in the love of Christ. Our hope was that the children might feel that their Lord is not a tyrant, hungry for boys and girls, but the good heavenly Father ready to welcome children with His blessing hands. With gratitude I remember many experienced catechists who were charismatic educators and impressive imitators of Christ.

The hostile climate toward us Christians during the last twenty years of East Germany became more and more inconsistent: on the one hand, it was easier for many in their everyday life; on the other hand, it was more bureaucratic, even dull, without new impulses and with barely acknowledged concerns related to the growing economic and ecological disaster. Nevertheless, leading functionaries showed self-confidence in the well-known traditional way through mass-media propaganda and speeches. The difference between propaganda and the people's experience became evident and provoked protests, particularly among the young adults. In truth, the rulers of East Germany in their last decade were rattled and anxious. Rattled rulers are difficult people, prone to panicky actions (which they finally took) and unpredictable. Many of the reliable parish members were exhausted by the continual head-wind and the difficulties of everyday life; they were tempted to resignation. Many people, Christians and non-Christians alike, asked, "Where is the living hope for us?"

But the Lord also raised new spiritual perceptions and experiences among us. Once again the open Bible, the Gospel itself, shone and invited us to new discoveries. For instance, we heard the message of Deutero-Isaiah, chapters 40 to 43: "Comfort, comfort my people, says your God. Speak tenderly to Jerusalem and cry to her that she has served her term" (40:1–2). "In the wilderness prepare the way of the Lord. . . . Then the glory of the Lord shall be revealed" (40:3, 5). We saw a certain analogy between God's people during their exile in Babylon in the sixth century before Christ and our situation waiting for the Lord's saving revelation among us.

We read: "Do not fear, you worm Jacob, you insect Israel! I will help you, says the Lord; your Redeemer is the Holy One of Israel" (41:14). And we read further on: "He gives power to the faint, and strengthens the powerless. Even youths will faint and be weary and the young will fall exhausted; but those who wait for the Lord shall renew their strength, they shall mount up with wings like eagles" (40:29–31). We learned that it is essential for "Christian hope" to see God's invisible but indestructible reality beyond the worldly things and facts.

In the 1970s, we often spoke about the short parable in John 12:24, where the Lord says: "Very truly, I tell you, unless a grain of wheat falls into the earth and dies, it remains just a single grain, but if it dies, it bears much fruit." We tried to accept both: if a Church is reduced in size and possibilities by a secular power, that is no joke—it reminds us of death. But the threat posed by secular power never means the end of the Church; indeed, it is the beginning of a new authentic life. Christ's Church cannot be destroyed by the secular violence of the Gentiles but can die only through the sin and disbelief of Christians themselves.

In the New Testament we pondered some passages of St. Paul's letters, especially those dealing with strength and weakness. We learned anew his exposition in 2 Corinthians 12:9–10, where God says: "My grace is sufficient for you, for power is made perfect in weakness. . . . for whenever I am weak, then I am strong." To put this in our own words: God established a helpful correlation between our spiritual temptations and his encouragements, a correlation not like a mechanical order, but as a consequence of his free mercy.

Later on, in the last years of East Germany's isolation, the New Testament's passages about Easter came to the fore. This was truly exciting because our traditional intellectual European difficulties about Christ's resurrection lost their importance. For instance, the famous story about the two disciples returning home after Good Friday to Emmaus assumed a new luster. The disciples are sad; an "unknown" man speaks to them, but they do not recognize him as their Lord. Not until Christ sits at their table, breaking and blessing the bread, and giving it to them, are their eyes opened: "and they recognized him; and he vanished from their sight. They said to each other, "Were not our hearts burning within us while he was talking to us on the road?" (Luke 24:31–32). The "burning hearts" became key words for us, for they assured us that God was near to us.

As a final example, the overwhelming promise of the New Heaven and the New Earth at the end of the Book of Revelation (21:1–6) fascinated us. Even with this special promise, we had no intellectual difficulties in understanding and translating the narrative into our modern way of thinking. We were struck by their relevance to the unsolved economic and ecological problems worldwide, to human brutality, and to the growing disparity between poor and rich. We listened to the challenging encouragement: "I

saw a new heaven and a new earth . . . and I saw the holy city, the new
Jerusalem, coming down. . . . He will wipe every tear from their eyes.
Death will be no more; mourning and crying and pain will be no more;
for the first things have passed away." We heard both: the Lord Himself will protect His creation, including mankind, from their selfish ambi-
tion, and He wants us to be His responsible helpers. We understood that
neither socialism nor any other economic system can replace the Lord's
saving acts. Christ is the only reliable hope for our future, for the New
Millennium.

This has nothing to do with any kind of Christian "merit" on our part.
With gratitude I must confess that, while the sometimes gentle and sometimes severe oppression of Christians under Communist rule in East Germany reduced the number of parishioners, it did not eradicate the Christian faith. Rather, it deepened its witness by recalling the biblical message
of the victorious coming of the Kingdom of God. I remember the day in
the 1980s when the youth groups began to sing: "We shall overcome."
Christ's Church is not a human enterprise but a fruit of God's superior
activity. Often enough we feel fear, but God's promises, our hope, prove
to be stronger.

Meanwhile—by God's grace—Germany has been reunited for seven
years. We feel joyful gratitude for this fact. However, we have new problems, and some of them are worldwide—for example, mass unemploy-
ment, the sad economic heritage of past decades in East Germany, the
growing disparity between the few rich people and the many who live at
subsistence level, and the lack of financial resources in private firms. Fear
and hope are realities among us at a new level.

We are living together in one Evangelical Lutheran Church in Germany.
That is joyful. We have come together after different journeys, with different experiences. So we are waiting together in fearful hope for the New
Millennium. We can and we must do a lot to protect our people and all
mankind from deadly disaster. But we are not strong enough—nor good
enough—to solve all the problems around the globe through our human
wisdom and power. Without any doubt, we will need God's advice, guid-
ance, illumination, and help in the New Millennium. We need the everlasting support of God's coming to us now and every day and the hope in His
coming at the end of all days. We need the Lord before us. But He is before
us. Nobody will prevent Him from coming to us again and again—as we
read in Revelation 22:20: "The one who testifies to these things says:
'Surely I am coming soon': Amen. Come, Lord Jesus."

Appendixes: Reports from the Workshops

Index

A Fannie J. LeMoine

Apocalyptic Experience and the Conversion of Women in Early Christianity

Perpetua and other early Christian martyrs assumed powerful roles as mediators within the Christian community. As the *Passion of Saints Perpetua and Felicity* demonstrates, the apocalyptic sense that "time is running to its close" contributed to unexpected transformations of expected roles in second- and third-century Roman society. Far from withdrawing from the world, these martyrs assumed responsibility for recording their experiences, converting those willing to hear their message, settling disputes within their religious community, and confronting their enemies. Conversion, at least for a woman like Perpetua, involved a dramatic departure from her expected roles as daughter and mother to that of a skillful and effective intercessor.

This chapter (like the conference workshop on which it is based) is devoted to a study of the text of the *Passion* and a close examination of Perpetua's visions and confrontations. It has three aims: (1) to introduce the *Passion of Saints Perpetua and Felicity* to a wider audience and illustrate how expectations of the end of time and imagery drawn from the Apocalypse reinforce the martyrs' authority as mediators between time and eternity; (2) to argue that Perpetua assumes the "quasi-legal" role of an advocate or intercessor before the Roman authorities, in direct violation of laws against women performing such mediating and advocacy roles; and (3) to demonstrate how expectations of an imminent end of time can result in active participation in the world rather than a passive retreat from it. The study of the early Christian community is undergoing tremendous changes, as indicated by the workshop itself and the short list of relevant new publications that follows this appendix.

In 203 Vibia Perpetua, a well-born mother of twenty-two, was killed in Carthage as part of the birthday games for the emperor Septimius Severus' younger son, the Caesar Geta. The date of the execution was probably March 7, the day Septimius' son turned fourteen. March 7 remains the traditional liturgical date commemorating Perpetua, her fellow martyr, the slave Felicity, and their companions Revocatus, Saturninus, Secundulus, and Saturus. Before her martyrdom in the arena, Perpetua wrote an account of her arrest, trial, and visions while in prison. An editor, probably a Christian Montanist, added a preface to the account, joined it with a vision recorded by Saturus, and appended an eyewitness report of the deaths of all six at the document's conclusion.

The apocalyptic frame of the *Passion of Saints Perpetua and Felicity* is set at the very beginning of the text by the author of the preface. In the introduction to Perpetua's prison journal, he challenges his contemporaries' excessive veneration of antiquity (old texts and old prophecies). Instead he asserts (1.3) that "more recent events are to be considered greater because they come nearer to the final fullness of time" ("Ut nouissimiora secundum exuperationem gratiae in ultima saeculi spatia decretam"). And he supports that claim with this Old Latin version of Acts 2:17 (itself a recalling of Joel 2:28):

> In nouissimis diebus, dicit dominus, effundam de Spiritu meo super omnem carnem, et prophetabunt filii filiaeque eorum;
> et super seruos et ancillas meas de meo Spiritu effundam; et iuuenes visiones uidebunt, et senes somnia somniabunt.

In the last days, says the lord, I shall pour forth from my Spirit over all flesh, and their sons and daughters will prophesy; and over my men servants and my maid servants shall I pour from my Spirit; and young men will see visions, and old men will dream dreams. [Author's translation]

Allusions to scripture are not especially prominent in the *Passio,* but the influence of Revelation seems notable in two of the three visions recorded by Perpetua and in the vision of Saturus. The visions themselves illuminate the prison diary and dissolve the martyrs' actual and metaphorical confinement through powerful images of triumphant ascent and spacious joy. The scriptural references also deepen and expand the text in a different way. They not only confirm the reliability of the visions and the visionaries; they link the martyrs' experience of imminent execution with a divine realm guaranteed by sacred text and witnessed by testimony from all five senses: sight, taste, hearing, touch, and smell.

Perpetua records three major visions. In the two that relate directly to the coming martyrdom, apocalyptic imagery is prominent. For example, her first vision (4.3–9) reveals a ladder that extends upward from a dark pit. At the foot of the ladder lurks a huge serpent, and every rung is covered with hideous instruments of torture. Perpetua crushes the head of the viper, climbs the ladder, and enters into a bright, pastoral landscape where a gray-haired old man is milking sheep; others clothed in white are standing near. The old man welcomes her and gives her a sweet taste that remains in her mouth after she wakes.

This vision centers upon a serpent, *draco,* and could well remind hearers and readers of the text of the *draco magnus* of Revelation 12:3. The gray-haired old man and the others clothed in white (*candidati*) suggest Revelation 1:13–14 and Revelation 7:13–14. White is the color of the "candidates for martyrdom," and that clothing image dominates Revelation 7:13–14: "These who are dressed in the white robes, who are they and where did they come from? . . . These are the ones that come out of the great tribulation, and they have washed their robes and made them white in the blood of the Lamb" (New World translation).

Perpetua's last vision, recorded on the day before the games (10.1–14), also repeats the white-clothing imagery. Here Pomponius the deacon, dressed in an unbelted white robe, comes and beats on the door of the prison. Perpetua goes out to meet him and is led through tortuous and winding places to the middle of the arena. There she encounters a hideous Egyptian, his supporters, and a huge crowd intently watching. Her own supporters rub her down with oil, while her enemy rolls in the arena sand in preparation for combat.

After Perpetua is transformed into a man, she wrestles with the enemy and crushes his head. As her reward she receives a branch bearing apples and a kiss from a figure like the leader of a gladiatorial troup. Yet this figure is so large he towers over the highest seats of the amphitheater. He directs her to the Sanavivaria gate, the gate out of which the living pass from the games. Here Perpetua centers her vivid imagery of the fight around the figure of Satan as an Egyptian, an identification familiar from Revelation 11.8.

Allusions to Revelation are even more explicit in Saturus' one recorded vision (11.2–13.8). When he and Perpetua come to a place with walls seemingly made of light and four angels standing before the door, they hear the united voice of the white-robed choir singing, "Holy, Holy, Holy" without cease and a seated figure like a man with white hair and a youthful face, both reminiscent of passages in Revelation (4:8, 1:14). The angels lift Perpetua and Saturus, they kiss the seated figure, and "with his hand he passed over their faces" (12.5: "de manu sua traiecit nobis in faciem"). The action recalls God's wiping away of every tear in Revelation 7:17.

Saturus' vision ends with reconciliation of church factions in a rose garden and the nourishment of an indescribably satisfying perfume.

The allusions to Revelation, the strong appeals to the senses, and the relevance of the visions to the immediate experience establish a bridge between the stifling oppression of the prison, its accompanying terrors, and the promise of joyful peace. The narrative of the *Passion* moves ineluctably toward death. The text covers the anxious period of waiting before the end of the martyrs' lives or, following the words of the preface, of time itself. The text illustrates how divine grace transforms that "waiting time" into freedom and fulfillment for the martyrs and, by extension, for their willing listeners.

Perpetua's second two-part vision is one of the most famous in the text. It involves her brother Dinocrates, who had died of a terrible cancer of the face when he was seven years old. She first sees Dinocrates with the frightful sore on his face, dry and thirsty and unable to drink from a pool whose rim was far too tall for his small frame (7.3–8). After her intercessory prayers, she again sees her young brother, now clean, with a healed scar on his face, happily drinking from a golden cup and playing in the pool of water, now with a low rim, easily accessible to small children (8.1–4). This vision demonstrates Perpetua's intercessory power in aid of the dead. It foreshadows later medieval assumptions about the efficacy of prayers of intercession for souls of the departed, and also Perpetua's and Felicity's continuing roles as major intercessors whose prayers for sinners are sought in the Mass.

The second vision contains no readily identifiable apocalyptic imagery, but it does demonstrate Perpetua's powerful role as advocate. As such, it provides a spiritual example of the worldly confrontations Perpetua manages with equal success and skill. Two key intercessions recorded in the *Passio* (16.1–4, 18.1–8) illustrate an extraordinary departure from fundamental restrictions applied to women in Roman law and a new attitude toward the nexus of religious and civic sacrifice in the Roman state. Perpetua, speaking for her fellow martyrs, successfully undermines the authority of civic and religious institutions in Severan North Africa.

The authority Perpetua assumes, to speak for others (not simply for herself) and to act as an *intercessor* in a legal sense, challenges the traditional conception of female capacities in Roman law and civic life. Although women could handle their own affairs, they were denied the right to take legal or political action on behalf of others, even their own children. The constitution of Septimius Severus clearly states: "The affairs of others cannot be entrusted to women unless, through the actions they are directed to bring, they are pursuing their own interest and profit."[1]

In several instances in the narrative, Perpetua wields an authority that exceeds her personal interest and directly affects others, interceding on behalf of her brother Dinocrates, acting as mediator between two church factions in Saturus' vision, representing the interest of the group when they request better treatment and when they refuse to enter the arena for their execution garbed in the robes and sacrificial fillets that priests and animal victims traditionally wore before immolation.

Two of these intercessions illustrate how firmly public execution was identified in ancient society as both a secular and a religious act. In her first confrontation with the prison tribune (16.1–4), she turns his assumption that the convicted prisoners are like sacrificial animals into a humorous appeal to his self-interest and his religious superstition: "Quid utique non permittis nobis refrigerare noxiis nobilissimis, Caesaris scilicet, et natali eiusdem pugnaturis? Aut non tua gloria est, si pinguiores illo producamur." [Why don't you let us freshen up? After all we are most distinguished criminals of Caesar—about to fight on his birthday. Won't it be to your credit if we are led out fattened up?]

The title that Perpetua applies to the convicted criminals, *noxiis nobilissimis*, is a recurring epithet for Caesar, even applied to Geta in inscriptions. By transferring the epithet to the convicted criminals, Perpetua dramatizes who are the authentic holders of the *nobilissimus* title. *Pinguiores* ("better fattened") makes an uncomfortable comparison between convicted criminal and animal victim in ritual sacrifice. The tribune's reaction (16.4: "horruit et erubuit tribunus"—the tribune shook with fear and blushed with shame) is a telling sign of his superstition and his loss of face.

Perpetua's last confrontation with the authorities also reveals the close ties between the secular and sacred, and illustrates two pervasive attributes of honorable men of authority (and of these honorable women): the honorable fulfill their duties with decorum and control their own destinies by courageous action.

This section of the *Passio* (18.1) opens with a description of the procession from the prison into the amphitheater. The martyrs were forced to put on costumes: the men, robes of priests of Saturn; the women, robes of the priestesses of Ceres. Fillets, streamers of ribbons, were normally worn by priests taking part in sacrifices and by animal victims, and were used as decorations on sacred places such as altars. They mark the close association between victim and priest in ancient Roman religion. By refusing to don the robes and ribbons, Perpetua and the other martyrs reject participation in the sacred. To make her case, she uses the language of Roman legal contracts (18:5):

Ideo ad hoc sponte peruenimus ne libertas nostra obduceretur; ideo animam nostram addiximus, ne tale aliquid faceremus; hoc uobiscum pacti sumus. (18.5)

We came to this of our own free will in order not to lose our liberty. We have pledged ourselves not to do any such thing. We have entered on this contract with you.

Perpetua succeeds by asserting the group's legal right to enter into a contract binding on both parties. The tribune is forced to acknowledge the essential justice of her claim. His assent dramatizes the victory; the bonds of legal contracts are shown to have greater force than the coils of sacrificial garlands. Perpetua clearly acts here as intercessor and advocate for the group.

All the martyrs demonstrate their freedom in a spectacular way. When they freely choose death in the arena, they enact the principle expressed in Seneca's famous aphorism that the foulest death is better than the fairest servitude (*Epistulae* 70.21). Thus, the martyrs assert their intrinsic control over their future in the most conspicuous forum available to them: they refuse to play the role of willing victims. They actively confront injustice in the world and, with divine grace, create the sense of completion and fulfillment so frequently denied those who only wait.

Note

1.   Yan Thomas, "The Division of the Sexes in Roman Law," in Pauline Schmitt Pantel, ed., and Arthur Goldhammer, trans., *A History of Women in the West*, vol. 1: *From Ancient Goddesses to Christian Saints* (Cambridge: Harvard University Press, 1992), 83–138.

Selected Bibliography

Feldman, Louis H. *Jew and Gentile in the Ancient World*. Princeton: Princeton University Press, 1993.

Gardner, Jane F. *Women in Roman Law and Society*. Bloomington: Indiana University Press, 1986.

Kraemer, Ross Shepard. *Her Share of the Blessings: Women's Religion among Pagans, Jews and Christians in the Greco-Roman World*. New York: Oxford University Press, 1992.

MacDonald, Margaret Y. *Early Christian Women and Pagan Opinion: The Power of the Hysterical Woman*. Cambridge: Cambridge University Press, 1996.

Salisbury, Joyce E. *Perpetua's Passion: The Death and Memory of a Young Roman Woman*. New York and London: Routledge, 1997.

Stark, Rodney. *The Rise of Christianity: A Sociologist Reconsiders History*. Princeton: Princeton University Press, 1996.

Trevett, Christine. *Montanism, Gender, Authority, and the New Prophecy*. Cambridge: Cambridge University Press, 1996.

Wilken, Robert L. *The Christians As the Romans Saw Them*. New Haven and London: Yale University Press, 1984.

Abbot Joachim of Fiore
A Reformist Apocalyptic

"Reformist apocalyptic" designates a person who applied the characteristics that were expected to occur at the end of history to reform of the church, most especially clerical reform. An unprecedented struggle against anti-Christian powers and a crisis of turbulence and suffering that surpassed anything that had previously occurred were to be indications of the imminent coming of a holier, purer church, not of the end of history.

Reformist apocalypticism first emerged in the thinking of Pope Gregory VII. Bernard of Clairvaux (1090–1153) was its major proponent in the first half of the twelfth century. His *Five Books on Consideration,* addressed to Pope Eugene III and written between 1148 and 1153, strongly influenced both Gerhoh of Reichersberg (1093–1169) and Joachim of Fiore (c. 1135–1202), and perhaps Hildegard of Bingen (1098–1179). These three were the chief proponents of reformist apocalypticism in the second half of the twelfth century.

Like Bernard of Clairvaux, Joachim was a Gregorian, one who argued that the pope had been made the vicar of Christ in order to carry out thoroughgoing clerical reform, not to usurp the military duties or the jurisdictional rights of lay rulers. If Bernard was worried by the trends that he perceived in Eugene's pontificate, Joachim, who was at least two generations younger, had been convinced by the popes of the second half of the twelfth century that reform could only happen after an "apocalyptic" crisis.

The key to understanding Joachim's thought is the *Liber de Concordia Novi ac Veteris Testamenti,* books 2 through 4. The system of concords that Joachim elaborated in these three books began with Augustine, who utilized the generations of Christ from Matthew and Luke to demarcate the five *etates* (ages) from creation to the incarnation.[1] The exodus paradigm is the key to understanding Joachim's theology of history. This is best illustrated in figure 2 of the *Liber de Concordia,* which is found in book 2, part 2 (pp. 163–72 of my edition), where the three circles each have three subcircles describing the works of the patriarchs of the first *status,* the apostles of the second *status* (stage, period) and the future *viri spirituales* (spiritual men) of the third *status.* The Babylonian exile was conceived by Joachim as a second captivity in Egypt that led to another exodus led by Zorobabel and to the construction of the second temple. Joachim carefully constructed the concords so that the generations of the second *status*—that is, of the church, from the accession of Pope Leo IX (1049–1154) to the year 1200—paralleled the Old Testament generations from Josiah to the exile. Thus Joachim made Josiah's attempted reform, his death at the hands of Pharaoh Necho, the conquest of Jerusalem by the Babylonians, and the Babylonian exile the parallel to the history of the papacy from the beginning of the Gregorian reform to the commencement of the pontificate of Innocent III (1198–1216). The church had begun to relax its rules and to permit more wealth and luxuries to the clergy and to the religious since the eighth century (the opening of the fifth seal according to Joachim), and at the end of the twelfth century this had resulted in such overwhelming corruption among the clergy and religious that symbolically the church was once again exiled to Babylon. At some point not long after 1200, twin persecutions would afflict Latin Christendom—the Old Testament concords were recorded in Judith and Esther. These were also the sixth and seventh heads of the dragon, or sixth and seventh in the series of Antichrists. The persecutions and sufferings would purify the clergy and the orders, and under the leadership of a holy pontiff the Christians would return to Jerusalem. Hence the third *status* would be the era of a reformed, holier church.

This third "exodus" had already commenced in Bernard, whom Joachim depicted as the Moses of this last exodus. Joachim identified Cîteaux and its four daughter houses as the five tribes that had received their inheritance first in this final "conquest of Canaan." Perhaps his own order was meant to produce the seven houses that would receive their share after the purification.

Reformist apocalyptics continued to envision a reformed church after

1200, and John Calvin must be seen in the light of reformist apocalypticism. Reformist apocalypticism was a significant factor leading to the
sixteenth-century reformations.

Note

1. In their studies on Joachim, Marjorie Reeves focused on the intricate figures, especially those in the *Liber Figurarum,* as the key to understanding Joachim,
while Bernard McGinn approached him through the *Expositio in Apocalypsim.*

Selected Bibliography

Bernard of Clairvaux. *Five Books on Consideration: Advice to a Pope.* Trans. John
D. Anderson and Elizabeth T. Kennan. The Works of Bernard of Clairvaux, vol.
13. Cistercian Fathers Series, no. 37. Kalamazoo: Cistercian Publications, 1976.
Czarski, Charles. *The Prophecies of St. Hildegard of Bingen.* Ph.D. dissertation,
University of Kentucky, 1983.
Daniel, E. Randolph. "Joachimism and John Calvin: New Approaches." In Ro-
berto Rusconi, ed., *Storia e figure dell'Apocalisse fra '500 e '600,* 163–73. Atti
del 4° Congresso internazionale di studi gioachimiti, San Giovanni In Fiore,
14–17 September 1994. Roma: Viella, 1996.
Daniel, E Randolph. "Reformist Apocalypticism and the Friars Minor." In Mi-
chael F. Cusato, OFM and F. Edward Coughlin, OFM, eds., *That Others May
Know and Love: Essays in Honor of Zachary Hayes, OFM,* 237–53. St. Bonaven-
ture: Franciscan Institute, 1997.
Hildegard of Bingen. *Book of Divine Works with Letters and Songs,* ed. Matthew
Fox. Santa Fe: Bear, 1987.
Hildegard of Bingen. *Scivias.* Trans. Mother Columba Hart and Jane Bishop. Classics of Western Spirituality. New York: Paulist Press, 1990.
Joachim of Fiore. *Liber de Concordia Novi ac Veteris Testamenti: Books One
through Four,* E. Randolph Daniel. Transactions of the American Philosophical
Society, vol. 73, pt. 8. Philadelphia: American Philosophical Society, 1983. Also
published at Venice, 1519, edited and reprinted by Minerva G.M.B.H., Frank-
furt am Main, 1964.
Kerby-Fulton, Kathryn. *Reformist Apocalypticism and 'Piers Plowman.'* Cam-
bridge Studies in Medieval Literature, vol. 7. Cambridge: Cambridge University
Press, 1990.
McGinn, Bernard. *Antichrist: Two Thousand Years of the Human Fascination with
Evil.* San Francisco: Harper San Francisco, 1994.
McGinn, Bernard. *The Calabrian Abbot: Joachim of Fiore in Western Thought.*
New York: Macmillan, 1985.
McGinn, Bernard, ed. *Apocalyptic Spirituality.* Classics of Westsern Spirituality.
New York: Paulist Press, 1979.
Reeves, Marjorie. *The Influence of Prophecy in the Later Middle Ages: A Study in
Joachimism.* Oxford: Clarendon Press, 1969; reprinted Notre Dame: University
of Notre Dame Press, 1993.

Reeves, Marjorie. *Joachim of Fiore and the Prophetic Future.* New York: Harper Torchbooks, 1977.

Reeves, Marjorie, and Beatrice Hirsch-Reich. *The Figurae of Joachim of Fiore.* Oxford: Clarendon Press, 1972.

Walzer, Michael. *Exodus and Revolution.* New York: Basic Books, Inc., 1985.

Wessley, Stephen E. *Joachim of Fiore and Monastic Reform.* New York: Peter Lang, 1990.

C Robert M. Kingdon

Early Protestant Views
of the Book of Revelation

The most important source of thought about the millennium, even in our own days is the Book of Revelation. Since the earliest Protestant Reformers tried to base their entire interpretation of Christianity on their reading of the Bible, they must have something of interest to say about this book.

Two documents serve as the basis for our discussion here (as at the conference workshop).[1] One comprises the copious marginal annotations attached to the Book of Revelation as translated in the Geneva Bible of 1560; the other is Luther's preface to the version of the Book of Revelation included in the second edition of his translation of the entire Bible into German.

At the beginning of the Reformation, many experts on the Bible expressed serious doubts about the Book of Revelation. Lorenzo Valla, the great fifteenth-century Latinist, and his admirer and disciple Erasmus, doubted its canonicity. So did Ulrich Zwingli, the reformer of Zurich and an admirer of Erasmus. John Calvin, the reformer of Geneva, accepted its canonicity but nevertheless complained that he found it obscure. None of them prepared commentaries on Revelation.

The first Protestant who took the Book of Revelation seriously was Martin Luther, and even he did not take it seriously at first. In his *second* preface to Revelation in the 1530 edition of his translation, he presented a quick analysis of what he took to be the meaning of the book.

211

The first Protestant leader who prepared a detailed commentary on the Book of Revelation was Henry Bullinger, Zwingli's successor as director of the Reformed Church in Zurich and a theologian with enormous influence all over Europe in the second generation of the Reformation, an influence that rivaled that of Calvin in many areas. During his long and prolific career, Bullinger prepared commentaries on all the books of the New Testament. When he had finished the others, in 1546, he turned to Revelation. He took his time with it, but finally he delivered a series of sermons on the book and had them published in book form in 1557.

What seems to have provoked Luther and Bullinger to take the Book of Revelation seriously was the beginning of persecution of Protestants by Catholics. The book at the time it was first written seems designed to console Christians suffering from persecution and give them hope that their cause will ultimately triumph. These early Protestants believed that they could find similar consolation in the Book of Revelation in their own day. They did this in good part by finding in it a prediction that the Roman Catholic church to which they were so sharply opposed would become corrupt and cruel and persecuting. They convinced themselves that the head of that church, the pope, had himself become the Antichrist predicted in the Bible, one of the beasts predicted in Revelation.

Meanwhile, English Protestants had discovered the Book of Revelation and found in it consolation in periods when they faced persecution—at first during the Anglo-Catholic reign of Henry VIII, and even more emphatically during the Roman Catholic reign of Mary Tudor (1553–1558). A group of English exiles in Geneva decided to prepare a fresh translation of the Bible into their language. It was first published there in 1560, and thus is called the Geneva Bible. It became in the following years the most popular Bible in all English-speaking countries, including the new colonies of America, until it was superseded by the Authorized (King James) translation. The Geneva Bible was militantly Protestant; its partisan intentions are most clearly revealed in the marginal annotations that accompany every book, interpreting texts in rigorously Protestant directions.

Close technical study of the annotations attached to the Book of Revelation in the Geneva Bible, specifically by Richard Bauckham, professor of New Testament Studies at the University of St. Andrews, reveals that most of these marginal comments come straight from Bullinger's commentary, sometimes using almost the same words. They do not make the book primarily a forecast of things to come; they make it rather a forecast of things that happened shortly after it was written, not long after the death of Christ. Thus the millennium proper, the period of one thousand years in which Satan is bound, described in chapter 20, is believed to be the period between the birth of Christ and the pontificate of Sylvester II, 999–

1003 (see 20:2, note c). During this period the Roman Catholic Church was reasonably faithful to Christian truth. Only after Sylvester II did it become so corrupt that its leaders became Antichrist. Similarly, Luther's preface to the Book of Revelation dated the thousand years as beginning when John drafted the book and ending in the eleventh century, when the papacy became corrupt.[2]

Both Luther and the redactors of the Geneva Bible also find in this text predictions of other events that came to pass. Both identify the two beasts in Revelation 13 as the Roman empire and the Roman papacy. Both find predictions of the rise and spread of Islam, especially in the references to Gog and Magog. Neither dwells at length on the end of the world that is to come. To a degree they are reacting against the Anabaptist predictions of an imminent apocalypse (see chapter 6, by H. C. Erik Midelfort), just as they reacted against almost everything else the Anabaptists taught. While these interpretations reveal much of the mentality of the earliest Protestants, they are not of much value in our ecumenical age.

Notes

1. This well-attended workshop included H. C. Erik Midelfort, several Lutheran clergymen, a Jesuit priest, a retired justice of the Wisconsin State Supreme Court, the director of the State Humanities Council, and a number of graduate students and other scholars.

2. Workshop participants discussed in detail some specific notes in the Geneva Bible, including ones that suggest that the forecast of a thousand-year reign of Christ does not mean a literal period of one thousand years (e.g., chapter 20: 6, n. 1).

Selected Bibliography

Backus, Irena. *Les sept visions et la fin des temps: les commentaires genevois de l'Apocalypse entre 1539 et 1584, Revue de théologie et de philosophie* no. 19 (Lausanne, 1997).

Barnes, Robin B. *Prophecy and Gnosis: Apocalypticism in the Wake of the Lutheran Reformation.* Stanford: Stanford University Press, 1988.

Bauckham, Richard. "Heinrich Bullinger, the Apocalypse, and the English," in Henry D. Rack, ed., *The Swiss Connection: Manchester Essays on Religious Connections between England and Switzerland between the Sixteenth and Twentieth Centuries.* Manchester: University of Manchester, 1995.

Bauckham, Richard, ed., *Tudor Apocalypse: Sixteenth Century Apocalypticism, Millenarianism, and the English Reformation.* Appleford, England: Sutton Courtenay Press, 1978.

D   *Sargent Bush, Jr.*

The American Puritans and Millennialism

I will deal plainly with you. As sure as God is God, God is going from England. . . .

Well, look to it, for God is going, and if he do go, then our glory goes also. And then we may say with Phineha's wife, 1 Sam. 4:22: '[The] glory is departed from Israel.' So glory is departed from England; for England hath seen her best days, and the reward of sin is coming on apace; for God is packing up of his gospel, because no one will buy his wares. . . . God begins to ship away his Noahs, which prophesied and foretold that destruction was near; and God makes account that New England shall be a refuge for his Noahs and his Lots, a rock and a shelter for his righteous ones to run unto.

Thomas Hooker, "The Danger of Desertion" (1631)

And then considering our English plantations of late, and the opinions of many grave divines concerning the Gospel's fleeting westward, sometimes I have had such thoughts, why may not that be the place of the New Jerusalem?

William Twisse to Joseph Mede, 4 March 1634

The idea that America offered a new—and perhaps last—hope for the world had begun to appear in English discourse by early in the seventeenth century. Some believed America would be the site of the promised kingdom of God in the last times. Millennialism was certainly much in the air in England at the time of the Great Migration to America (1620–1640). Yet specifically millennialist prophecy was first preached in Puritan New England only in the 1640s, by such powerful voices as John Cotton and John Eliot, after which it took root in the faith of many. Later in the seventeenth century the strain became more pronounced, finding popular appeal in the sermons and other writings of Increase and Cotton Mather, among others. Samuel Danforth's famous election sermon of 1670 represents, for many interpreters of this early American period, a key statement: "*To what purpose then came we into the Wilderness? And what expectation drew us Thither? Was it not the expectation of the Pure and Faithful Dispensation of the Gospel and the Kingdom of God?*" (*A Brief Recognition of New England's Errand into the Wilderness,* 1670). Even the great Jonathan Edwards, though not an insistent millennialist, offered the thought that "we may well look into the discovery of so great a part of the world as America and bringing the gospel into it, is one thing by which divine providence is preparing the way for the future glorious times of the church, where Satan's kingdom shall be overthrown not only throughout the Roman empire but throughout the whole habitable globe. . . . When those times come, then doubtless America shall have glorious success" (*History of the Work of Redemption* [1739/1774]).

As these selections suggest, millennialist thinking found a home in America; on that historians agree. But there is no longer agreement on the question as to whether or not millennialism was an actual motivation for the first generation's migration. Did the hope and expectation of achieving the kingdom on earth in a pristine America drive the thinking of those first emigrants? In a very influential essay (see Selected Bibliography below), J. F. Maclear suggests an affirmative answer: "Preoccupation with Last Things seems to have been a selective factor drawing many eschatologically sensitive Puritans to the New World" (p. 230). Mason Lowance, with others, agrees: "In New England emigrant Puritans viewed their crossing of the Atlantic as a preparatory stage in the drama of world redemption through their errand into the wilderness, whose mission would be realized in the future glory of an American millennium" (p. 117).

Certain historians have recently disagreed. Theodore Dwight Bozeman argues that "millennial hope was a far more modest factor in early American Puritan theology than usually assumed" (p. 194). Andrew Delbanco insists that there was *not* a millennial consensus among the first New Englanders: "Our present vision of the Puritan founders as hungry for the millennium and convinced that their journey was typed out in scripture needs to be revised" (p. 351).

What is not in doubt is that, early on, the Puritans introduced the idea of America as a special place, a location where God's word might thrive and thus where virtue and goodness might reign. Churches were established on a new footing, with demanding membership requirements of godliness and gracious experience. Settlers were admonished by no less a leader than John Winthrop to bind themselves in a body politic held together by the bonds of love. Only thus could they be a beacon to the world, a "Model of Christian Charity," a "city on a hill."

This early construction of images of an inspired and godly people proved highly adaptable over many generations of American experience. The project or idea of America at some point was allied with a forward-looking, hope-engendered way of thinking. Our earliest historians—Edward Johnson, in the climactic chapter of his *Wonder-Working Providence of Sion's Saviour in New England* (1653), for example—sometimes saw

American settlement in terms of "the Forlorne of Christs Armies" (Puritan emigrants) doing battle against "Antichrists Army" (English prelates) (p. 271).

As one era gave way to another, one set of intellectual/political/social assumptions about American civilization merged into another; the decidedly religious, and specifically Calvinist Puritan, notions about the colonial enterprise gave way to increasingly secular modifications of the idea of a chosen people. This idea has been employed at various critical moments—some would say nearly apocalyptic moments—in American history, including but not limited to the Revolutionary War, the Civil War, and various conflicts in the twentieth century. Woodrow Wilson's post–World War I comment, which provides the epigraph for Ernest Tuveson's *Redeemer Nation,* summarizes modern uses of these ideas of America: "America had the infinite privilege of fulfilling her destiny and saving the world." Perry Miller, employing Samuel Danforth's adoption of a biblical phrase, described the Puritans' "errand into the wilderness," with its suggestion of future glory and special destiny; this concept blossomed, in Wilson's and others' minds, into a mission of salvation for the world. It was no longer a spiritual salvation and certainly not a specifically millennialist expectation, but it was rooted in such ideas from earlier times.

Selected Bibliography

Bercovitch, Sacvan. *The American Jeremiad.* Madison: University of Wisconsin Press, 1978.

Bercovitch, Sacvan. *The Rites of Assent: Transformations in the Symbolic Construction of America.* New York: Routledge, 1993.

Boyer, Paul. *When Time Shall Be No More: Prophecy Belief in Modern American Culture.* Cambridge: Harvard University Press, 1992.

Bozeman, Theodore Dwight. *To Live Ancient Lives: The Primitivist Dimension in Puritanism.* Chapel Hill: University of North Carolina Press for the Institute of Early American History and Culture, 1988.

Delbanco, Andrew. "The Puritan Errand Re-Viewed," *Journal of American Studies* 18 (1984), 343–60.

Hatch, Nathan. *The Sacred Cause of Liberty: Republican Thought and the Millennium in Revolutionary New England.* New Haven: Yale University Press, 1977.

Lowance, Mason I. *The Language of Canaan: Metaphor and Symbol in New England from the Puritans to the Transcendentalists.* Cambridge: Harvard University Press, 1980.

Maclear, J. F. "New England and the Fifth Monarchy: The Quest for the Millennium in Early American Puritanism," *William and Mary Quarterly,* 3d ser., 32 (1975), 223–60.

Smolinski, Reiner. "Introduction," *The Threefold Paradise of Cotton Mather: An*

Edition of "Triparadisus," ed. Reiner Smolinski. Athens: University of Georgia Press, 1995.

Stein, Stephen J. "Transatlantic Extensions: Apocalyptic in Early New England," in C. A. Patrides and Joseph Wittreich, eds., *The Apocalypse in English Renaissance Thought and Literature: Patterns, Antecedents, and Repercussions,* 266–98. Manchester: Manchester University Press, 1984.

Tuveson, Ernest Lee. *Redeemer Nation: The Idea of America's Millennial Role.* Chicago: University of Chicago Press, 1968.

Zakai, Avihu. *Exile and Kingdom: History and Apocalypse in the Puritan Migration to New England.* Cambridge: Cambridge University Press, 1992.

Index

Ælfric of Eynsham, 60
Adso of Montier-en-Der, 60, 83*n74; Epistola de Antichristo,* 72; *Libellus de Antichristo,* 87–88, 95, 102–103
Akhmatova, Anna, 140, 144
Aldegrever of Soest, Heinrich (engraver): portraits of Jan of Leiden and Bernd Knipperdolling, 128
Alighieri. *See* Dante Alighieri
Anabaptists, 116–129 *passim,* 213; opponents of Luther, 117; refugees from the Duchy of Jülich-Cleves and the Netherlands, 119; ascendency in Münster, 120–121
Antichrist, 49, 54, 71–73, 99, 151, 153, 157, 160, 172, 175, 208; in manuscript illuminations, 86–114 *passim*
Antiochus IV Epiphanes, 26, 36, 39, 48
Anti-Semitism, 156–157, 175, 178
Applewhite, Marshall, 149; and Bonnie Lu Nettles as Two Witnesses, 149. *See also* Heaven's Gate
Armageddon, 151, 153–154, 159, 171, 175, 179
Aryan Nation, 149
Atomic bomb, 155, 166*n21*
Augustine, Saint, 188; *City of God,* 53; letter to bishop of Salona, 53–54; *Literal Commentary on Genesis,* 64

Babel, Isaak, 140
Babylon, 160
Babylonian exile, 26, 29, 208
Bancroft, George, 153
Barnabas, 49
Beast of Revelation: seven-headed, 8, 88; two-horned ram-like, 88; mark of, 89, 95, 157, 174; number of (666), 89, 95, 157–

158; as Roman empire and Roman papacy, 213
Beatus of Liébana, 60
Belinsky, Vissarion, 141
Bely, Andreiz: *Petersburg,* 138, 144
Bernard of Clairvaux, 68, 207–208
Bible, apocryphal books
   2 Esdras, 124
   Judith, 208
   1 Maccabees, 40; *ch. 1* and *4,* 38
Bible, general: Geneva Bible, 211–212; Luther's preface to Revelation, 211
Bible, individual books of the New Testament
   Matthew: *ch. 3,* 47; *ch. 5,* 51; *ch. 24,* 96, 151; *ch. 24–25,* 195; *ch. 26,* 51–52
   Mark: *ch. 1,* 4; *ch. 12,* 47
   Luke: *ch. 4,* 47; *ch. 13,* 47; *ch. 19,* 47; *ch. 24,* 197
   John: *ch. 7,* 47; *ch. 10,* 115; *ch. 12,* 197; *ch. 18,* 47
   Acts: *ch. 2,* 202; *ch. 14,* 195
   Romans: *ch. 13,* 46
   1 Corinthians: *ch. 1,* 63; *ch. 3,* 53; *ch. 12,* 195; *ch. 13,* 46
   2 Corinthians: *ch. 4,* 194; *ch. 12,* 197
   Galatians, 49; *ch. 4,* 53
   Ephesians, 186, 190; *ch. 4,* 185, 195
   1 Thessalonians: *ch. 4,* 151
   2 Thessalonians: *ch. 3,* 46
   Hebrews: *ch. 4–6,* 49–50; *ch. 11,* 49, 196; *ch. 13,* 49
   2 Peter: *ch. 3,* 46, 155
   1 John: *ch. 4,* 129
   Revelation, 50, 186, 188; *ch. 1,* 64, 66; *ch. 6,* 145; *ch. 7,* 122, 203; *ch 11,* 73, 87; *ch. 12,* 203; *ch. 13,* 95, 157, 191, 213; *ch. 15,* 191; *ch. 17,* 99; *ch. 19,* 193; *ch.*

20, 63, 212–213; *ch. 21,* 197–198; *ch. 22,* 67, 198
Bible, individual books of the Old Testament
Genesis: *ch. 1,* 46, 123; *ch. 6,* 30; *ch. 15,* 156; *ch. 16,* 161
Exodus: *ch. 28* and *39,* 50
Deuteronomy: *ch. 30,* 49; *ch. 15* and *28,* 52
Esther, 208
Psalms: *ch. 90,* 46
Isaiah: *ch. 13,* 25; *ch. 24–27,* 26, 29; *ch. 40–43,* 196–197; *ch. 56–66,* 27–28
Jeremiah: *ch. 4* and *9,* 49; *ch. 25* and *29,* 37
Ezekiel: *ch. 38,* 155–156; *ch. 40–48,* 27–28
Daniel, 186; *ch. 1–12,* 34–40 *passim; ch. 2,* 45–46; *ch. 9,* 48
Joel: *ch. 2,* 202
Amos: *ch. 5,* 25
Habakkuk: Dead Sea Scrolls commentary on, 37
Haggai: *ch. 2,* 26
Zechariah: *ch. 1–8,* 27–28; *ch. 13,* 157, 167*n27; ch. 14,* 155
Bible, pseudepigrapha
Book of Jubilees, 30, 46
Book of Enoch, 29–34, 38–40
Testament of Moses, 36–37
Birgitta, of Sweden, 61; *Revelations,* 66
Blok, Alexander, 140, 144; *The Twelve,* 138
Branch Davidians (Waco, Texas), 4, 149, 179. *See also* Koresh, David
Brezhnev, Leonid, 192
Brodsky, Joseph, 140
Bucer, Martin, 129
Buchanan, Pat, 176–177
Bulgakov, Mikhail, 140, 142, 144; *The Master and Margarita,* 138
Bullinger, Henry: commentary on Revelation, 212
Burton, Robert: views on behavior at Münster, 128, 129, 133*n61*
Bush, George, 173–174

Calvin, John, 209, 211–213
Celsus, 51
Charles V, 119
Chernyshevsky, Nicolai, 140, 142; *What Is to Be Done?,* 137, 141

Chester Mystery Cycle: "Coming of Antichrist," 100
Christian Identity movement, 149, 173
Cicero: and rhetoric, 4
Cold War, 156, 159–163, 170–172
Communism: and oppression in East Germany, 191–198 *passim*
Conspiracy theories, 170–179 *passim*
Constantinople: fall of, 54
Corvinus, Antonius, 129; interviews with leaders of Münster, 126–127
Cotton, John, 214

Danforth, Samuel, 214–216
Dante Alighieri: *Paradiso,* 7–8; and illustrations by Gustave Doré, 8; *Inferno,* 8; *Purgatorio,* 8; *Divine Comedy,* 39
Darby, John, 150–151, 153, 156
Dead Sea Scrolls, 26, 29, 31
Denys Exiguus ("Denys the Tiny") (monk), 44; and date of Easter, 44–45, 52
Deventer, Johann van: disputation with Rothmann, 119
Dionysius (Bishop of Alexandria), 53
Dispensationalism, 150–151, 153, 161. *See also* Premillennial dispensationalism
Dobrolyubov, Nikolai: "What Is Oblomovism?" 141; "When Will the Real Day Come?" 141
Donation of Constantine, 8
Doomsday: Fifteen Signs of, 96, 105
Dostoevsky, Fyodor, 140, 144; *The Brothers Karamazov,* 137–138; *The Idiot,* 137–138; *The Devils,* 138
Dürer, Albrecht, 18
Dusentschur, Johann: prophet of Jan of Leiden, 124–125

Easter: date of, 44–45
Ecclesia: figure of, 99
Edwards, Jonathan, 158
Elijah, 72, 83*n77; Apocalypse of Elijah,* 83*n78*
Eliot, John, 214
Elisabeth of Schönau: as female prophet, 75*n2*
Enoch, 72, 83*n77;* Enoch and Elijah as the Two Witnesses, 87, 103
Ephrem (church Father), 60
Epiphanius (church Father), 60

Erasmus, 211
Erofeev, Venedikt: *From Moscow to the End of the Line*, 145
Esenin, Sergei, 140
Eugene III (pope), 68, 207

Falwell, Jerry, 152
Felicity, Saint (Christian martyr), 201–206 *passim*
Freemen (Montana), 179

Gebeno of Eberbach: collects Hildegard's apocalyptic writings (*Pentachronon*), 69
Gerardo of Borgo San Donnino, 71; *Introductorius in Aeternum Evangelium*, 71
Gerhoh of Reichersberg, 62, 207
Germany, East: church life in, under Communism, 191–198 *passim;* unification of, 198
Gladkov, Fyodor, 142
Gog and Magog, 89, 100, 102–103, 155–156, 213
Gogol, Nicolai, 140; *Dead Souls,* 138, 145
Goncharov, Ivan, 142
Gorbachev, Michail, 155, 193
Gorky, Maxim, 142; *Mother,* 137, 138
Great Tribulation, 151, 153–154, 157, 159
Gregory I the Great (pope): *Moralia* on Job, 95
Gregory VII (pope), 68, 207; ecclesiastical reforms of, 62–63
Griboedov, Alexander, 142

ḥārēdîm ("tremblers"), 27
Heaven's Gate, 5, 149
Henry IV (emperor), 59, 67–68
Henry of Halle: assists Mechthild in writing *The Flowing Light,* 69
Herrad of Landsberg: *Hortus Deliciarum,* 72, 83n76
Herzen, Alexander: *Who Is to Blame?,* 141
Hesiod: *Works and Days,* 35, 45
Hilarion (c. 1037–1050): "Sermon on Law and Grace," 143
Hildegard of Bingen, 59, 61–69 *passim,* 74, 207; letter to Guilbert of Gembloux, 65; *Liber Vite Meritorum,* 65; *Liber Divinorum Operum,* 65, 66–69; *Scivias,* 65, 67, 99; *Explanatio Symboli S. Athanasii,* 66; break with Gregorian reforms, 68; *Phys-*

ica, 68; rebuke to the clergy of Cologne, 68; as first *sibylla* in Christian history, 68; approval of, from Pope Eugene III, 68–69; collection of apocalyptic texts (*Pentachronon*) made by Gebeno of Eberbach, 69; preaching campaigns of, 69, 80n54
Hoffman, Melchior, 118; Melchiorite Christology, 127, 128
Holy fool, fool-in-Christ (*iurodivyi*): in Pushkin (*Boris Godunov*), 138; in Olesha (*Envy*), 138
Honecker, Erich, 192
Hope: message of the millennium, 185–190 *passim*
Hufschmidt, Jakob: predictions of, concerning Münster, 122
Hugh of Strassburg: *Compendium Theologicae Veritatis,* 95

Innocent III (pope), 208
Irenaeus (Bishop of Lyon), 51, 52
Israel, state of: founding of the, 151; and recapture of Old City of Jerusalem, 151

Jacobus de Voragine: *Légende dorée,* 105–108, 113n56
Jan of Leiden, 119, 122–128; king of Zion and of whole world, 123; madness, 124
Jenkins, Jerry, 159, 162–163. *See also* "Left Behind" series
Jerome, Saint: commentary on Daniel, 53; Fifteen Signs of Doomsday, 96, 105
Jerusalem: Temple of, 46, 50; recapture of Old City of, in 1967, 151; destruction of the Temple by the Romans in 70 c.e., and its rebuilding, 156; Yad Vashem Holocaust memorial, 156
Jesus: as Son of Man, 35; Second Coming of, 96, 105, 108
Joachim of Fiore, 7, 63, 70–71, 74, 207–209 *passim; Liber de Concordia Novi ac Veteris Testamenti,* 208
Joan of Arc, 61
Johnson, Edward, 158, 215–216
Jones, Jim, 149; Jonestown (Guyana), 4
Josephus (Jewish historian), 47
Jost, Lienhard and Ursula (evangelical visionaries), 118
Justin: dialogue with Trypho, 51, 52

Kairos, 185
Kerssenbroch, Hermann von: account of Anabaptists in Münster, 126
Khlebnikov, Velimir, 140
Khodasevich, Vladislav, 140
Klyuev, Nikolai, 140
Knipperdolling, Bernd: madness and ecstatic dancing of, 123–124, 126
Koresh, David, 149
Krechting, Heinrich, 126
Kronos, 185
Kymeus, Johann: interviews with leaders of Münster, 126–127

LaHaye, Tim, 159, 162–163. *See also* "Left Behind" series
Langland, William: *Piers Plowman,* 96
Last Judgment, 5–6
"Left Behind" series, 163
Leo IX (pope), 208
Lermontov, Mikhail, 140
Libellus de Antichristo. See Adso of Montier-en-Der
Liber Chronicarum. See Nuremberg Chronicle
Liber Floridus, 95; compiled by Lambert of Saint-Omer, 111n27
Lindsey, Hal: *The Late Great Planet Earth,* 152, 160; *Planet Earth—2000,* 160–161
Ludus de Antichristo, 73
Luther, Martin, 116, 118; criticism of his spiritualist and Anabaptist opponents, 117; and Lutheran ideas in Münster, 119–120; reactions to Münster, 127–129

Mad Friedrich: in Schleswig-Holstein, 118
Mandelstam, Nadezhda, 141
Mandelstam, Osip, 140, 141
Manuscripts: Mozarabic Beatus Apocalypse (Pierpont Morgan Library M.644), 87; Wellcome Apocalypse (Wellcome Library, MS 49), 87–90, 100; *Jour de Jugement* (Besançon, Bibliothèque Municipale 579), 90–93; *Omne Bonum* (British Library Royal 6.E.vi), 93–96, 100, 108; *Piers Plowman* (Bodleian Douce 104), 96–99; *Carthusian Miscellany* (British Library MS Additional 37049), 99–102; *Livre de la Vigne notre Seigneur* (Bodleian Douce 134), 102–105; *Légende*

dorée (Fitzwilliam Museum MS 22), 105–108
Marcion, 50–51
Mather, Cotton and Increase, 214
Matthijs, Jan, 119, 121–122, 128; death of, 122; as Second Enoch, 122
Maurois, André: "The War against the Moon," 171
Mechthild of Magdeburg, 59, 61, 63–64, 69–74; *The Flowing Light of the Godhead,* 69–74; composition of works, 69, 81n57; as a reformist, 70
Methodius, 60; Pseudo-Methodius, *Revelationes,* 95, 100, 102
Millenarianism: in America, 171; "catastrophic" millenarians, 172
Millennium: pop-culture exploitation of, 149–150
Millerite movement, 38, 176
Mohammed: as character in the *Jour de Jugement,* 91
Montanism, 52, 60, 202
Mormons, 158
Moses, 29–30
Münster, 115–134 *passim*
Müntzer, Thomas: criticism of Luther, 116
Muspilli (Old High German poem), 73, 83n78
Mussolini, Benito: as redeemer, 8; as Antichrist, 153

Nebuchadnezzar. *See* Bible, individual books of the Old Testament, Daniel
New World Order, 172–179. *See also* Robertson, Pat; Bush, George
Nuremberg Chronicle, 10, 18

Olesha, Yury: *Envy,* 138
Order of the Solar Temple, 149
Origen, 52–53

Papias, 50
Passion of Saints Perpetua and Felicity, 201–206
Pasternak, Boris, 140; *Doctor Zhivago,* 138, 144
Peasants' War (1525), 120
People's Temple, 149
Perpetua, Saint (Christian martyr), 201–206 *passim*

Petrarch, Francis, 8–10; *Triumphs,* 9–10
Philipp of Hesse, Landgrave, 120, 127
Physiologus, 95
Planets: determinism of, 45
Platonov, Andrei: *Chevengur,* 138
Plenitudo temporis ("fullness of time"), 3
Plymouth Brethren, 150. *See also* Darby,
    John
Polycarp of Smyrna, 51
Porphyry, 51
Premillennial dispensationalism, 150–152
Prigov, Dimitri, 145
Protestantism: views of Revelation, 211–213
Pseudo-Methodius. *See* Methodius
Puritans, New England, 158; and millenni-
    alism, 214–217 *passim*
Pushkin, Alexander, 140, 142, 144; *Boris
    Godunov,* 138; *Prorok,* 140

Radishchev, Alexander, 140
Rapture, 151, 152, 159. *See also* Great
    Tribulation
Reagan, Ronald, 155, 158
Roberts, Oral, 152
Robertson, Pat, 152, 172–173; *The End of
    the Age,* 159, 161–162; *The New World
    Order,* 161, 163, 174–175, 178
Robine, Marie, 61
Rome: Scipios, 4; war with Carthage, 4;
    millennium in 248 C.E., 44
Rothmann, Bernhard, 119–121, 125, 127
Rubinstein, Lev, 145
Rupert of Deutz, 62
Russia: in apocalyptic interpretations, 155–
    156, 159, 160

Scandal of the Eternal Gospel (1254–57),
    71
Schleswig-Holstein, 118
Scofield, Cyrus, 150, 153, 156
Seneca: *Epistulae* 70, 206
The Seventh Seal (film), 10
Shalamov, Varlam, 140
Shinriko, Aum, 149
Sibyl: Erythraean Sibyl, 60; Tiburtine Sibyl,
    60; prophesies, 60, 68

Sinyavsky, Andrei, 140
Skurdal, Rodney. *See* Freemen (Montana)
Solomon, 29–30
Solzhenitsyn, Alexander, 140
Sorokin, Vladimir, 145
Stalin, Joseph, 192
Stepnyak-Kravchinsky, Sergei: *Andrei Koz-
    hukhov,* 137
Strasbourg (Strassburg): home of Lienhard
    and Ursula Jost, 118
Sylvester II (pope), 212–213

Tertullian, 52
Thiota (prophetess), 60–61
Tolstoy, Lev, 137, 144, 145
Trediakovsky, Vasily, 140
Tribulation. *See* Great Tribulation
Trypho, the Jew. *See* Justin
Tsvetaeva, Marina, 140, 144
Turgenev, Ivan, 142; "Living Relics," 137
Twelve Monkeys (film), 6
Tyconius (Donatist theologian): lost com-
    mentary on Apocalypse, 53

Ulbricht, Walter, 192
Utenhoven, Wolfgang von (chancellor), 118

Van Impe, Jack, 152; *2001: Countdown to
    Eternity,* 160
Viri spirituales, 71–73, 82n68

Waco, Texas. *See* Branch Davidians
Waldeck, Franz von (Bishop of Münster),
    120, 126
Walesa, Lech, 193
Wieck, Johann von der (Lutheran leader),
    120
Winthrop, John, 215
Women: as seers, 59–61; literacy of, 61
World: ages of, 45; in Hesiod, 45; in
    Daniel, 45

Zamyatin, Evgeny, 140; *We,* 138
Zealots, 47
Zwingli, Ulrich, 116, 211; and doctrine of
    Eucharist, 120, 127

www.ingramcontent.com/pod-product-compliance
Lightning Source LLC
Chambersburg PA
CBHW060046100426
42742CB00014B/2713